The Challenge of God

The Challenge of God

Continental Philosophy and the Catholic Intellectual Tradition

Edited by

Colby Dickinson, Hugh Miller, and Kathleen McNutt

LONDON • NEW YORK • OXFORD • NEW DELHI • SYDNEY

T&T CLARK
Bloomsbury Publishing Plc
50 Bedford Square, London, WC1B 3DP, UK
1385 Broadway, New York, NY 10018, USA
29 Earlsfort Terrace, Dublin 2, Ireland

BLOOMSBURY, T&T CLARK and the T&T Clark logo are
trademarks of Bloomsbury Publishing Plc

First published in Great Britain in 2020
Paperback edition first published 2021

Copyright © Colby Dickinson, Hugh Miller, Kathleen McNutt and contributors, 2020

Colby Dickinson, Hugh Miller and Kathleen McNutt have asserted her right under the Copyright, Designs and Patents Act, 1988, to be identified as Editors of this work.

Cover design: Terry Woodley
Cover image: Andriy Popov / Alamy Stock Photo

All rights reserved. No part of this publication may be reproduced or transmitted in any form or by any means, electronic or mechanical, including photocopying, recording, or any information storage or retrieval system, without prior permission in writing from the publishers.

Bloomsbury Publishing Plc does not have any control over, or responsibility for, any third-party websites referred to or in this book. All internet addresses given in this book were correct at the time of going to press. The author and publisher regret any inconvenience caused if addresses have changed or sites have ceased to exist, but can accept no responsibility for any such changes.

A catalogue record for this book is available from the British Library.

Library of Congress Control Number: 2019946180

ISBN: HB: 978-0-5676-8990-0
PB: 978-0-5676-9896-4
ePDF: 978-0-5676-8992-4
eBook: 978-0-5676-8991-7

Typeset by Integra Software Services Pvt. Ltd.

To find out more about our authors and books visit
www.bloomsbury.com and sign up for our newsletters.

Contents

Notes on Contributors		vi
Preface *Colby Dickinson, Hugh Miller, and Kathleen McNutt*		ix
Introduction: God as Challenge: The Past and Future of Continental Philosophy of Religion *Bruce Ellis Benson*		1
1	Is God a Challenge for Philosophy? *Adriaan T. Peperzak*	23
2	On the Infinite: A Response to Adriaan Peperzak *David Tracy*	31
3	God and the Ambivalence of Being *Jean-Luc Marion, Translated by Kathleen McNutt*	37
4	Being, God, Nihilism, Love: On Marion's "Ambiguity of Being" *Hugh Miller*	55
5	A Phenomenology of Revelation: Contemporary Encounters with Saint Ignatius Loyola *Robyn Horner*	69
6	"Consolation without Previous Cause"? Consolation, Controversy, and Devotional Agency *J. Michelle Molina*	87
7	Tradition and Event: Radicalizing the Catholic Principle *John D. Caputo*	99
8	Theological Thinking and John Caputo's *Tradition and Event: Radicalizing the Catholic Principle* *John McCarthy*	113
9	Epic and the Crucified God *Thomas J. J. Altizer*	127
10	Scripture, Epic, and Radical Catholicism: A Response to Thomas J. J. Altizer *Adam Kotsko*	135
11	Anatheism: A Theopoetic Challenge *Richard Kearney*	143
12	The God Machine: Techno-Theology and Theo-Poetics *John Panteleimon Manoussakis*	161
Index		170

Contributors

Thomas J.J. Altizer was Professor Emeritus of Religious Studies at State University of New York at Stony Brook. During his long and distinguished career, Altizer published numerous books working out the implications of a theology of the "Death of God," recently including *Living the Death of God, The Apocalyptic Trinity*, and *The Call to Radical Theology*.

Bruce Ellis Benson is Senior Research Fellow at the University of St. Andrews. He is Executive Director of the Society for Continental Philosophy and Theology. He taught for over twenty years at Wheaton College. His research interests include the "theological turn" in phenomenology and work at the intersection of Continental philosophy and theology as well as hermeneutics and interpretation theory.

John D. Caputo is the Thomas J. Watson Professor of Religion and Humanities Emeritus at Syracuse University and the David R. Cook Professor of Philosophy Emeritus at Villanova University. Caputo specializes in Continental philosophy of religion, working on approaches to religion and theology in the light of contemporary phenomenology, hermeneutics and deconstruction, and also the presence in Continental philosophy of radical religious and theological motifs. He is known especially for his notions of radical hermeneutics and the weakness of God.

Colby Dickinson is Associate Professor of Theology at Loyola University Chicago. He has published and researches on the relationship of contemporary Continental thought and systematic theology, focusing on the works of Theodor Adorno, Jacques Derrida, Michel Foucault, Giorgio Agamben, and Paul Ricoeur. He is the author of *Agamben and Theology, Between the Canon and the Messiah, Words Fail*, and *Theology and Contemporary Continental Philosophy*.

Robyn Horner is Associate Professor in the Office of the Dean of Theology and Philosophy at Australian Catholic University. Her work is focused on the contributions of phenomenology and post-structuralism, especially the work of Levinas, Derrida, and Marion, to the field of Christian theology and philosophy of religion, particularly on the topic of r/Revelation.

Richard Kearney holds the Charles B. Seelig Chair in Philosophy at Boston College and has served as Visiting Professor at University College Dublin, the University of Paris-Sorbonne, and the Australian Catholic University. He is the author of over twenty books on European philosophy and literature (including two novels and a volume of poetry) and has edited or coedited fifteen others, many on the intersection of hermeneutics and the problem of God.

Adam Kotsko is on the faculty of the Shimer Great Books School at North Central College, where he teaches widely in the humanities and social sciences. His research focuses on political theology, continental philosophy, and the history of Christian thought. He is the author, most recently, of *The Prince of This World* and *Neoliberalism's Demons*.

John Panteleimon Manoussakis is Associate Professor of Philosophy at the College of the Holy Cross. His research interests include philosophy of religion, phenomenology (in particular Heidegger and Marion), ancient Greek philosophy (especially Plato and the Neo-Platonic Tradition), Patristics, and psychoanalysis.

Jean-Luc Marion is the Andrew Thomas Greeley and Grace McNichols Greeley Professor of Catholic Studies and Professor of the Philosophy of Religions and Theology at the University of Chicago; Dominique Dubarle Chair of Philosophy at l'Institut Catholique de Paris; Professor Emeritus at the University of Paris-Sorbonne; and a member of the Académie française. His work is well known in the history of philosophy and in philosophy of religion, in which he has initiated and written extensively on the phenomenology of givenness.

John McCarthy is Associate Professor of Theology at Loyola University Chicago. His teaching and research focus on fundamental theology and hermeneutics, with research interests in the intersection of philosophy and theology, especially modern and contemporary, and literary theory.

Kathleen McNutt is a Ph.D. candidate in Theology at Loyola University Chicago. Her research currently focuses on the relationship between theosis and ecofeminist theology. She has translated two essays by Jean-Luc Marion, including the one in the present volume.

Hugh Miller is Assistant Professor of Philosophy at Loyola University Chicago. His areas of specialization are philosophy of religion, philosophical theology, history of metaphysics, and contemporary French philosophy. Dr. Miller is the author of several articles and conference papers, and is presently at work on two book-length manuscripts: the first on the philosophy of Emanuel Levinas and the second on Hegel's system.

J. Michelle Molina is the John and Rosemary Croghan Chair and Associate Professor in Catholic Studies at Northwestern University. She studies the Society of Jesus in the early modern period. Molina is the author of *To Overcome Oneself: The Jesuit Ethic and the Spirit of Global Expansion*, which examines the impact that the Jesuit program of radical self-reflexivity had on the formation of early modern selves in Europe and New Spain.

Adriaan T. Peperzak is Professor Emeritus of Philosophy at Loyola University Chicago, where he held the Arthur J. Schmitt Chair from 1991 to 2015. His research in the history of philosophy has focused on Hegel (six books and numerous articles) and Levinas (two books and three others edited). He also published on Plato, Aristotle, Bonaventura, Descartes, Heidegger, and Ricoeur, and on thematic questions in ethics, social and political philosophy, metaphilosophy, and philosophy of religion.

David Tracy is the Andrew Thomas Greeley and Grace McNichols Greeley Distinguished Professor Emeritus of Catholic Studies and Professor of Theology and the Philosophy of Religions at the University of Chicago. His many publications include *The Analogical Imagination: Christian Theology and the Culture of Pluralism* and *On Naming the Present: Reflections on God, Hermeneutics, and Church*.

Preface

Colby Dickinson, Hugh Miller, and Kathleen McNutt

Some of the many recent volumes on the intersection of Continental philosophy and theology have included an essay or two on the relationship of Catholicism to Continental philosophy, but none have centered themselves on these two traditions that have been mingled together for millennia. No volume of essays has yet sought to address directly this major lacuna in scholarship and bring both Continental philosophy of religion and the Catholic intellectual heritage into dialogue. From this point of view, the uniqueness of this volume lies in its direct engagement with many perspectives within the Catholic intellectual tradition from a variety of philosophical, theological, spiritual, literary, and artistic dimensions. As the Introduction by Bruce Ellis Benson will demonstrate, continental thought has a core strongly influenced by Catholic thought and that connection needs to be teased out in a much more in-depth way.

It is indeed somewhat surprising that Catholic intellectual traditions have not been singled out specifically for their influence on Continental philosophical lines of thought. So many of the French, German, and Italian philosophers commonly referenced in Continental circles were either raised in or conversant with Catholic scholarship and traditions, and yet surprisingly little has been written to bring this context to the forefront of contemporary scholarship. Quite simply, the Catholic Church permeates Continental thought, especially in the modern period, from René Descartes and Blaise Pascal to the likes of a Jacques Maritain, an Étienne Gilson, or a John Henry Newman. Figures as diverse as Edith Stein and Gabriel Marcel played important roles in establishing phenomenological and existentialist movements, and many more were formed within a Catholic context, though not formally being a part of Catholicism or having any desire to join the Catholic Church.

In addition to this obviously Catholic backdrop, the past few decades have seen a number of significant continental thinkers engage with religious themes in ways both productive and insightful. Nevertheless, the recognition of just how Catholicism has shaped continental thought continues to elude scholars. And with fewer philosophers overtly identifying as Catholic these days, it is often difficult to get a sense of the influence that Catholicism continues to wield upon philosophical writings and debates. Despite this trend, however, thinkers as diverse as Charles Taylor, Alasdair MacIntyre, Jean-Luc Marion, Adriaan Peperzak, John Caputo, Gianni Vattimo, Mario Perniola, Richard Kearney, and Michel Henry circulate around the Catholic Church as it informs their respective works in significant ways. In particular, debates within those parts of contemporary continental philosophy which have been concerned with what Dominique Janicaud termed the *"tournant théologique"*—primarily the phenomenological school, and especially in the work of Marion—have seen extensive contributions and participation by Catholic intellectuals.

The present international and interdisciplinary volume aims to address these questions from a variety of angles, hoping to produce a deeper and more sustained engagement with both Continental philosophical discourses and the Catholic intellectual heritage. At the same time, however, it constitutes only an initial foray into what we hope might be a much more fruitful inquiry taken up by many others who have sensed the lack of engagement between these two traditions in our current context, and wish to pursue the intricate networks of influence that are much in need of sorting out.

Our first thanks are due to Andrew Cutrofello and Stefano Giacchetti for taking the initiative for this project and envisioning it from the start. Thanks are also due to the Hank Center for the Catholic Intellectual Heritage at Loyola University Chicago, under the guidance of Fr. Mark Bosco, S.J. and Michael P. Murphy, for suggesting and generously funding a collaborative effort like this one, something that was conceived as a conference co-sponsored by the Hank Center and the Philosophy Department at Loyola University Chicago. Without the support of the Hank Center, as well as its many industrious workers, including Gabi Steponenaite, John Crowley-Buck, and Guy Valponi, the initial conference that led to the present collection of essays would not have been possible.

We would also like to thank Mark Waymack, Hanne Jacobs, Hille Haker, John McCarthy, Susan Ross, Tom Regan, S.J., and Michael Garanzini, S.J., for the support they showed us throughout the duration of the events that followed. The Loyola University Chicago Philosophy Department, which has long been the home of scholars interested in the issues discussed in this volume, deserves our thanks as well for the wholehearted support they showed from day one.

Our thanks are extended especially to Jacob Torbeck and Chen Xin for organizing all of the practical details of the conference and for all of the hard work they contributed throughout the event. Kathleen McNutt and Marcos Norris were also dedicated to the task of making the conference a successful one and we are grateful for their participation as well.

We would also like to extend a special thank you to Bettina Bergo and Hugh Miller for reviewing Kathleen McNutt's translation of Jean-Luc Marion's article—and Kathleen for her very able translation, of course.

Introduction: God as Challenge: The Past and Future of Continental Philosophy of Religion

Bruce Ellis Benson

Upon seeing the Call for Papers with the title of "The Challenge of God: Continental Philosophy and the Catholic Intellectual Heritage," I wondered exactly how these papers, particularly those of the keynote addresses included here, would approach such a topic. I think it's safe to say that they (the authors and their papers in this volume) quite nicely work out the challenge in different and yet complementary ways. Further, one can see these different ways of considering such an issue as providing an outline both for the current state of the sub-discipline of "continental philosophy of religion" (CPR) and for its future. In what follows, I first wish to provide a kind of genealogy of CPR. After all, that there is something that can be called CPR is a relatively recent development that required a particular set of events. Moreover, if we pay attention to the phenomenon indicated by the subtitle of the conference—Continental Philosophy and the Catholic Intellectual Heritage—we can see that the Catholic intellectual tradition has been a (and probably even the) prime mover of CPR (not necessarily continental philosophy in general but CPR). Indeed, the keynote speakers at the conference have been some of the chief movers and shakers of CPR. Second, I wish to attend to the various ways in which these chapters articulate the "challenge." As I see it, they provide a glimpse of the spectrum of the options available to continental philosophers of religion. While some of these options are simply incompatible with one another, none of them (given the way CPR has developed) are out of line with CPR per se. Third, after considering those variations on the question, I then turn to how I see CPR playing out in the future. I believe these papers provide important indicators of how CPR can develop, but I want to suggest that there are some aspects which should need to find a greater place in CPR if it is going to continue to be a vital force in the world of philosophy of religion more broadly construed.

The introduction of phenomenology to the Catholic academy

Not all that long ago, the very idea of "continental philosophy of religion" (CPR) didn't really exist. To be sure, there were thinkers like Gabriel Marcel and Paul Ricoeur (one Catholic; one Protestant; both French) who were in effect *doing* CPR.

But they were in no sense part of a "movement" that could be called CPR. On the other hand, they were both inheritors of the phenomenological tradition, in their respective ways. Marcel was known as a "Christian existentialist" (a category that for some seemed like an oxymoron) and existentialism, at least of the twentieth-century variety (for such a term has been applied to such figures as St. Paul, Augustine, and Shakespeare), is deeply indebted to phenomenology. There are multiple important links that connect CPR to phenomenology. Yet CPR has, in its own way, moved from the kind of phenomenology associated with Husserl to something that claims to be more Husserlian than Husserl—we might say more "orthodox." Further, while much of CPR is related to and grows out of phenomenology, not all thinkers working in CPR arise directly from that tradition. For CPR to emerge, though, a new conception of phenomenology was required, one that built upon Edmund Husserl and Martin Heidegger but likewise went beyond and even contradicted them. Early key thinkers in this movement were Jacques Derrida, who effectively blazed a trail (with the help of his North American interpreter, John D. Caputo) and Emmanuel Levinas (who, though older than Derrida, wasn't introduced to the North American context until later, though then with the help of scholars like Adriaan Peperzak). These thinkers helped usher in the era of the full flowering of CPR.

It is not too much to say that the establishment of the Husserl Archives at the Catholic University of Louvain in Belgium was a key moment in changing Catholic thinking and education, in philosophy to be sure but also in other disciplines. Father Leo Van Breda, O.F.M. then a doctoral student at Leuven, visited Husserl's widow not long after his death and discovered 40,000 pages of unpublished manuscripts. Through a process that reads somewhat like a spy novel, he was able to smuggle those manuscripts out of Germany with diplomatic immunity.[1] Why this represented such an important move is that, at the time, Leuven was heavily Neo-scholastic in terms of teaching and research interests. While Van Breda was not alone in his interest in Husserl, the climate of the Institute of Philosophy was hardly phenomenological in nature. Despite this, the Neo-scholastics found a kind of ally in Husserl, whose emphasis on "the things themselves" fit well with Thomist realism.[2]

Because of the highly international nature of the university, promising students came from throughout the world to study philosophy and theology. Of course, it would be too simple to trace phenomenology from Louvain to North America. Many of the early proponents of the movement in North America were at best distantly related to Louvain. For one thing, Husserl had a number of North Americans come to study with him in Göttingen and Freiburg, such as Marvin Farber, Dorion Cairns, and Charles Hartshorne. Further, given the upheaval of the Second World War in Europe, some phenomenologists emigrated to North America, such as Moritz Geiger, Aron

---

[1] See Leo Van Breda, "The Rescue of Husserl's *Nachlass* and the Founding of the Husserl Archives," in *History of the Husserl-Archives* (Dordrecht: Springer, 2007), pp. 39–69.

[2] The great divide in Husserlian texts would seem to be *Ideas I*, in which Husserl seems to turn to an explicitly idealistic position. But this would be an oversimplification. My own view is that Husserl rejects the realist–idealist divide as commonly posited, though I can't argue for that here. For a brief but insightful discussion of this, see Dan Zahavi, *Husserl's Phenomenology* (Stanford, CA: Stanford University Press, 2003), pp. 68–72.

Gurwitsch, and Alfred Schütz. In North America, centers for phenomenology early on were places like the New School for Social Research (NYC), SUNY Buffalo, Toronto, and McGill.

Yet there were many Roman Catholics who studied with Husserl and found his work congenial to their faith or as a kind of springboard to conversion. One is Dietrich von Hildebrand, who studied with both Husserl and Max Scheler, and credits the influence of Scheler in his conversion to Catholicism. Another is Edith Stein, who served as one of Husserl's assistants, and worked to bring about a kind of synthesis between Husserl and medieval thought. In Scheler, she found a Catholic who was nevertheless a highly respected philosopher. Given her then current identity as an atheist, this was a revelation. While she was particularly influenced by Thomas, her positions on various matters are not strictly Thomistic in nature.[3] Although there are differing views regarding the success of her project, there is no question that the notion of intentionality—central to phenomenology—is taken over from the Scholastics through Franz Brentano, with whom Husserl studied. However, there were others, including philosophers influenced by Husserl though not his students per se, such as Martin Heidegger and Scheler (both of whom eventually left the church). It is not incidental that Heidegger wrote his *Habilitationsschrift* on Dun Scotus.[4] The early phenomenologist Roman Ingarden was a teacher of John Paul II, who himself was a phenomenologist and was influenced by Husserl, Scheler, and von Hildebrand.

It comes as no surprise to discover that this trajectory is likewise true of Louvain, particularly in the 1960s. Two of the most influential thinkers in phenomenology and CPR are Msgr. Robert Sokolowski at the Catholic University of America, who finished his PhD in 1963 at Louvain, and Father William Richardson, S.J. who earned the PhD and *Maître agrégé* and taught at Fordham University and then Boston College. Whereas the former is renowned as a Husserl scholar, the latter wrote a magisterial work on Heidegger that was supervised by Alphonse de Waelhens, who had published a very early work on Heidegger.[5] One can find numerous Catholic institutions with faculty who studied at Louvain and have spent time at the Husserl Archives. Yet, in recent decades, many Catholic institutions in North America have themselves become centers for CPR. Such institutions include Boston College, Duquesne University, Fordham University, Gonzaga University, Loyola University Chicago, Loyola University Maryland, Loyola Marymount University, the University of Dallas, and Villanova University. Georgetown University and the University of Notre Dame are notable exceptions to this description. There are, of course, quite a number of non-Catholic universities that have faculty working in continental thought, though they

---

[3] See Sarah Borden Sharkey, "Edith Stein and Thomas Aquinas on Being and Essence," *American Catholic Philosophical Quarterly* 82 (2008), pp. 87–103.

[4] For more on these connections to Scholasticism, see Dermot Moran, *Introduction to Phenomenology* (New York: Routledge, 2000), particularly the chapters on Brentano and Heidegger.

[5] These texts were, respectively, Robert Sokolowski, *The Formation of Husserl's Concept of Constitution* (The Hague: Martinus Nijhoff, 1964) and William J. Richardson, S.J., *Heidegger: Through Phenomenology to Thought* (The Hague: Martinus Nijhoff, 1962). Both of these texts were published in the *Phaenomenologica* series put out by the Husserl Archives. Also see Alphonse De Waelhens, *La philosophie de Martin Heidegger* (Louvain: Éditions de L'Institut Supérieur de Philosophie, 1942).

generally do not work in CPR.[6] In any case, continental philosophy (and thus CPR) has never been mainstream. It has always been on the fringe of the philosophical world (in English-speaking countries) and it has been particularly prominent in Catholic institutions.

One explanation for the proliferation of CPR in Catholic institutions is the genealogy that I've offered above, even though it is hardly complete. That genealogy can be extended to include Paul Ricoeur, a Huguenot Protestant who taught at the Sorbonne and then Nanterre (now Paris X) before taking a post at Louvain for three years.[7] It is a significant part of our story that his assistant in the early 1960s was Jacques Derrida. While at Louvain, Ricoeur was offered the position of John Nuveen Professor of Philosophical Theology at the University of Chicago Divinity School, a chair that had been occupied by Paul Tillich. He served in that capacity until his retirement in 1992, though during this time he also taught at the Husserl Archives in Paris. His successor in that chair was Jean-Luc Marion, someone we will turn to later.[8]

Another explanation for the growth of CPR is that Catholic universities in North America often found themselves in similar situations to that of Louvain. In short, they were largely Thomist in orientation and phenomenology provided a way of thinking that was both different from and compatible with such an orientation. Further, phenomenology provided something that was deeply satisfying *existentially*, something that touched the individual in a personal way. Consider what John D. Caputo says of his early years of study:

> Having come of age intellectually in the bosom of the Catholic Church, having had the good fortune to be educated by a handful of intelligent, progressive Catholic teachers in high school and professors in college, it was the intellectual culture of Continental Europe, German and French, that most spoke to our hearts, addressing what we called in those days—and the word still has a use— the *existential* questions. Those questions show up pointedly in art, religion, and philosophy, and make up the passion of my life. They search for truth existentially conceived, which Søren Kierkegaard—a lifelong hero of mine—called a truth "to live and die" for. It was not an accident that so many Catholic graduate programs in philosophy—surrounded on all sides by an Anglo-Saxon Protestant culture and a philosophical climate that had abandoned American Pragmatism and adopted a more positivist, empiricist, and logicist approach to philosophy—went "Continental". After Vatican II, which was spearheaded by French and German

---

[6] A listing of programs "interested in, supportive of, or specializing in continental philosophy" can be found at the Society for Phenomenology and Existential Philosophy website. See: http://www.spep.org/resources/graduate-programs/.

[7] When Ricoeur taught at Louvain, he would have taught on the French faculty there. At that time, there were Flemish and French faculties. In 1968, at the insistence of the Flemish students who wanted to have their own university, the university was officially split into the Flemish-speaking Katholieke Universiteit Leuven and the French-speaking Université catholique de Louvain, located in Louvain-la-Neuve. This division took place over a number of years. In keeping with the historic usage of using the term Louvain in English, I follow that convention.

[8] Marion currently holds the Andrew Thomas Greeley and Grace McNichols Greeley Professor of Catholic Studies, a position that had been held by David Tracy until his retirement.

theologians, Continental philosophy was the discourse of choice for most Catholic and recovering Catholic philosophers who were looking for an alternative to the austere scholasticism on which they were raised.[9]

Here I think Caputo lays out what would have been likely the two alternatives of the time and argues that neither seemed like good choices. Regarding scholasticism, his own take was that it was "austere," which I take to mean that (among other things) it was theoretical and detached from everyday life. Yet the alternative of positivism that had invaded most of the centers of higher learning—certainly the "Ivy League"—was not really an option. One can't forget that positivism ruled out the possibility of either ethics or religion making truth claims. In fact, as long as positivism reigned in North America (up until the 1980s), it really wasn't respectable to be a religious believer in philosophical circles such as the American Philosophical Association (APA). The proof for that claim is simple: once logical positivism had been thoroughly discredited, religious believers started to make significant inroads into such circles, and many of them explicitly cited this change. It also led to the rise of the Society of Christian Philosophers (SCP) in 1978. Officially, the SCP endorses no particular school of philosophy, though most of its members work in the analytic tradition (doing what I will term here analytic philosophy of religion, APR). The success of APR is signaled by the nearly 1,000 members of SCP and that their publications appear with prestigious journals and university presses.

A somewhat different take on being exposed to continental philosophy can be found in Adriaan Peperzak, who writes:

> While studying at the Institute for Philosophy at the University of Leuven in Belgium, I continued to discover the spiritual world of old and new philosophers. Kant, Hegel, Heidegger, Husserl, and French phenomenology were interpreted and admired by my professors, several of whom were priests; but, although the Institute had been founded as a school for Neo-Thomism, most of them refused to speak about the links between philosophy, faith, theology, and spirituality .... Although the climate of Leuven was Catholic, the theoretical assumptions on which most professors in philosophy based their teaching were hardly different from those that ruled the University of Paris, where I obtained my doctorate. There the only professor who thematized the links between philosophy and theology was Paul Ricoeur, whom I got to know and greatly admire while he was the director of my dissertation.[10]

What Peperzak is talking about here becomes clear when he says that his professors both in Louvain and Paris had "accepted the modern postulate that separates autonomous reason, as displayed in philosophy and the sciences, from a theology that appeals not only to historical sciences and philosophical thought, but also, and principally, to the

---

[9] John D. Caputo, *Hope against Hope: Confessions of a Postmodern Pilgrim* (Minneapolis, MN: Fortress Press, 2015), p. 5.

[10] Adriaan Theodoor Peperzak, *Philosophy between Faith and Theology: Addresses to Catholic Intellectuals* (Notre Dame, IN: University of Notre Dame Press, 2005), p. 17.

authority of Scripture and the Church." He rightly connects this view with modernity, though he claims that "'postmodern' is a word with so many meanings, including several vague and confused ones, that its utility has become minimal."[11] I agree that we are at the place where the word "postmodern" doesn't seem to do enough work, though no one has come up with a better term to replace whatever it is that comes after modernity (itself a fraught term), assuming that modernity is really over (itself a fraught assumption). At least the term "postmodern" reminds us that we are still connected to modernity in deep ways.

However, what I find interesting about these two accounts is that they are so *similar*. This might not be apparent at first glance. Caputo speaks highly of the appearance of continental philosophy because it spoke to him existentially. Similarly, Peperzak speaks of philosophy as being "a way of life." Peperzak's worry is that, all too often, scholars both secular and Catholic disconnect their lives and traditions from their philosophizing. In so speaking, Peperzak is following Pierre Hadot's emphasis that ancient philosophy *was* a way of life. Hadot quotes Plutarch as saying: "Socrates did not set up a grandstand for his audience and did not sit upon a professorial chair; he had no fixed timetable for talking and walking with his friends .... He was the first to show that at all times and in every place, in everything that happens to us, daily life gives us the opportunity to do philosophy."[12] If philosophy truly is a way of life, then *everything* in our lives is connected to it. Another way of putting this is that all philosophy is autobiographical. Peperzak speaks of "the existential elements of life" as conditioning our thinking.[13] This is one of the great mistakes of modern thinking—that one's everyday life and one's scholarly work are two different things. If anything, it is exactly the opposite. *Who* we are, *how* we live, and *what* circumstances we find ourselves in are all very much connected to our thinking and writing. In this respect, Caputo and Peperzak fundamentally agree.

This recognition that philosophy is a way of life may seem new—or, at least, *new to us*. As it turns out, it's a very ancient notion. Whereas modern thinking disconnects everyday life from thought, pre-modern thinking sees them as deeply connected. Moreover, modern thinking puts forth the idea that we can know the world "objectively," which essentially is a claim that we can know in such a way that our subjectivity—that we are subjects—can be left behind. Yet we always see the world from a point of view, something that both Husserl and Heidegger realize. Yet even this language is problematic, for it fails to take into account our existential being (which is not reducible to anything like a mental "view"). This is why talking about "world views" [*Weltanschaungen*] is, at the very least, problematic. For philosophy to be a way of life it must not simply be thought but *lived*. Or, better, it can only be thought *by* being

---

[11] Ibid., p. 195.
[12] Plutarch, *Whether a Man Should Engage in Politics When He Is Old*, quoted in Pierre Hadot, *What Is Ancient Philosophy?* (trans. Michael Chase; Cambridge, MA: Harvard University Press, 2004), p. 38. Also see Pierre Hadot and Arnold Davidson, ed., *Philosophy as a Way of Life* (Oxford: Blackwell, 1995), p. 38.
[13] He also claims that even much "postmodern" philosophy can still be characterized as "autonomous, theoretical, thematic, and disengaged" (*Philosophy between Faith and Theology*, p. 4), though he mentions no specific names.

lived. This is, as it turns out, what both Søren Kierkegaard and Friedrich Nietzsche make very clear. And this is also what makes their writings so interesting and inspiring, whether one agrees. It's not hard to see why Caputo would name Kierkegaard his hero. Both Kierkegaard and Nietzsche play a prominent role in CPR. It is not merely that their works are discussed but also that it is hard to overstate their influence on thinking being done today.

I have discussed the importance of Husserl for CPR, but here we need to turn to Heidegger. Among the important texts for the development of CPR are the lecture courses that Heidegger gives in the 1920-1 academic year, "Introduction to the Phenomenology of Religion" and "Augustine and Neoplatonism." He makes it clear that he is describing religious life, not "dogmatic or theological-exegetical concerns." Instead, he wants to provide "guidance for phenomenological understanding," for it is only with this that "a new way for theology is opened up."[14] What Heidegger provides are readings of Galatians and Thessalonians that attempt to return to what he terms "primordial Christian religiosity."[15] His goal is not to find something like the "essence" of religious experience but to describe it and yet still acknowledge its historical and subjective features. It becomes clear in these courses that religious experience for Heidegger becomes paradigmatic for experience in general, though what he means is a kind of primordial Christianity that has not yet been covered over by Neoplatonic and Augustinian thought.

That paradigm of religious experience is clearly in evidence in Heidegger's *Being and Time* (BT), a text which has proved highly influential in directing the course of continental philosophy in general and CPR in particular. Ostensibly, the text is about the question of the meaning of Being, yet Heidegger ends up studying the being of a particular being—Dasein. As such, BT becomes a deep phenomenological investigation as to how Dasein exists, in a very similar way to the way one experiences religiosity. To be sure, the work is truly phenomenological in nature. And yet Heidegger himself, the former seminarian, reminds us that he could have never embarked on this path apart from his theological background.[16] In the years leading up to BT, he spent time studying the medieval scholastics and mystics, Luther, Hegel, Schleiermacher, Otto, and Dilthey. Yet a thinker who remains very close to Heidegger—and to whom he comes even closer over time—is Kierkegaard. Although Heidegger does not take up Kierkegaard's notion of "spirit," which he thinks entangles Kierkegaard in Hegelian metaphysics, in BT he does take much over from Kierkegaard's ontology of the human being.[17] Like Kierkegaard, Heidegger believes that Dasein can only be understood by the way of its relations both to the world and to others. The Kierkegaardian features of Heidegger's thought—some of

---

[14] Martin Heidegger, *The Phenomenology of Religious Life* (trans. Mattias Fricsch and Jennifer Anna Gosetti-Ferencei; Bloomington: Indiana University Press, 2004), p. 47.
[15] Ibid., p. 57.
[16] For a masterful treatment of Heidegger's relation to theology, see Theodore Kisiel, *The Genesis of Heidegger's Being and Time* (Berkeley and Los Angeles: University of California Press, 1993), particularly the chapter titled "Theo-logical Beginnings."
[17] Martin Heidegger, *What Is Called Thinking* (trans. Fred D. Wieck and J. Glen Gray; New York: Harper & Row, 1968), p. 213.

which he acknowledges and others of which he hides—are many. Heidegger follows Kierkegaard in relating everyday, historical life to thought. The existential themes that concerned Kierkegaard likewise concern Heidegger, though these are transformed into non-religious themes. Whereas authenticity and fallenness for Kierkegaard are explicitly Christian notions, for Heidegger they are simply descriptions of how Dasein exists. Regarding authenticity, Heidegger employs the Kierkegaardian themes of anxiety, repetition, and the moment. He likewise is influenced by Kierkegaard in speaking of "leveling down" and such phenomena as idle talk, curiosity, and ambiguity.[18] Finally, Heidegger follows Kierkegaard in emphasizing death and anticipation as basic to human existence.

The development of CPR in North America

One of the key moments on the way to CPR was the appearance in 1984 of Mark C. Taylor's text *Erring*, in which Derrida is presented as a thinker that has something significant to say about religion.[19] That this was a view that seemed novel at the time is an understatement. For Derrida had been deemed by many as someone who promoted an agenda that was anti-realist, relativistic, and even simply nihilistic (though many who made these charges were often unclear as to what they really meant). Those who embraced such views saw Derrida as an ally; those who eschewed them saw Derrida as the enemy. Early on, Derridean reception in North America was mainly in English departments at Johns Hopkins, Yale, and Cornell universities, though he was also read in philosophy and theology departments to a lesser extent. For many in English departments, his notion of "deconstruction" provided a model of textual reading that that was often more destructive than helpful. It would not be too much to say that such a "method" resulted in some interesting readings of texts but just as often readings that were hard to take seriously, such as the "explication" I once heard at a prominent university that Thomas Paine's *Common Sense* showed that the American Revolution was about *food*.[20]

Another important milestone for Derrida's reception as someone who has theological interests and is not easily put into a neatly packed box marked "deconstruction" is Kevin Hart's book *The Trespass of the Sign*, which appeared in 1989.[21] What is particularly important about Hart's book is that it displays a deep theological knowledge combined with a sophisticated understanding of Derrida. Similarly, while Caputo's book *Radical Hermeneutics* (1987) is more philosophical than theological, it likewise shows that Derrida's thinking is not only not nihilistic but lends itself to many religious themes.[22]

---

[18] These particular themes come from Søren Kierkegaard, *Two Ages* (trans. Howard V. Hong and Edna H. Hong; Princeton, NJ: Princeton University Press, 1978).
[19] Mark C. Taylor, *Erring: A Postmodern A/theology* (Chicago, IL: University of Chicago Press, 1984).
[20] Derrida makes it clear that deconstruction is not a method but something that naturally occurs.
[21] Kevin Hart, *The Trespass of the Sign: Deconstruction, Theology and Philosophy* (Cambridge: Cambridge University Press, 1989).
[22] John D. Caputo, *Radical Hermeneutics: Repetition, Deconstruction, and the Hermeneutic Project* (Bloomington: Indiana University Press, 1987).

However, before Caputo became explicitly Derridean, he had published various books that bring Heidegger together with Aquinas, provide both an account and critique of Heidegger's theological turnings, and deconstruct standard ethical views by drawing on Kierkegaard, Nietzsche, and Derrida.[23]

The year 1997 was a pivotal year for the development of CPR in North America. It was the first year of Caputo's postmodernism conferences at Villanova, this one titled "Religion and Postmodernism" and held in September. It drew a crowd of about 400 participants. That conference included Marion, Richard Kearney, Merold Westphal, David Tracy, Michael J. Scanlon, Mark C. Taylor, Edith Wyschogrod, Françoise Meltzer, and John Dominic Crossan. Yet many of these talks had responses by Derrida, who also participated in a roundtable discussion with Marion on the nature of the gift. In October of that same year, at a meeting at the Society for Phenomenology and Existential Philosophy, Norman Wirzba and I announced the formation of the Society for Continental Philosophy and Theology. We had simply placed flyers at the registration table, not knowing if anyone would show up, but the room was packed. One couldn't say at this point that CPR now existed, yet these conferences and society meetings brought together a critical mass of people interested in doing what came to be known as CPR. The initial board of the society included Caputo, Peperzak, Tracy, Westphal, Wirzba, Wyschogrod, and myself. Yet another event of that year was a publication in which Caputo also truly baptizes Derrida as a theological thinker in *The Prayers and Tears of Jacques Derrida: Religion without Religion*.[24] His text builds upon his previous work on Kierkegaard, Heidegger, and Levinas, yet decisively demonstrates that Derrida is a theological thinker who is somewhere between his Jewish upbringing and Christianity. And he also publishes *Deconstruction in a Nutshell: A Conversation with Jacques Derrida*, a text that provides as clear an introduction to deconstruction as can be imagined.[25]

That Derrida can be read as quasi-religious thinker—or even as a religious person—can be explained by looking at his texts.[26] One of these is titled "How to Avoid Speaking: Denials." Derrida begins with the notion of the trace, a notion that goes back to a much older text of Levinas. This immediately gets him to the question of negative theology (*apophasis*) and he links it to the use of such ideas in his corpus as *différance*, the supplement, and the pharmakon. Already in his essay titled "*Différance*," he notes that difference resembles negative theology "occasionally to the point of being

---

[23] John D. Caputo, *Heidegger and Aquinas: An Essay on Overcoming Metaphysics* (New York: Fordham University Press, 1982); *Demythologizing Heidegger* (Bloomington: Indiana University Press, 1993); and *Against Ethics: Contributions to a Poetics of Obligation with Constant Reference to Deconstruction* (Bloomington: Indiana University Press, 1993).

[24] John D. Caputo, *The Prayers and Tears of Jacques Derrida: Religion without Religion* (Bloomington: Indiana University Press, 1997).

[25] John D. Caputo, *Deconstruction in a Nutshell: A Conversation with Jacques Derrida*, ed. and with a commentary by John D. Caputo (New York: Fordham University Press, 1997).

[26] A reading of Derrida's texts vis-à-vis their relation religion that very explicitly does *not* see them as quasi-religious but strongly atheistic is Martin Hägglund, *Radical Atheism: Derrida and the Time of Life* (Stanford, CA: Stanford University Press, 2008). I find this reading unconvincing on multiple levels, though I cannot make a sustained critique here. For Caputo's (highly critical) response, see John D. Caputo, "The Return of Anti-Religion: From Radical Atheism to Radical Theology," *Journal for Cultural and Religious Theory* 11 (2011), pp. 32–125.

indistinguishable" from it. Yet he qualifies this by saying that the "aspects of *différance* which [he delineates] are not theological."[27] For Derrida, theology and deconstruction are separated in that the former is concerned with God's hyperessentiality that goes beyond predication and being. So he tells us that negative theology is not simply the same as deconstruction and yet the two are not completely separable either, for they both partake of the logic that says and yet unsays precisely at the moment of saying.

Another text is Derrida's autobiographical reflections titled "Circumfession," which takes the pattern of Augustine's *Confessions* as its model. He speaks of

> my religion about which nobody understands anything, any more than does my mother who asked other people a while ago, not daring to talk to me about it, if I still believed in God ... but she must have known that the constancy of God in my life is called by other names, so that I quite rightly pass for an atheist.[28]

What is Derrida's religion and who is Derrida's God? He is unwilling or unable to delineate either, though they are "unorthodox" enough that he would seem to be an atheist. Yet, like Augustine, he asks: "*Quid ergo amo, cum Deum meum amo?* [what therefore do I love, when I love my God?]," something which Augustine asks in his *Confessions* but *after* his conversion. Finally, Derrida claims "not only do I pray, as I have never stopped doing all my life, and pray to him, but I take him here and take him as my witness."[29]

A third text is *The Gift of Death*, which contains a sustained reading of the story in which Abraham nearly kills Isaac. Derrida leads up to this story by discussing the logic of sacrifice. In French, the text is *Donner la mort*, a euphemism for committing suicide. But his reading is that the logic of sacrifice is that one gives up something of oneself—or even oneself—on behalf of someone else. Such a logic—which one finds in love, the gift, and other figures—is one that can never really explain itself. His reading of Christianity is that it revolves around this logic of sacrifice, which always involves a secret. Abraham cannot tell Sarah or Isaac what he is about to do. Further, he cannot really explain his action. Following Kierkegaard, Derrida invokes the tension between the ethical duty of "giving reasons" for what one does versus an absolute responsibility that cannot explain itself. To do so would be to revert to the ethical, which Kierkegaard insists that Abraham must not do if he is going to be true to God and his responsibility. To give reasons for an action is not, thinks Kierkegaard, to take an absolute responsibility for what one does. Derrida closes the text by invoking Mt. 6.14, which advises giving in secret (not letting the left hand know what the right one is doing). Is this, as Nietzsche would argue, just a ruse to get an even bigger reward, a calculation much more shrewd than giving in the open? Or can one truly give a gift without entering an economy of reward and return? Derrida leaves this question regarding Nietzsche open, though he calls gift-giving and love not impossible but

---

[27] Jacques Derrida, "Differánce," in *Margins of Philosophy* (trans. Alan Bass; Chicago, IL: University of Chicago Press, 1982), p. 6.

[28] Jacques Derrida, "Circumfession," in Geoffrey Bennington and Jacques Derrida, *Jacques Derrida* (trans. Geoffrey Bennington; Chicago, IL: University of Chicago Press, 1993), pp. 154–155.

[29] Ibid., pp. 56–58.

the impossible. That gift giving—as well as love, hospitality, friendship—are in an important sense never fully pure is no reason not to pursue them.

Yet there is an important figure in the development of CPR that I have so far left out. In terms of reception history in North America, Derrida comes first and Emmanuel Levinas second. And this is not merely a North American phenomenon for, while Levinas published *Totality and Infinity* in 1961, it took quite some time before his thought became influential among French intellectuals. Of course, already in an early, lengthy essay (1962) Derrida pays deep attention to Levinas.[30] Although he is critical of Levinas, there is a deep appreciation for his project. Indeed, as Derrida matures as a philosopher, his thought becomes progressively more Levinasian. In an interview in 1986, he says "before a thought like that of Levinas, I never have any objection."[31] So what is this thought? One can read Levinas as responding (largely negatively though not entirely) to Husserl and Heidegger, yet his critique is really of the entire Western philosophical tradition. In brief, the criticism is that Western metaphysics is all about mastering (in one way or another) "otherness" so that there is "the rigorous coincidence between the thought" and the object "which this thought thinks."[32] That charge comes in a text about God and the point is that Western metaphysicians have attempted to "reduce" the otherness of the other to coincidence with the sameness of the same.

How does one overcome this basic problem, or can it even be overcome? Levinas calls for a rethinking of the very structure of philosophy. In place of the freedom of the "autonomy" of the subject called for by Immanuel Kant, Levinas calls for a "heteronomy" in which the other curbs my freedom. In effect, one becomes free by serving the other. Yet the question arises as to just who is this "other." If Levinas is correct, then the other can never be properly circumscribed and to attempt such is deeply unethical, for the otherness of the other escapes our grasp. Given Levinas's religious perspective, the paradigmatic figures for the other are the powerless: "The Other who dominates me in his transcendence is thus the stranger, the widow, and the orphan, to whom I am obligated."[33] Given how Levinas draws upon Hebrew Scriptures for his philosophy, it should come as no surprise that his is not merely an ethics but likewise a philosophy of religion. For Levinas, we encounter God *through* the other. "In the other, there is a real presence of God. In my relation to the other, I hear the Word of God. It is not a metaphor; it is not only extremely important, it is literally true. I'm not saying that the other is God, but that in his or her Face I hear the Word of God."[34] Of course, Levinas also makes clear that God is not merely another other but, instead, "other than the other, other otherwise, other with an alterity prior to the alterity of the other … to the point of his possible confusion with the agitation of the

---

[30] Jacques Derrida, "Violence and Metaphysics: An Essay in the Thought of Emmanuel Levinas," in *Writing and Difference* (trans. Alan Bass; Chicago, IL: University of Chicago Press, 1978).

[31] Jacques Derrida and Pierre-Jean Labarrière, *Alterities* (Paris: Osiris, 1986), p. 74.

[32] Emmanuel Levinas, "God and Philosophy," in *Of God Who Comes to Mind* (trans. Bettina Bergo; Stanford, CA: Stanford University Press, 1998), p. 55.

[33] Emmanuel Levinas, *Totality and Infinity: An Essay on Exteriority* (trans. Alphonso Lingis; Pittsburgh, PA: Duquesne University Press, 1996), p. 88.

[34] Emmanuel Levinas, *Entre Nous: On Thinking-of-the-Other* (trans. Michael B. Smith and Barbara Harshav; New York: Columbia University Press, 1998), p. 110.

there is [*il y a*]."[35] Yet it is precisely on this point—the lack of identity of the other—that Derrida is critical of Levinas. If we cannot identify the other, then how do we make a distinction between a human being and a stone? Further, Derrida points out that it is precisely the tradition of Greek philosophy that Levinas criticizes that makes his own project even possible. The problem is that, and here Derrida is simply quoting Levinas, one cannot "arrest philosophical discourse without philosophizing."[36] Not surprisingly, Levinas resists this charge. He begins the essay "God and Philosophy" by quoting what Derrida says at the end of "Violence and Metaphysics": "Not to philosophize is still to philosophize" and then goes on to insist that he can escape from the Greek *logos* of philosophy. Whether such a project could be successful is a matter that I cannot discuss here.

The idea that the *logos* of philosophy has dominated theology is one that Heidegger takes up in a late text, "The Onto-theo-logical Constitution of Metaphysics." While the term "ontotheology" goes back to Kant, the concern for ontotheology has been a central theme driving CPR. Heidegger claims that "metaphysics is theology, a statement about God, because the deity enters into philosophy." In effect, God serves as the ground or ultimate foundation for philosophy by being the first or highest being and the first cause. *This* God is often termed "the god of the philosophers." As Heidegger points out, though, "the deity can come into philosophy only insofar as philosophy, of its own accord and by its own nature, requires and determines that and how the deity enters into it." The result is that "man can neither pray nor sacrifice" nor "fall to his knees in awe nor can he play music and dance before this god."[37] Instead, this is a thoroughly domesticized version of "God," one entirely within the domain of philosophy and there to do its bidding.

For Marion, the death of God proclaimed by Nietzsche is long overdue, since Marion reads Nietzsche as describing the death of the god of the philosophers. As such, it was merely an idol that "does not have any right to claim, even when it is alive, to be 'God.'"[38] In response to Heidegger's rhetorical question "will Christian theology one day resolve to take seriously the word of the apostle and thus also the conception of philosophy as foolishness?"[39] Marion responds by saying "to take seriously that philosophy is a folly means, for us, first (although not exclusively) taking seriously that the 'God' of onto-theology is rigorously equivalent to an idol."[40] Central to his text *God without Being* is the contrast of between the idol, which is merely a reflection of us and so like a mirror, and the icon, which is like a window through which we gaze and so it "summons sight in letting the visible ... be saturated little by little with the invisible."[41] Marion takes Paul's conception of Christ (as the "icon" of God, Col. 1.15) and claims

---

[35] Levinas, "God and Philosophy," pp. 55–78.
[36] Derrida, "Violence and Metaphysics," p. 152.
[37] Martin Heidegger, "The Onto-theo-logical Constitution of Metaphysics," in *Identity and Difference* (trans. Joan Stambaugh; Chicago, IL: University of Chicago Press, 2002), pp. 55, 56, 72.
[38] Jean-Luc Marion, *The Idol and Distance* (trans. Thomas A. Carlson; New York: Fordham University Press, 2001), p. 1.
[39] Martin Heidegger, "Introduction to 'What Is Metaphysics?'" trans. Walter Kaufmann, in *Pathmarks* (ed. William McNeill; Cambridge: Cambridge University Press, 1998), p. 288.
[40] Marion, *The Idol and Distance*, p. 18.
[41] Jean-Luc Marion, *God without Being: Hors-Texte* (trans. Thomas A. Carlson; Chicago, IL: University of Chicago Press, 1991), p. 17.

that Christ is the model of all icons, which he terms "saturated phenomena." Whereas Husserl's "principle of all principles" states that the object of consciousness appears "within the limits" of consciousness, Marion argues that some phenomena simply *exceed* those limits, which means that intuition is overwhelmed by that which is given. In such a case, the ego is no longer in control and is "mastered" by the object. In effect, Marion (following Levinas) is turning Husserlian phenomenology on its head. Marion is particularly concerned with the phenomenon of revelation, which is similar to the experience of going outside of Plato's cave. He terms this experience "bedazzlement," in which the intuition of intentionality is simply overwhelmed by sheer excess. Much like Levinas's idea of thinking "otherwise," Marion attempts "to think God without any conditions, not even that of Being," a God who is *agápê*, who appears to us as gift. The result is that "predication must yield to praise," so that "faith neither speaks nor states."[42] Marion asserts that there is a "language" that goes beyond the true and false language of predication.

Given all that we have seen so far, it is no wonder that Dominique Janicaud writes a text on the state of philosophy in France with the title *The Theological Turn of French Phenomenology*. In that text, he accuses Levinas and Marion (as well as Jean-Louis Chrétien and Michel Henry) of hijacking phenomenology for theological purposes. Although Levinas and Marion (like Ricoeur) make a point of publishing their "theological" works with one publisher and their "phenomenological" works with another, Janicaud's verdict is that the phenomenological texts are just as theological as the theological ones. As he puts it, "despite all the denials, phenomenological neutrality has been abandoned." Instead of providing "scientific" analysis, Janicaud accuses Marion and Chrétien of "theological veering" that "leads to analyses that verge on edification." Similarly, he accuses Levinas of "theological hostage-taking."[43] There are two obvious responses to Janicaud. One is that these "new phenomenologists" are actually trying to be *more* true to the principles of phenomenology than were Husserl and Heidegger. In this they may not succeed, but that is what they are trying to do. Second, the question has to be asked: why is some sort of scientific "neutrality" held up as the standard? Other than simply proclaiming it to be the standard, there is no *argument* that can be adduced that this is the way things must be. Of course, Janicaud is right that these religious thinkers—Levinas, a Jew; Henry, Marion, and Chrétien, Roman Catholics—have used phenomenology for causes that are at least partly, if not more, religious. But it's hard to see why focusing on religious phenomena—or even using religious phenomena (after all, we have seen that Heidegger takes primitive Christian experience as the model for experience in general) as guiding principles—is somehow *bad* or unscholarly.

Once we realize that there is no such thing as neutrality—which is what those who followed the logical positivists realized—then it becomes merely a matter of assumptions made that guide further analysis. To believe that there is no God is hardly any more "neutral" than to believe that God exists. Both are starting points. After all, one has to start *somewhere*—and that somewhere is never neutral. So one

---

[42] Ibid., pp. 106, 183.
[43] Dominique Janicaud, *The Theological Turn in French Phenomenology*, in *Phenomenology and the "Theological": The French Debate* (trans. Bernard G. Prusak; New York: Fordham University Press, 2000), pp. 68, 69, 43.

can never say "I am simply doing phenomenology" without any further qualification. However, once one makes such a recognition, then it is possible for CPR to bloom, as has been the case. It is no surprise that CPR in North America has blossomed precisely because of the reception of these decidedly religious figures. One of the reasons for this creative energy is that old assumptions regarding the relation of faith and reason have been strongly put into question. It is Derrida who reminds us that faith and reason always go together, that there is no reason that is without faith, whether scientific, philosophical, or theological.[44] But this, then, puts into question Kant's move of reason "making room for faith." Is it reason that is in control here, or does faith graciously make room for reason? It's not clear which has the upper hand. This is a central point in Levinas's "God and Philosophy," but it is likewise the theme of Marion's most recent book, *Believing in Order to See*.[45]

The challenge of God

The chapters in this volume illustrate where CPR stands today. Although not every chapter makes explicit mention of "the challenge of God," each can be read as dealing with this question in one way or another. We need to examine each in turn.

To begin, all of these authors are interested in giving up on the onto-theological project. Although only David Tracy's response to Peperzak and Caputo's paper mentions onto-theology explicitly, this concern is implicit in every chapter. Of course, we have already seen that Marion thinks that the death of God is that of the metaphysical God, the "god" of the omnis, the *causa sui*, the unmoved mover. Such a "god" was merely an idol before whom, Heidegger reminds us, one cannot dance and to whom one cannot pray. Consider the following denunciations of such a god. Peperzak puts it as follows: "As Plato already knew, no play of finite beings, essences, or ideas, and no combination of *universalia*, particularizations, and individual *concreta* can yield any God outside the gods of ancient Greece or the idols of modern and post-modern mythologies." Tracy speaks of a totality that leaves no room for God. Starting from the question of Being and how Being relates to God, Marion gives us the choice of "either Being as something to be possessed like property, or else Being as something to be received and given as a gift." Clearly, Marion prefers the latter. For Altizer, the metaphysical God is certainly dead, but there is no substitute, no "other" God to put in "god's" place. Kearney speaks of "losing the illusion of God," which he goes on to define as "sovereign superintendent of the universe."

So where does one go from here? I find it quite instructive that the authors in this text move in a very similar direction. Having shown that the theoretical, metaphysical god is problematic, they turn to an understanding of God that begins in religious experience. This is perhaps the single most important thing that they have in common. For instance, after having shown how the modern paradigm exalts the

---

[44] See Jacques Derrida, "Faith and Reason: The Two Sources of 'Religion' at the Limits of Reason Alone," in *Acts of Religion* (ed. Gil Anidjar; New York: Routledge, 2002), pp. 42–101.

[45] Jean-Luc Marion, *Believing in Order to See: On the Rationality of Revelation and the Irrationality of Some Believers* (trans. Christina Gschwandtner; New York: Fordham University Press, 2017).

solitary ego that creates a totality that leaves no room for God, Peperzak points to Jesus's challenge to any disciple who wishes to become great. He wonders whether "'Jesus' critique could also be applied to philosophers who not only want to follow Jesus as disciples but also desire to be founders of the highest wisdom". Since Jesus is concerned about the kingdom of heaven, his concern is not for building systems or empires "but the absolute dignity of each single person." Not surprisingly, Peperzak turns to Jesus's singling out of a child and comparing his reception to that of a child. Thus, the challenge of God becomes vocative—God calls us to follow. That call deeply resonates with Jean-Louis Chrétien's emphasis on the call and response structure that he believes is present in life in general and Christian faith in particular. To realize that we are called long before we theorize is humbling. To realize that, in treating the least of these with the greatest respect we are treating Jesus, gives us a formula that is perhaps the greatest challenge of all.

Marion takes a remarkably similar departure from the metaphysical god to that of Peperzak. He points out that, unlike the prodigal son who demands his *ousia* (being) and so is like "us all, who are spontaneously metaphysicians," Christ does not consider his *ousia* as something to be possessed. Instead, he empties himself (Phil. 3.7) "even to the point of taking on another ousia, the morphe doulou [the form of a servant]," which is exactly what the *returning* prodigal son is forced to take on voluntarily. Instead of the child here, we have the servant. But the principal is the same. Jesus rightly recognizes that he is "master and lord" (Jn. 13.13), but this is a form that he also rightly recognizes is a gift that cannot be possessed. Marion's analysis here is driven by multiple forces, but strongly by Nietzschean ones. Early on in his chapter, Marion quotes Nietzsche as saying that "Christ remains outside of metaphysics." And he picks up this Nietzschean thread toward the end of his chapter by noting that Zarathustra "only says *yes* to what *his* own will can want and endure," whereas "Christ says *yes to all* that the Father wants." Of course, one should add here that Nietzsche eventually (much later than *Thus Spoke Zarathustra*, indeed only in his last year of sanity) came to realize that giving up one's will really is the only course available.

In her chapter, Robyn Horner also begins in the realm of religious experience. She cites Jean-Yves Lacoste to the effect that our knowledge of God must be "in the domain of affection." That is, to understand God aright we must start with our experience of God. She insists (quite rightly) that "we must understand revelation in relational terms and relationships based on personal experience." Knowing God is not some abstract exercise; instead, it is deeply connected to our being. Accordingly, she turns to the Spiritual Exercises of Ignatius of Loyola. While these exercises are designed to accomplish many different things, they are clearly about coming to know God. In the process of becoming discerning, we come to understand who God is. In her response to Horner, J. Michelle Molina points out that the exercises are "a process, one knows them by making them, not by reading them." Along with Peperzak and others that we have considered so far, Molina reminds us that "self is a problem!" And the self has many different ways of getting in the way of knowing God. Like love, knowing God is something one *does*.

Caputo begins his chapter by reference to a current event in which "calling" plays an important role. Regarding a lesbian teacher at a local Catholic school, an op-ed appears in which the authors say "we are convinced that this is a moment when insistence on doctrinal adherence is clashing with what we believe the Spirit is unfolding in our history." At the heart of Caputo's chapter is the belief that Christianity is first and foremost a movement of the Spirit rather than a set of doctrines. He says that "the Spirit inspires by calling." Indeed, the doctrinal parts of the "way," which eventually comes to be known as "Christianity," are completely preceded by the *living* out of the teachings of Jesus. Scripture comes into being precisely by lived tradition. Caputo emphasizes that our conception of God is one that is continually being formed and that "tradition is an ongoing process of auto-correction." At stake here is what truly proves to be the driving mechanism of Christian faith. Surprisingly enough, Caputo could cite someone rather unexpected to bolster his point. While he was still Cardinal Ratzinger, Pope Benedict writes the following about Christianity: "Christianity is not an intellectual system, a collection of dogmas, or a moralism. Christianity is instead an encounter, a love story; it is an event."[46] Of course, this is not to say (and, no doubt, Ratzinger can hardly be thought of as saying) that doctrine or dogma has no place. Instead, it is question of *emphasis*. Yet Caputo's point is that, if it is the Spirit that brings about tradition and ultimately the scriptures and the hierarchy, the challenge of God is to continue to listen to the Spirit. Toward that end, Caputo quotes Pope Francis: "If the Christian is a restorationist, a legalist, if he wants everything clear and safe, then he will find nothing. Tradition and memory of the past must help us to have the courage to open up new areas to God." Or, to put this in terms of Caputo's respondent John McCarthy, it is "the constant challenge of the prophetic." Of course, for Caputo the "Spirit" is ultimately *us*—there is not some "other" entity. Further, "the challenge of God is that God is not about *winning*." In other words, when Paul talks about the wisdom of God as being foolishness and the strength of God being weakness, there is no Gnostic move that turns it back into a kind of wisdom and strength.

Although Altizer is best known for his "Death of God" theology, in line with what we've seen so far I find it interesting that he says that "the truth is that all of our great Christian epic visionaries are far more deeply theological than are our theologians." The danger for Altizer is that theologians, who are understandably hemmed in by certain Christian commitments, tend not to be all that visionary. Thus, Adam Kotsko makes the point (echoing Altizer) that "literature—much more than the institutional church or traditional academic theology—is where the most radical theology is happening." One might make that point another way. Apart from David Tracy (who taught at the University of Chicago Divinity School) and John McCarthy (who is in the theology department at Loyola), all of the other authors are not in theology departments. Perhaps that is at least one reason why they are able to say more visionary things than one might expect from someone in a theology department. In any case, I think Altizer is right that "one of the ultimate failures of Christianity is the failure of its thinkers and theologians to enter the depths of Christianity itself." While one might ask what exactly it means for him to say that "nothing is more revealing about Christian theology than its deep inability to know the crucified Jesus as the Crucified God," one can certainly

---

[46] Joseph Ratzinger, "Homily for Msgr. Luigi Giussani," *Communio: International Catholic Review* 31 (2004), p. 685.

agree that, all too often, theologians have not sufficiently taken seriously enough how God crucified (and even simply God as *human*) must challenge any onto-theological conceptions of God.

In the final chapter, Kearney gives us a conception of God that "anatheistic," in which the "ana" points us to what comes after the death of the metaphysical god, a "returning to God after God" or an "after-faith." Whereas for Altizer God is simply dead and for Caputo the Spirit ends up being us, Kearney claims that the human and the divine are involved in a "play of mutual recreation" between them. He begins by noting that *poiein* [creation] in Genesis is framed as "let *us*" [*Elohim*], so that creation from its very beginning is relational in nature. The seventh day, on which God does not create, is left for human creation. In so doing, Kearney is drawing upon Jewish tradition that maintains that "finite creatures [are] called to collaborate with God in the completion of tradition." What he calls "*theopoiesis*" [divine making] is precisely this mutual recreation. As he makes clear, "anatheism has nothing to do with Alpha-Gods or Omni-Gods." Instead, "it is about re-imaging- and re-living—the sacred in the 'least of these.'" Anatheism for Kearney is what comes after the metaphysical god.

As should be clear at this point, there is a rather deep-seated agreement in these papers, even despite their differences. Peperzak points to the figure of the child and the least of these as calling us to be servants. Marion continues this emphasis by reminding us that Jesus takes on the form of a slave and thus is able to provide an ultimate "yes" to that which the Father wills. Horner reminds us that receiving revelation means that we put ourselves in a position to hear. Caputo emphasizes the calling of the Spirit that both brought the church into existence and continues to support it. Altizer reminds us that too often we cling to a "standard" view of God and do not question our own assumptions. Kearney likewise returns us to the least of these as the basis for rethinking God. All in all, these papers are driven by their desire to escape from metaphysics and to rethink God from the perspective of practice. Where they differ is in how far one needs to go in order to avoid onto-theology.

The future of CPR

These are the main two alternatives in CPR at this point, at least in Catholic theology. One way of putting this is by way of the difference between two figures. On the one hand, there is Marion, who despite his startling ways of looking at Christian ideas remains conservative and orthodox. On the other hand, there is Caputo, who has taken the route of Derrida's "religion without religion" and so moved away from orthodoxy (here I am reluctant to say just how far that is the case; I would prefer to let Caputo speak for himself). Of course, there are many who work in CPR who write with no explicit religious commitments, scholars such as Thomas Carlson, Jeffrey Kosky, Tyler Roberts, and Mary-Jane Rubenstein. Moreover, there is an entire group of scholars who are part of CPR, but don't fit as neatly into the genealogy that I've given in the first section. French thinkers like Stanislas Breton, Emmanuel Falque, and Jean-Yves Lacoste naturally follow in this trajectory. But things are less clear-cut when we think of Giles Deleuze or Alan Badiou. Italian thinkers like Giorgio Agamben and Gianni Vattimo have played important roles in CPR, and the latter has written about his own take on religion and faith. In fact, if we consider the introduction to *The Future of Continental Philosophy of Religion* (a text containing papers from the last conference Caputo held at Syracuse), we might conclude there isn't any clear "future" because there is no homogenous past. CPR has been influenced by far more figures than the ones considered here. The editors of that text claim the following: "What we are suggesting, therefore, about the future of continental philosophy of religion is that we have come to a time when it is more about its different futures."[47] So the future remains varied, open to different directions.

But let me close by suggesting two ways of thinking the future of CPR and its openness to different directions. One suggestion concerns how CPR is done. Over the years, I've come to see that CPR in North America is largely *expository* in nature. Papers and books tend to be along the lines of "Heidegger on such and such" or "Levinas's view of X." In one very important sense, this is a key strength of CPR. Those who work in CPR are generally well-grounded in tradition. They have a sense of the historical place of a thinker, how that thinker's ideas relate to the time period, and how that time period relates to the history of philosophy more broadly. There is much to commend here. Derrida speaks of the importance of a "doubling commentary" in which the reader attempts to provide a reading that is as close to the text as possible. Without this "guardrail," as he calls it, "critical production would risk developing in any direction at all and authorize itself to say almost anything."[48] Careful exposition, then, is crucial.

However, as you probably realized while I was formulating the previous point, there is a "but" coming. Derrida goes on to say that "this indispensable guardrail has always only *protected*, it has never *opened*, a reading."[49] Exactly what counts as a "doubling" rather than "constructive" commentary is somewhat difficult to parse out, except at the extremes. Clearly, there is a continuum between the two. The most remarkable doubling commentary I have ever read is one on Heidegger's *Origin of the Work of Art*. It tries to stay so close to the text that, at points, it literally simply repeats what Heidegger writes. What makes this commentary so strange is that it constantly shifts back and forth between quoting Heidegger (without any quotation marks) and commenting, with no separation of the two. Of course, most commentaries have a little bit more room between the text and the commentary. In fact, it's safe to say that even authors who are attempting something like a doubling commentary still end up adding their own point of view. It is like the classical music performer who simply wants to "get it right" and thinks that she is *merely* repeating the score when in reality there is no such thing as pure repetition. Those of us who are jazz musicians are much more aware of the fact that we are constantly improvising upon pieces and the tradition. In other words, we know that tradition is not static and that we cannot help but add to it. Put another way, to honor and carry on a tradition *is* to add to it.

---

[47] Clayton Crockett, B. Keith Putt, and Jeffrey W. Robbins, eds., *The Future of Continental Philosophy of Religion* (Bloomington: Indiana University Press, 2014), pp. 2–3.

[48] Jacques Derrida, *Of Grammatology* (corrected, ed., trans. Gayatri Chakravorty Spivak; Baltimore, MD: Johns Hopkins University Press, 1998), p. 158.

[49] Ibid.

Of course, the authors in this volume do not represent those who merely exposit texts of other thinkers. They are among the thinkers whom other people exposit! Still, the general tendency in CPR is respectful commentary that hews rather close to the text. One may be critical at points, even seriously disagree with the author, but still stay within the bounds of commentary. As I say, this is a *tendency*, not anything like an absolute generality. However, the result is that, in CPR, while there are important authors who move in constructive ways beyond the established boundaries and push the dialogue forward (like the authors in this volume), most everyone else comments on these thinkers and that commentary often is about "getting it right." Having spent significant time at both the Hegel and the Husserl archives, I was often astounded how little anyone asked "but is Hegel or Husserl right?" as opposed to simply "what did they mean?"

What would it look like for CPR to become truly constructive in nature? Here is what I have in mind. A while back, I was speaking with a friend of mine who works on a particular topic in one of the philosophers represented in this volume. My comment was: "This is all very interesting, but what's *your* view of this particular topic?" A way of getting at this—as well as a way of moving forward—is by considering APR. Given my work, I am often asked to explain the difference between CPR and APR, or the difference between continental and analytic philosophy. We are familiar with the usual stereotypes. Continental philosophers write unclear prose (what the Brits call "woolly"); they don't make arguments; they use weird jargon. In contrast, analytic philosophers tend to be clearer and use arguments, but they often talk about wholly theoretical things that have nothing to do with real life—more like some kind of logical puzzle. Although stereotypes often have some degree of truth to them, I think that these stereotypes are largely unhelpful. For example, APR has its own weird jargon and CPR is hardly devoid of argument. Yet I think the real difference between CPR and APR is the latter's *tendency* is to be much more constructive in nature. There is much to praise about that. Having the courage to state one's own views, to actively put together a theory about some topic, to put something out there that is clear enough to be criticized is commendable.

Yet I'm sure you can hear that there's a "but" coming here too. Practitioners of APR all too often appear to be creating ex nihilo. They aren't, of course, but it often seems that way since they tend to write in a non-historical fashion. If practitioners of CPR sometimes get lost in history, APR tends to be disconnected from it or, at the very least, not aware of how much their work is indebted to tradition. Of course, one doesn't have to be aware of tradition to be influenced by it. Yet, since one is always embedded in a tradition—and multiple ones at the same time—it is much better to be aware of what that tradition is, at least to the extent one *can* be aware. However, the challenge is also to have tradition serve us rather than to simply serve tradition. Nietzsche writes in his essay on history: "We want to serve history only to the extent that history serves life: for it is possible to value the study of history to such a degree that life becomes stunted and degenerate."[50] While I'm not suggesting that CPR is filled with "stunted and degenerate" philosophers, it strikes me that CPR can be easily become a ghetto in which one is

---

[50] Friedrich Nietzsche, *On the Uses & Disadvantages for Life*, in *Untimely Meditations* (trans. R.J. Hollingdale; Cambridge: Cambridge University Press, 1983), Foreword.

preaching to the choir. That is *not* to say that APR is not ghetto-like in its own way, but the ghetto of APR happens to be considerably larger. Indeed, one need only think of the very category "philosophy of religion" to see that, without any further qualification, it almost always means *analytic* philosophy of religion (and this becomes clear if one considers listings in PhilJobs or looks at the catalogue from most university presses).

How, then, does tradition serve life? Nietzsche opens that same essay with a quotation from Goethe: "I hate everything that merely instructs me without augmenting or directly invigorating my activity."[51] According to the OED, the term "construct" means "to make or form by fitting the parts together."[52] This is not ex nihilo construction, but one that is grounded in tradition. In her wonderful book, Catherine Keller reminds us that ex nihilo creation is a highly *masculine* way of thinking about creation and belongs to a discourse of power.[53] Thinking of construction in this way reminds us of our debt to tradition. Yet it also pushes us beyond mere tradition preservation, for construction is what enables us to keep tradition alive and growing. One can't help but think of the parable of the talents here, in which one person is given five talents and doubles these and another is given one talent but buries it in the ground out of fear (Mt. 25:14-30). Construction, then, takes us beyond mere exposition and doubling commentary, but still keeps us connected to tradition. To go back to a musical example, classical music tends to emphasize "originality" (or Bloom's anxiety of influence) but Baroque music and jazz are deeply connected to tradition. With this awareness, one may set out to be constructive by drawing on a wealth of resources, using historical texts to advance thought. This gives us a very different notion of "creativity," in the sense that it becomes about how one uses one's past. Instead of making the study of history an end in itself, one uses history as a springboard to the future.

Yet there is something further that CPR can do. If one thinks about the current situation of CPR and APR, one sees that they are divided less by thought than by institutions. Earlier, I mentioned the phenomenon of respective ghettos or silos. So CPR has the Society for Continental Philosophy and Theology; APR has the Society of Christian Philosophers. Work in CPR tends to be published with presses like Indiana and Fordham, which produce volumes that people in APR generally don't read. Of course, CPR returns the favor by neglecting publications by those in APR. So why might now be a good time to change this? One of the things that has *begun* to take shape in APR is a move away from almost exclusive concern with questions of justification of belief to questions of practice. CPR has always been less interested in questions of belief than those of practice (or, better, how belief actually gets lived out). Such an emphasis should be abundantly clear from the papers in this volume. However, for instance, that Nicholas Wolterstorff has recently been publishing on liturgy is one indication of this move in APR. Further, I think we are at a time in which younger scholars, in particular, are less invested in the artificial distinction between continental and analytic. They don't see any reason to limit their projects to the boundaries of just

---

[51] Ibid.
[52] *The Oxford English Dictionary*, 2nd ed., s.v. "construct."
[53] Catherine Keller, *The Face of the Deep: A Theology of Becoming* (New York: Routledge, 2003).

one or the other. And these changes are likewise mirrored even in the APA, which now regularly accepts papers on continental figures (something that would have been unthinkable a couple decades ago).

What I would like to see happen is the development of a dialogue between CPR and APR. I have no naïve ideas that this will be easy. Yet I think it is quite possible. One of the things that we (folks in CPR and APR) can do is write in such a way that people on both "sides" can understand. While that means giving up some beloved jargon, what is gained is, I think, more than worth it. For the result will be that those among us who are authors will find that there are many more people reading their work and able to enter into dialogue with it. If I am forced to say "I don't think you understand me" when someone criticizes my work, then perhaps I need to write in such a way that I can be understood. I have heard Westphal say numerous times something along the lines of "I like to be clear enough so that people who disagree with me know exactly what they're disagreeing with." Another thing we can do is to be willing to read beyond the narrow confines of our respective silos. That is not always easy. But I would venture to say that, once one begins reading the work of the folks on the other "side," it becomes less and less clear that there really *is* another side. For instance, if one looks into work being done in APR on divine hiddenness, it soon becomes apparent that there is significant overlap between this topic and that of otherness (or the Other) in CPR. That is simply one example. No doubt, most folks in CPR are not going to be very interested in "perfect being theology." Yet there are many more topics that will resonate with CPR. And the other way around.

Or perhaps I should close my meditation on moving forward in a different way. Having just mentioned the topic of otherness, it seems only appropriate that, if we really care about those who are other—as opposed to merely posturing—we have a responsibility to take "them" (the other) seriously. If belief in God requires living in a certain way and not merely assenting to a set of doctrines, if philosophy truly is a way of life, then that will have to be reflected in our engagement with other philosophers— including philosophers whom we deem as "other." *That* is truly a challenge. Not the challenge of God as other, but the challenge of the other as Other whom I'm called to serve. But, otherwise, all we have is empty rhetoric.

1

Is God a Challenge for Philosophy?

Adriaan T. Peperzak

Perhaps the word "challenging," with its summoning, testing, and contesting connotations, is not the most adequate word to characterize God's basic relation to us, but if we may hear in it also other verbs like calling, inviting, alerting, reaching out, and so on, "challenging" seems acceptable as a point of departure for reflecting about God's presence and our answer to it.

All religious relations, especially the most fundamental ones, are initiated by God's creation. Creation, however, implies a *vocative* that, beginning from nothing, calls the ensemble of all creatures into existence, while redemption reveals not only the deficiencies of our responses to that creative vocative, but also God's compassionate forgiving in the realm of his graciously (re-)established peace. During our unfolding from nothing to a life that, in the end, disappears into another nothing, God's ongoing care is concretized in human persons who—already formed by predecessors in particular varieties of growth, language, culture, and history—save us from death and destruction by giving us birth and education.

Becoming fully human implies that we, by learning from others, make our own what of their experiences and works should be incorporated into our lives. Insofar as they and we are successful, human history can be understood as the reality in which we are associated by the Creator to participate in God's ongoing care and grace.

Can we challenge God?

That depends. Our relation to the Creator cannot take the form of a sovereign summons, because the mode of our relating to God is never an absolutely autonomous initiative, but always a provoked response: since we can neither command nor create the one God, who is not any god, our answer to the initial vocative is always a form of adoration, gratitude, and praise.

Our response to God's vocative is more or less adequate insofar as our adoration allows us to confide in God's incomparable generosity. We cannot approach God as a rival or antagonist, or even as someone with whom we could compete from another space or time or horizon within one shared universe. Since God is infinite and thus does not fit any place or link within the existing totality, competition between the creation and its Creator must be a logical and ontological mistake. Because each possible universe is as finite as its composing elements, God's infinity fits neither any finite reality or component, nor the *totality* of all finite realities. God is therefore neither greater than nor identical with any finite being, not even with the universe of all universes, because every universe has a horizon, which is the finite border of some whole.

Since Jesus, the human Christ, who is also the "Son" or "Word" of God, is the total and transcendent sacrament of all human—cosmic, social, cultural, and historical—realities, God "challenges" all humans "in Christ," while offering God's infinitely loving presence to them. If we welcome this extravagant gift in an appropriate way, this is our basic response to the original Vocative that awakens us to life.

If the double vocative of God's creative addressing is received by our responsive vocative to God and realized in Christ, it sets the initial and ultimate stance for our living thanks to, within, and toward God's infinity.

Philosophy

Before we can answer the question of how philosophers in their philosophical endeavors can speak about a challenge that reaches them from God, and how they can formulate a response of their own to such a challenge, I want to briefly sketch a perspective and manner of speaking that still functions as a standard framework for most philosophers from Descartes to our times. It seems almost inevitable to me that such a compressed sketch risks offering a caricature; but even that might be useful for proposing a different setup of philosophy. But first, I want to formulate two theses concerning the meaning of "philosophy" that I will use in this chapter.

Let me begin by stating a deep conviction that I share with a very long and well-argued period of "philosophia": the separation between *philosophy* and *theology*, and the split between theology and spirituality, are two fatal mistakes that have badly impoverished all three domains mentioned here. *Philosophy, theology,* and *spirituality* must be experienced and thought as three complementary perspectives on one reality. In a radically new way, we must retrieve the old, radical union of *philosophia* as an experiential, emotional, imaginative, and reflective exploration in search of understanding, when we focus on the essential elements that compose a fully unfolded human life.

Having studied both philosophy and theology, I am familiar with the separate modes that have developed in modern and postmodern Academe. But I also believe that it is high time to submit these modes to a radical critique. Although I cannot presently unfold a specific new method that should replace the standard view, I can at least outline a sketch of the deficient framework with which I became acquainted during my study of modern classics from Descartes to Hegel and Heidegger, to which I will then add some critical remarks.

Modern philosophy as reconstruction

The "modern" type of philosophy might be evoked through the following characteristics:

1. The philosopher enters the scene as an "ego" that "thinks," i.e., as a single self-consciousness in abstraction from its individual and particular connections with other egos and without presupposed relations to God or gods.
2. This ego is *universal*, insofar as it is supposed to be *identical* in all real philosophers. All of them had and have very different lives, destinies, characters, interests, passions, preferences, and properties. To be seen or conceived as universally equal or even identical, their egos must be stripped of all particular and individual differences in experience, age, attachment, character, preference, erudition, and so on.
3. The philosopher's philosophical ego is a solitary self-consciousness without particular social, cultural, or historical determinations. It overviews the universe of things and experiences, while completely ignoring their concrete and individually different involvements in natural, cultural, and historical events and experiences. From his universalized and elevated position, the singularized and "purified" philosopher is then able to systematically construct a common and universally valid blueprint of each one's basically human universe.
4. The philosopher has to remove all "subjective" impressions and opinions concerning the given data in order to establish an *objective* and thus a *universally valid* picture of the *universe* insofar as the common ego must perceive and think it.
5. It is the task of the philosopher to discover not only the basic and unadulterated *data* shared by all, but also the fundamental *logic* that governs "the" thinking "ego" in its naked universality and its relationship(s) to the onto-logical order of the universal ego's ascetically reduced objectivity.
6. The ideal of the "modern" philosopher, most clearly expressed in Spinoza's and Hegel's systems, lies in the conceptually provable constitution of the displayed universe, which can be seen as the realization of an all-encompassing and everywhere valid map or blueprint of creation. Insofar as the technical possibilities of the modern sciences permit it, we are then able to realize that blueprint or correct it in cases where our reconstruction discovers anomalies, whereas the logical regularity of the existing structures and phenomena justifies our admiration and provides us with laws for our scientific, ethical, and political behavior.
7. When the philosopher can convince the scientists that the sciences are subordinate parts of or appendices to the philosopher's dominating cogito, and when progress is made in describing or (re-)constructing what is thought correctly, then audacious plans for remaking, correcting, perhaps even for re-"creating," can be launched. Let's send exploratory machines to the planets in order to check whether our speculative reconstructions correspond indeed with the laws and movements by which they are ruled.
8. Hegel's *Encyclopaedia of the Philosophical Sciences* is the expression of an enlightened philosopher who indeed tried, by means of objective experience and

logical thought, to (re-)produce the essential plan of the universe, insofar as we, humans, can objectify and conceptually reconstruct it. When he had finished his book, he thought that he had captured the secret of the natural and spiritual cosmos in the syllogistic structures of the Spirit that unfolds itself in that cosmos. He even identified this universe with God and saw his *Encyclopedia* as the intelligent and learned description and exhaustive explanation of God's own self-comprehensive identity of Substance and understanding Subject—or, in other words, as the Absolute in the full differentiation of its essential determinations.

But how did Hegel's philosophical ego (which exists in all egos) relate to the "God" who coincides with Hegel's totality?

On the one hand, the solitary ego of the philosopher who, through a judicious combination of all-encompassing logic with presumably unbiased experiences, has discovered the truth of the entire universe, must be tempted to see itself as a kind of god and (re-)creator of the universe. Couldn't he apply to himself the first line of a Dutch sonnet that was famous when I was an adolescent: "I am a god in the deepest of my thoughts"? On the other hand, God cannot find a place in any universe, because universes (or totalities) are as finite and limited as all their components and connections.

As Plato already knew, no play of finite beings, essences, or ideas, and no combination of *universalia*, particularizations, and individual *concreta* can yield any God outside the gods of ancient Greece or the idols of modern and postmodern mythologies. Should we not return to Plato's insight that the *universe* of beings and *their* being (*ousia*) is neither the last nor the first word, because the Absolute, as this One Condition of all conditions, is not definable, not an essence, no *Hen kai Pan* and not any being or Being either, but instead the Infinite "beyond" or "before" all totalities?

9. If, however, God is the absolute and non-finite Beginning or unconditional Condition of all conditions, then God can neither challenge us nor *be* the one unique and true God at all *within* the horizons of a universe whose philosophical stage director is too finite to introduce Godself into it.

10. From Descartes to Hegel we can study how the philosophical scene becomes richer in a variety of objectified experiences and logical complications, whereas Godself does not appear in any of the universal overviews, because there is no place or time for Infinity *within* the network that is maintained by some philosophical ego, even if such an ego is the manager of the entire stage. Instead of God, some idols might be proposed and explored such as Nature, Life, Matter, History, or Being Itself; but in the end and despite the excitement of repeated explorations, the totality of the All remains the same, as long as the all-seeing manager has not been struck by an overwhelming experience that comes from "beyond" or "behind" or "before" the "One and All." The All of the explored universe even becomes too repetitious and dull, or at least quite dissatisfactory, for someone whose explorations were motivated by the undefinable but impetuous and irresistible Desire for That which resists all reduction to things, entities, essences, contrasts, structures, ideas, ideals, gods, or totalities.

A first, still dark, hint might flicker within the panoramic horizon of a philosophical system, when it disappoints the philosopher's unstoppable search for that ("the Good," "the One," "the Unique") which could not be joyfully welcomed if it were no more than "more of the same." Is such disappointment already a suggestion that we are driven beyond all universes and their horizons toward the unconditioned Condition which, as their first and ultimate secret, gives without measure? Are we ourselves—within our own finite possibilities, worlds, and histories—driven by a Desire whose reach and urgency *surpasses the All?*

Plato understood that the question of our most radical urgency drove him beyond the limits of the Academy toward a God-fearing priestess, Diotima, who served the sanctuary of Dodona. And many God-seeking philosophers—from Plotinus and Proclus through Gregory of Nyssa and Augustine of Hippo to Anselm, Scotus, and Nicholas of Cusa—retrieved that wisdom within the Christian context of their own existential and meditative praxis.

Through Socrates, Plato justified his radical recourse to "religion" by inviting Diotima to give her inaugural lecture on *method* as the culmination of a conference about *Eros*, but their medieval friends began their most fundamental treatises by invocations of God's guiding voice in order to set their philo-theo-logical stage. Even Descartes himself changed the objectifying perspective of his metaphysical scrutiny when, at the end of his third *Metaphysical Meditation*, he responded to his own speculative proof of God's existence by adopting the radically different perspective of a sudden turn to the vocative of adoration.

Whereas the mapping out of universal blueprints seems to symbolize all kinds of philosophy in which a quasi-divine Ego reconstructs what (s)he has discovered about the human universe, we need the double *vocative* of a *dialogical* relation between God and human egos in order to perceive any challenge that reaches out from beyond all blueprints to move us to a more adequate mode of response.

Jesus's voice

While musing about the difference between types of characteristically modern perspectives of philosophy, I was struck by the difference between the idea of an abstract, universally present but isolated and lonely ego without religious or social attachments, on the one hand, and some basic aspects of the attitude that Jesus recommends to his disciples in a few passages of Luke's Gospel and its parallels in Mark and Matthew.[1]

Luke tells us that, shortly after Jesus's apotheosis in the company of Moses and Elijah (Lk 9.30), his disciples are quarrelling about the question of who was the greatest among them. *Jesus*, however, challenges every disciple who wants to be great (*megas*) or even the greatest (*meizōn*) of all. While rereading those texts as hints to us, I wondered if Jesus's critique could also be applied to philosophers who not only want to follow Jesus as disciples but also desire to be founders of the highest wisdom, glimpses of which they had just seen. Perhaps we could then learn how to philosophize from a different

---

[1] Lk. 9.46-48; Mt. 18.1-5; Mk 9.33-37; but see also Lk. 22.24-28; Mt. 20.25-27; Mk 10.41-45.

perspective and in a different spirit than the one that might fascinate us by primarily holding out hopes of obtaining prestige and recognition.

To put an end to the fight among his disciples, Jesus does not appeal to any law or established authorities. His admonition does not invoke any "great" or learned power. What counts for him—the coming of the *basileia*—is not another system or empire, but instead a most fundamental relation to an easily overlooked aspect of everyone's daily experience. It is, in truth, not just some aspect, but the absolute dignity of each single person, whatever degree of work or wisdom that person may or may not yet have developed. On their many trips, the disciples have of course seen many children, very young like babies, as well as older ones who might already have shown good work and fulfilled some promises. However, Jesus does not compare their merits, but shockingly draws a very young child (*paidion*) to his side and embraces it before he places it in the midst (*en mesōi*) of the twelve, while saying:

> Whoever receives this child in my name, receives me,
> and whoever receives me, receives him who sent me;
> for he who is the least among all of you, is the one who is great.

Many turns or returns (*straphēte*, Mt. 18.3) must be made to understand the various versions and explanations with which the synoptic gospels surround this important encounter of Jesus with a young child in the midst of his disciples. By stating that whoever receives (*dechesthai*) a barely developed child, is hospitable to Jesus, and in Jesus hosts the Father who sent him, he identifies himself with someone who does not offer more than a recently created promise. At the same time, however, he insists on each person's radical dignity of being born from God as an irreplaceable son or daughter of God in the Son. Shortly after the child's arising from nothing, Jesus thus associates the understanding disciples with the needs that are contained in this newly created person's destiny.

The child has not yet been responsible for remarkable utterances, works, or contributions to the material, social, or cultural life of humanity. Whatever it already has or has not yet done, it represents a human self that is unable to boast. It is certainly neither the first (*prōtos*) of all, nor *great* (*megas*) or greater (*meizōn*) than all the other individuals that populate the earth. However, Jesus is not looking for any "greatness"; not even for anyone who will make this child great enough to be proud or powerful. In this one and unique little person without exceptional qualities, whom he lovingly embraces, Jesus shows how poor, fragile, without merit, unimportant, and un-great every human person is, when we realize that *no* importance, greatness, or distinction is sovereign enough to present it as a creation of one's own. Indeed, all that is a beautiful success or a good product, is, first of all, a pure gift from God, whose Spirit has inspired charitable persons to serve others' sons and daughters in the realization of their destiny.

It is good to be reminded once in a while that each of us comes to existence as a welcomed gift, which separates us from drowning into pure nothingness. After conception and many months of being heeded in the mother's womb, and without responsibilities of our own, we come to existence in a situation of utter helplessness, immediately in danger of losing our existence. We were received and saved by a mother, father, nurses, brothers, sisters, family, teachers, the society, the nation, a culture, and so on. From the nothing of not-yet-being to the nothing of disappearance into death, my life owes everything to God and to those who are sent my way to summon out of me what is also burgeoning from within me. They take care—first *for* and then *with* me—of my becoming someone who I will have become before I lose my life by being welcomed again in God.

As *basileia* of *heaven*, the kingdom of God is immune against political, philosophical, or theological grandstanding. The basic condition for entering Jesus's realm is to *receive* and responsibly *accept* the vocatives of God's presence in the Spirit of Christ. Welcome to you, my little friend, in your singular destiny that does not have to be examined before you earn your divine right of being embraced by me.

By making the disciples face the poorest of all interlocutors (the child who cannot add anything to its *dignity*), Jesus gives his followers a destination: Instead of looking from the top down, while speaking *about* the depths and structures of the universe, turn your words and thoughts not to yourself, so rich in thoughts alone, but first of all to those who are incapable of recompensing you with recognition of your excellence.

God's challenge strikes us here. Instead of our excelling objectivity, God's vocative takes over by eliciting a response, even if we prefer to reject or resist its direction. The summoning Word of God presents itself in the eyes, the mouth, and the hands of the most unlearned baby, and it cannot be left unanswered. In the Son, who is the Word, Godself challenges my aptitude to dialogue. If, before turning to my own self and its busy thoughts, I receive and welcome the ones who need but cannot help me, I have already met the living Word, and in this Word I am embraced by the One who speaks from the Origin of God's Word to me. But then I have been called to service in a multilayered dialogue, where all neighbors visit one another in the Name of Jesus and the Spirit of God's presence.

Do not chase the little ones away! Do not avoid your own involvement in creation! Instead, engage in their preparation for an adequate fulfillment of every single destiny. Do what every father or mother would do to prevent their children to fall back into nothingness or corruption. By welcoming the destitute, we fulfill the promises of creation. Responding to the Vocative by becoming servants, we join voices in praising the very Beginning of "it all."

2

On the Infinite: A Response to Adriaan Peperzak

David Tracy

Adriaan Peperzak's meditative chapter is marked by his customary virtues: great erudition, acute philosophical reflection, sharp biblical awareness, and theological acumen. The chapter continues deep aspects of Peperzak's lifeworks on Hegel, on Plato, on Levinas and, above all, on the question of God at the border of philosophy and theology.

I fully agree with what I take to be his three main points:

First, on Peperzak's pointed and persuasive analysis of the modern as well as most postmodern philosophical frameworks whereby the philosophical ego constitutes an objectified panorama of all finite realities as a totality leaving no entry point for an Infinite God. As one of Professor Peperzak's mentors, Emmanuel Levinas, famously argued (against the panoramic position of Hegel), modern philosophy characteristically produces a closed totality of all realities even as it abhors an open Infinite.

Indeed, Peperzak, who is rightly considered one of the major interpreters of Plato, Levinas, and Hegel in both Europe and North America, in this chapter subtly employs these hermeneutical resources to rethink his own highly original position on the challenge of God. Peperzak's philosophy employed here has been articulated in his several groundbreaking works of the last thirty years.[1]

My second critical agreement: the critical argument Peperzak, in fidelity to his lifelong reflections on the turn of philosophy away from the modern self to the postmodern other, brilliantly appeals to the Jesus of Luke's Gospel rejecting the disciples' call for greatness in favor of the sheer goodness of the Christianity-preferred non-great others—the child, the marginalized, the poor, all those rejected by the "great" and ignored by most philosophers and theologians alike. Backed by his many studies of Plato (on the Good beyond Being) and Plotinus (on the One which is both

---

[1] All footnotes compiled by the editors. Adriaan Peperzak, *The Quest for Meaning: Friends of Wisdom from Plato to Levinas* (New York: Fordham University Press, 2003); *Modern Freedom: Hegel's Legal, Moral and Political Philosophy* (Dordrecht, Netherlands: Kluwer Academic Publishers, 2001); *Beyond: The Philosophy of Emmanuel Levinas* (Chicago, IL: Northwestern University Press, 1997); *Platonic Transformations: With and after Hegel, Heidegger, and Levinas* (Lanham, MD: Rowan and Littlefield, 1997); "The One for the Other: The Philosophy of Emmanuel Levinas," *Man and World* 24 (1991), pp. 427–459; *Philosophy and Politics: A Commentary on the Preface to Hegel's Philosophy of Right* (Dordrecht, Netherlands: Kluwer Academic Publishers, 1987).

the One and generous Good) in addition to the Christian most basic metaphor for God, 1 John's "God is Love," Peperzak notes the opening of the philosophical idea of the Infinite Good to the Infinite loving God (i.e., the Trinitarian understanding of God) occasioned by a turn to the other of an innocent child and all other officially "non-great" others—the marginal, the rejected, the poor.

My third critical agreement: Peperzak defends the idea of the Infinite as the primary idea for naming God rightly. Since my own work for the last ten years or so has also focused on naming God as Infinite and therefore on the Infinite in both philosophy and theology,[2] I will merely recall some historical thinkers who share this affirmation of the Infinite for naming God both philosophically and theologically. The different and sometimes contradictory understandings of the Infinite (philosophical, theological as well as spiritual) in our intellectual histories demonstrate that the idea of the Infinite should return to the critical attention of contemporary efforts to name God.

In my judgment, the category of the Infinite for naming God is a more adequate primary name for God than the now more prominent name of the Impossible or such traditional philosophical onto-theo-logical names as the Absolute, or as Being or *causa sui* or even *Ipsum Esse Subsistens* or *Ipsum Intelligere*. Moreover, the categories the "Infinite" and the "Impossible" are not contradictory categories but can be complementary if the category of the Infinite God is allowed to clarify how the Impossible God is the Infinite God just as, in the tradition, the category of the Infinite God (Gregory of Nyssa) clarifies why God is also rightly named the Incomprehensible God (Dionysus the Areopagite and the apophatic tradition). God is Incomprehensible because God is Infinite, not the reverse. God is the Impossible as possible because Infinite, not the reverse.

What has caused the relative neglect of the idea of the Infinite in contemporary discussions of God? I believe that the problem has been principally this: in the many contemporary discussions of the Infinite there is a widespread confusion between two notions of the Infinite first noted by Aristotle in the *Physics* and the *Metaphysics*. The most basic difference remains Aristotle's: that between a quantitative infinite of space, time, number—or in post-Cantor modern mathematics, quantitative infinities in the plural—and what Aristotle named the actual Infinite, i.e., a metaphysical infinite which Peperzak lucidly calls the absolute, unconditioned Infinite which is the source and end of all finitude.[3]

In part, the enormous and surely welcome success of the modern scientific and mathematical revolutions have occasioned most contemporary thinkers (including, it seems, philosophers and theologians) to construe the idea of the infinite as solely quantitative. With few exceptions (e.g., Emmanuel Levinas and Adriaan Peperzak in philosophy and Karl Rahner and, earlier, Friedrich Schleiermacher in theology)

---

[2] David Tracy, "The Ultimate Invisible: The Infinite," *Social Research* 83 (2016), pp. 879–902, 1062; "God as Infinite Love: A Roman Catholic Perspective," in *Divine Love: Perspectives from the World's Religious Traditions* (Westconhocken, PA: Templeton Publishers, 2010), pp. 131–162; "Form and Fragment: The Recovery of the Hidden and Incomprehensible God," in *The Concept of God in Global Dialogue* (Maryknoll, NY: Orbis Books, 2005), pp. 98–114.

[3] See especially Aristotle, *Physics*, Ed. and trans. Philip H. Wicksteed and Francis Macdonald Cornford. Loeb Classical Library (Cambridge, MA: Harvard University Press, 1934), III.4-8, 204b-208a.

any discussion of the actual absolute unconditioned Infinite has proved to be rare. Moreover, for Aristotle himself—who first named the two very different (but analogous) notions of the Infinite, an actual Infinite was an intellectual impossibility. This Aristotelian position influenced most medieval thinkers with the great exceptions of Thomas Aquinas and Duns Scotus.

Thomas Aquinas argued that the Infinite was an attribute of God. The attributes of God, of course, were medieval categories for what the earlier and later traditions more precisely called "the names of God." It is remarkable that Thomas Aquinas, in contradistinction to most of his fellow Scholastics and in serious disagreement with his and their principal mentor Aristotle, argued that there is an actual absolute Infinite which, in fact, is one of the attributes of God. Aquinas's position on the idea of the Infinite as an attribute of God was a cautious one. Thomas was straightforward in his criticism of Aristotle's denial of the possibility of an actual Infinite but cautious in relating the attribute Infinite to Thomas's primary name for God, *Ipsum Esse Subsistens*.[4]

Duns Scotus went further than Thomas Aquinas dared to go. Scotus argued that the Infinite is the primary attribute of God to which all other attributes should be logically and metaphysically related. Scotus's insistence on the primacy of the Infinite as the name of God was later deeply influential in naming God as Infinite not only in Scotist philosophy and theology but also in the great tradition of seventeenth-century French spirituality, usually related to a philosophy and theology of the Infinite: Benet of Canfield, Pierre de Bérulle, Francis De Sales and, above all, François Fénelon who in fact rethought not only Scotus's but also Descartes's idea of the Infinite for his and Jeanne Guyon's mysticism of Infinite Love.[5]

To return to the Greeks on the Infinite: Aristotle's difficulty in allowing the possibility of an Actual Infinite as actual partly concurs with that of Plato. For both Plato and Aristotle, like all classical Greek thinkers save Anaximander, denied the category Infinite to name ultimate reality. Plato's Good beyond Being in the *Republic* and Plato's One in the *Parmenides* were not named Infinite despite the logic which leads in that direction—i.e., in my judgment, Plato's Good beyond Being is more accurately named not as the highest Form (as by most interpreters) but as beyond all Form, i.e., the formless Infinite. For a classical Greek philosopher, ultimate reality (whether Plato's Good or Aristotle's Unmoved Mover) must, by definition, be perfect and therefore must have form. The Infinite by definition is formless. For Plato, Aristotle and all classical Greeks save Anaximander, the category of the Infinite cannot be used to name properly the Ultimately Real.

Not until seven centuries later in philosophy, with Plotinus in the third century CE, and in theology, with Gregory of Nyssa in the fourth century, did it become possible to call Ultimate Reality Infinite in Greek philosophical terms. Plotinus named the One-Good Infinite and most neo-Platonists followed him by arguing for the proper Actual Infinite as the Infinitely Good. The Infinite One of Plotinus was impersonally generous

---

[4] Thomas Aquinas, *Summa Theologiae* (Cambridge: Cambridge University Press, 2006), Ia. 3, 4.
[5] See François Fénelon, *The Complete Fénelon* (trans. and ed. Robert J. Edmonson; Brewster, MA: Paraclete Press, 2008) and Nancy C. James, *Divine Love: The Emblems of Madame Jeanne Guyon and D'Othon Vaenius* (Arlington, VA: European Emblems Publishing, 2016).

but not loving.⁶ For the Christian and neo-Platonist theologians, moreover, the Actual Infinite was not the impersonal generous Infinite One of Plotinus, but the personal, infinite love which for theologians is the Trinity.

In early modernity, Aristotle's position on the impossibility of the actual Infinite was seriously challenged on many fronts: for example, in the fifteenth century by the extraordinary mathematical–theological genius of Nicolas of Cusa for whom a mathematical quantitative infinity was to be affirmed as leading a thinker to a limit understanding of God as actually Infinite.⁷ In the sixteenth century, the amazing polymath, Giordano Bruno, a highly original thinker influenced both by Cusanus and Copernicus, was the first philosopher to maintain that the universe is infinite—and that God's infinity is somehow one with the infinite universe (more likely panentheism than pantheism: clearly not traditional theism).⁸

The early modern breakthrough on the import of the idea of the Infinite was a singular moment in the third meditation of Descartes. For Descartes, the idea of the Infinite is that idea which thinks more than it thinks; the idea of the Infinite shatters all closed totalities and opens the mind to the actually Infinite. To cite this unique moment in Descartes's otherwise completely modern framework so well analyzed by Peperzak is not to deny that Descartes never really developed his breakthrough idea of the Infinite any further. In fact, even by the fifth meditation Descartes retreated from naming God as Infinite to naming God as "*causa sui*" (a name, as Heidegger rightly argued, is the ultimate onto-theo-logical name for God).⁹

At the same time Descartes, aware of Bruno's position of an infinite universe as somehow one with an infinite God, insisted against Bruno and with Cusanus, that only God is Infinite; the universe is indefinite. Although Bruno's judgment that the universe is infinite dominated scientific thought for centuries, it has since been rejected by most physicists and cosmologists in contemporary post-relativity and post-quantum theory. In a similar manner, contemporary mathematical notions of plural infinities are (as Georg Cantor insisted) plural quantitative mathematical infinities that may be somehow related to the actual Infinite which is synonymous with God (so Cantor argued, probably unsuccessfully, in his later years).¹⁰ The ever-expanding universe is, as Cusanus and Descartes argued against Bruno, not infinite but indefinite. Only God as source, sustainer, and end of the universe and all reality including human beings is actually absolutely, unconditionally Infinite.

My all too brief account recalling to critical attention certain important moments in the complexity of Western thinking on the Infinite—both the quantitative Infinite

---

[6] See Plotinus, *The Intelligence, The Ideas, and Being* (V, 9 [5]) and *The Good or The One* (VI, 9 [9]).
[7] Jasper Hopkins, *Nicholas of Cusa on Learned Ignorance: A Translation and an Appraisal of De Docta Ignorantia*. Minneapolis: Banning, 2nd edition, 1985. I.1-20.
[8] See Paul Henri Michel, *The Cosmology of Giordano Bruno* (trans. R.E.W. Maddison; Ithaca, NY: Cornell University Press, 1962).
[9] René Descartes, *Mediations on First Philosophy*, ed. John Cottingham, Cambridge: Cambridge University Press, 1986. V.65-71.
[10] See Georg Cantor, *Contributions of the Founding of the Theory of Transfinite Numbers* (ed. Philip Jourdain; New York: Dover, 1955).

of mathematics and science and the Actual absolute, unconditioned Infinite of some metaphysics and theology—may, I hope, suggest the following thought: that philosophical, theological, and spiritual reflections, like that of those thinkers I cite above backing Peperzak's reflections on the idea of the Infinite, are correct. The idea of the Infinite is a major understanding that any thinker concerned with naming God should address.

3

God and the Ambivalence of Being

Jean-Luc Marion
Translated by Kathleen McNutt

I

In 1986, a few months before his death the following year, Dominique Dubarle O.P. gave Jean Greisch permission to assemble five studies (published between 1969 and 1981) under the title *God with Being*, in the Catholic Institute's collection "Philosophy." As preface writer, Jean Greisch asked me diplomatically if I saw any objection to this title. I would not have found fault with it in any event, if only out of friendship and admiration for Dominique Dubarle; for, even if the reference to my own book *God without Being* (1982) seemed obvious, and even if certain people think otherwise, there was, in fact, "no polemical intention" in the title chosen for this collection.[1] In addition to this good reason, I also had another for approving the title of this work, a reason marked by the avowed ambition in his subtitle: to attempt not an ontology (even an *ancilla theologiae*—a theological appendix—in the service of theology), but a theologal ontology. In fact, more essential than the inversion of the prepositions (from *without* to *with*), the addition of this adjective, "theologal," elsewhere unused, raises a totally different question, more subtle and more decisive. That is, when it comes to God, must not even the question of being, or, to put it bluntly, of ontology, receive a new qualification?

Dubarle posed the question and responded to it in his manner. He showed how, for St. Augustine and St. Thomas Aquinas, notably, the multiple senses of being underwent a reinterpretation according to the demands of revealed theology. First, the name of the One who is the *Is* for St. Augustine is neither *essentia*, nor *esse ipsum*; second, for St. Thomas Aquinas, the name of the One is neither *essentia*, nor *ens commune*, nor even the *ipsum esse* of a possible "metaphysics of the book of Exodus," but indeed an "impenetrable" act. These responses certainly do not correspond to mine in *God without Being*—God radically outside of being, in the name of ἀγαπή.

Yet we still have the question in common: if, perhaps, according to Exodus 3.14, the question of God cannot be posed or even understood without some relation with

---

[1] J. Greisch, Préface à *Dieu avec l'être. De Parménide à saint Thomas. Essai d'ontologie théologale* (Paris: Beauchesne, 1986), p. 5.

the *Seinsfrage*, perhaps enigmatic and disturbing—at least what we will ever be able to understand by the word "being," long sought but never found by philosophy according to Aristotle (up to Heidegger)—then it shall have to be sought in a different direction, even one absolutely distinct from what metaphysics believed it could say and do with it, from Duns Scotus to Nietzsche. The question of a "theologal ontology," even of a "*Christic ontology*,"[2]—for Dubarle went as far as this in commenting on St. Augustine—has to be posed.

Put otherwise, when it comes to God, what do we mean by "being"? What kind of ambivalence does the plurality of meanings of being (according to Aristotle, notably thematized by Brentano in 1862) take on when the question concerns God? Will not the debate between God *with* or *without* being sink into insignificance if we cannot identify this plurality? Thus, let us try to take a few steps in this direction.

II

The question does not consist in applying the predicate of being to God, as though it were simply a matter of discussing his existence or claiming to demonstrate it, without for a moment doubting that the verb *to exist* or the substantive *existence* could legitimately, in one way or another, concern God; in short, as though it were obvious that God, before all else, had to be. The true question, or rather the principal difficulty, consists first in determining what we mean by being in general, then especially in assessing the pertinence (if not the meaning) that being still has when we refer it to something like God.

Yet, if we persist in wanting to link God to being, directly and without preliminaries, ambiguities and imprecisions arise and immediately accumulate, like so many symptoms of the impropriety of the term "being" for God, even its inappropriateness. Let us raise the main ones.

The first is the imprecision of knowing if the answer to the question of Being can arise from a being. What is Being? If we answer, "God" ("God is Being," "Being is God"), do we not inadequately correlate some being or beings in general, with Being? Have we not, from the outset, misunderstood the ontological difference? That we qualify this supreme being (*summum ens, ens entium, ens supremum*) only *reinforces* the inadequacy of this response to the question, by highlighting, by means of dealing with a purely ontic transcendence, that we no longer understand Being itself at all in the question, that we forget it in substituting an ontic response for it. What do we say about Being, when we respond to the question with the word "God"? A being or nothing, something or nothing else. Hence the first "strike-through": a being is substituted for Being, attesting to the *ontological* deficit in responding "God" to the question of being.

Conversely, what are we really saying about God when we reply, "Being" to the question concerning God? What do we say about God, when we say, without further precision or precaution, that he *is*? Everything in the world *is*: the human being, the animal, the vegetal and the stone, the star and the particle, even those gods who died,

---

[2] D. Dubarle, *God with Being* (Paris: Beauchesne, 1986), p. 172.

like "the Great Pan," and who were, doubtless, and surely for some people, beings. In what sense does the claim, "the being who is" teach us anything whatsoever about God in his divinity? And if God came among us in the person of Jesus Christ to divinize us by loving us, and not by instructing us to love, how would the fact of his being (and, quite simply of his being, like us) teach us anything whatsoever of love and the divinity attested therein? And if, by chance and by hypothesis, Being sufficed to approach, if not express, the divinity of God, it would still be necessary to know what makes *this* Being, *this* mode of being, adequate to his divinity—and to that of love. But if, as the system of *metaphysica* has never ceased postulating it from Duns Scotus to Hegel, *Being* constitutes the most abstract and the most perfectly empty determination because it extends the most universally, how could it define the divinity of God as such? Nothing divine can come to us from the homology, loudly proclaimed by *metaphysica*, that covers what is, beings in general and even nothingness. Hence the second "strikethrough": the fact of *being* offers only nothingness itself, making of this the access to the divinity of God; it thus misses the divinity of God, since it misses *divinity* in regard to God.

Unsurprisingly, no theologian has seen this defect as well as St. Thomas Aquinas. We recognize the incomprehensibility of God in his essence and that his essence is summarized in *esse in actu*: it follows that the *esse* remains incomprehensible: "sicut Dei substantia ignota, ita et esse" ("As the substance of God is unknown, then so is His being").[3] At the very least, if God *is Being*, however we understand this, the *esse* will remain, precisely because divine, according to Thomas Aquinas himself, "profoundly unknown—*penitus incognitum*."[4] In other words, we have no (quidditative) concept that makes *ipsum esse* comprehensible from *actus essendi*, whereas, de facto and de jure, we have an immediate apprehension of the *ens commune* (which will soon become a *conceptus entis*):

> esse dupliciter dicitur: uno modo significat actus essendi; alio modo significat compositionem propositionis, quam anima adinvenit conjunguens praedicatum subjecto. Primo igitur modo accipiendo esse, non possumus scire esse Dei sicut nec ejus essentiam, sed solum secundo modo—"To be" can mean either of two things. It may mean the act of essence, or it may mean the composition of a proposition effected by the mind in joining a predicate to a subject. Taking "to be" in the first sense, we cannot understand God's existence, nor His essence; but only in the second sense.

It follows that as much as the predicative compound remains intelligible for us, so the act of divine being never becomes so: "hoc intelligitur de esse, quo Deus in se ipso subsistit, quod nobis quale sit ignotum est, sicut ejus essentiam—Being, by which God subsists, whatever it may be, remains for us as unknown as his essence."[5]

---

[3] Aquinas, *De Potentia*, q.7, a.2, *ad* 1m.
[4] Aquinas, *Summa Contra Gentiles* (Rome: Apud Sedem Commissionis Leoninae, 1934). III, c.49.
[5] Aquinas, *Summa Theologiae* (Cambridge: Cambridge University Press, 2006), Ia, q.3, a.4, *ad* 2m, also *Summa Contra Gentiles* I, c. 12.

Either God is a being, eventually understandable by concepts, though they cannot indicate his being (first defect, *ontological*); or the name "God" would eventually indicate Being as such, but God will remain in principle unknowable—and this *esse* as well. And this for at least two reasons: because God does not merit the title of God if he does not remain by definition incomprehensible to a finite understanding (according to the Augustinian principle that "If you understand it, it is not he");[6] and because Being cannot be conceived of by an ontic concept, since the concept only ever reaches precisely such and such a being in a clear and distinct representation (in respect of the ontico-ontological difference, which is doubtless as Thomist as it is Heideggerrian).

Ontology itself, understood in the historic sense of *metaphysica* (the only precise sense, which we will thus retain here exclusively) has never claimed to give access *as such* either to God or to the question of God. Evidently, in invoking a *theologal* ontology, Dominique Dubarle knew this perfectly well. Thus he clearly put in question, implicitly but radically, the strange affirmation assumed by Suarez, with no proof and as evident, in the opening of *Disputationes metaphysicae*:

> [As] metaphysical dogmas intervene in the discussion of divine mysteries, without the knowledge and intelligence of which these highest mysteries can barely, or not even barely, be justly treated (*vix, aut ne vix quidem pro dignitate tractari*), I have often been compelled [...] to mix inferior questions [sc. metaphysical questions] with divine and supernatural things [...]. For metaphysical principles and truths form a unity (*ita cohaerent*) with theological conclusions and reasonings, such that if we remove the science and the perfect knowledge of the first, the science of the second necessarily completely collapses as well (*si illorum scientia ac perfecta cognitio auferatur, horum etiam scientiam nimium labefactari necesse sit*).[7]

Would the thought of God then *necessarily* rely on that which *metaphysica* can say about Being? Could it "not even barely, *ne vix quidem*" dispense with Being? Should *theo*logy always conceive of itself as a metaphysico-theo*logy*? Must it resolutely neglect the warning of Athenagoras, to "learn the things of God starting from God—[παρὰ θεοῦ περὶ θεοῦ μαθεῖν],"[8] or, more modestly, the statement of Niezsche that "Christ remains outside of any metaphysics"?[9] To answer this question, we shall have to respond, if briefly, to two other questions. First, what does *metaphysica* say about Being? Next, what can theology say about Being?—if at least it can say something, and something *other than has been said*.

---

[6] St. Augustine: "Si enim quod vis dicere, capisti, non est Deus: si comprehendere potuisti, cogitatione tua decepisti. Hoc ergo non est si comprehendisti: si autem hoc est, non comprehendisti—For if could comprehend what you would say, it is not God; if you can comprehend it, you have comprehended something else instead of God" (*Sermon* 52.6.16, PL 38, col. 663).

[7] Suarez, *Disputationes Metaphysicae, Proemium*, O.o., (ed. C. Berton; Paris: Nachdruck der Ausgabe, 1866), t. 25, p. 1.

[8] Athenagoras, *Supplique pour les Chrétiens* (Paris: Editions du Cerf, 1992), p. 64.

[9] Nietzsche, *Nachgelassene Fragmente*, 11 [368] (ed. Colli-Montinari; t. VIII/2; Berlin: De Gruyter, 1970), p. 406 (tr. fr. P. Klossowski, *Fragments Posthumes*, automne 1887–mars 1888; Paris: Gallimard, 1976, p. 341).

III

What, in fact, does *metaphysica* establish in relation to the being of beings? What does it teach us about the mode of being of beings, *ens supremum* included? At first, the question seems without response. Or, more exactly, the response seems empty. First, because the question of knowing what Being means is not posed, as the response goes without saying: "In the present disputation, the question is thus to explain what is the *ens in quantum ens*; because, that the being might be is so well known that it requires no other declaration."[10] But if *that* the being is is not a "marvel" at all (to speak like Heidegger), must we conclude that the same definition of *ens in quantum ens* is obvious? In a sense, yes: this is a concept that "related to determinate beings as they are such and such, [remains] confused and indistinct in the representation of such or such a being (*confusus et indistinctum in repraesentendo*)."[11] In effect, it does not represent any being in particular (for this, only the concept of the essence of that being would suit), but its confusion and even its indistinctness allow it to reach, by pure abstraction, that is to say by pure *representation* (therefore without the presentation of any being in particular) the *ens ut sic*, the "onticity" (*étantité*) as such: "For the mind assumes (*sumit*) all these things only as similar among themselves by reason of being (*solum ut inter se similia in ratione essendi*), and, as such, forms an image by a single formal representation representing what is (*unica representatione formali repraesentantem id quo est*), which image is the formal concept [of the being] itself."[12] In other words, the concept of being (*étant*) (and let us notice, again, that it is no longer a matter of Being) does not present the being as such; it does not say *what* it is, but consists only in the *re*presentation of what any particular being is not, that is, the being *ut sic*, the being as such, which appears only as an unreal common point between all the beings that are themselves things. The objective concept, the object of this concept, in effect consists only in what corresponds to this abstraction by representation, consists in a pure and simple representations, devoid of all reality: "The objective concept [of a being][13] is nothing other than the object itself, as known or represented by such a formal concept." This decision, that of the unreality of the objective concept of a being, founded uniquely on its representation through the formal concept of a being, that is to say an abstraction of the mind, will find its complete confirmation and its flourishing in the definition of a being that allowed Clauberg to establish *ontologia* for the first time as the metaphysical science par excellence: "*Ens est quicquid quovis modo est, cogitari ac dici potest. Alles was nur gedacht und gesacht werden kann*—The being is everything that is in any manner possible, [everything that] can be thought and said." In other words, the being *as such* is not *ens cogitabile*, except as that which can think itself.[14] This

---

[10] Suarez, *Disputationes Metaphysicae*, II, *Proemium* (ed. C. Berton; Paris: Nachdruck der Ausgabe, 1866), p. 64.
[11] Ibid., II, s.1, n.8, p. 67.
[12] Ibid., II, s.1, n.8, p. 69.
[13] Ibid., II, s.1, n.8, p. 70.
[14] J. Clauberg, *Metaphysica de ente, quae rectius ontosophia* (Amsterdam: D. Elzevir, 1664), according to *Opera philosophica omnia*, Amsterdam, 1691, reedited Hildesheim, 1968, p.283. See the recent study by M. Savini, *Johannes Clauberg. Methodus Cartesiana et ontologie*, (Paris: J. Vrin, 2011).

decision, which in fact goes back to Goclenius and Timpler, allows us to understand why, in Wolff[15] as in Baumgarten,[16] the first (and only) determination of the concept of a being as such amounts to non-contradiction: that a concept does not contradict itself constitutes in effect the first condition of its possibility; and creates its possibility itself, but only from the point of view of its thinkability, precisely because it rests only on the thought that alone imposes it, insofar as it abstracts it from any real determination. The concept of a being says nothing about the being (since it remains indeterminate, empty, universal, as well as confused) but speaks in the name of representation, of the *cogitatio* from which it results exclusively. *Metaphysica* says nothing of such a being, so that it ends up identifying it with nothingness—both thinkable in the same way, as empty. Hegel made this diagnosis in the opening of *The Science of Logic*. We quite agree.

But, however, *metaphysica* does indeed think of the real characteristics of the being qua being, at least when it defines what it calls *substantia*. By *substantia*, *metaphysica* intends the most accomplished figure of being: beyond simple *cogitabile*, which encompasses nothingness, the rational being (*ens rationis*), the universals, and the accidents, *substantia* designates the *ens reale* par excellence, which Spinoza, with his habitual brutality and ambiguity, defined, without seeing the contradiction, as "that which is in itself and is conceived through itself."[17] What, then, would be unique to *substantia*? To remain in its Being (*être*), to be for itself, without dissolving into its accidents or passing from one mode of being to another; to resist corruption and thus to escape the origin, in which Aristotle anchored it invariably in the sublunary world (our own). Logically, it would be necessary to conclude that a single *substantia* merits this title, God. Like so many scholastics, Descartes was not far from admitting this; and Spinoza would draw the conclusion without hesitation. A substance subsists. Hobbes

---

[15] C. Wolff defined "a being" by possibility (*Ontologia*, 1730, §134: "*Ens dicitur, quod existere potest, consequenter cui existentia non repugnant*—Being is said to be what can exist, therefore it is that to which existence is not contradictory"), but he based possibility upon non-contradiction for thought: "*Eam experimur mentis nostrae naturam, ut, dum ea judicat aliquid esse, simul judicare nequeat, idem non esse*—We have this experience of the nature of our mind, that while it judges some thing exists, it cannot judge at the same time that the same thing does not exist" (*Ontologia*, §27). Non-contradiction follows from an experience of the nature of thinking spirit, before the very nature of the being and in order to define it.

[16] A.G. Baumgarten, *Metaphysica*, I,1, §8: "nonnihil est ALIQUID: repraesentibile, quicquid non involvit contradictionem, non est A et non-A, est POSSIBILE—Not-nothing is *something*: whatever does not involve a contradiction (i.e., is not 'A and not-A'), is *possible* and representable." This "non-nothing" depends, therefore, on the nothing, itself defined by the epistemological impossibility of thinking it: §7 "*Nihil* negativum, irrepraesentabile, impossibile, repugnans (absurdu) contradictionem involvens, implicans contradictorium, est A et non-A. [...] Haec propositio dicitur *principium contradictionis*, et *absolute primum*—There is nothing negative, unrepresentable, impossible, absurd, involving a contradiction, implying a self-contradictory statement ('A is not-A') ... *This proposition is called the principle of contradiction, and it is absolutely first*" (Magdebourg, 17574, Historische-kritische Ausgabe, hrsg. G. Gawlick & L. Kreimendhal, Stuttgart, 2011, p.56). Hence the absolute point of departure resides, as far as a being is concerned, in a rule of *cogitatio*, in accordance with the principle of the *ens ut cogitabile*.

[17] Spinoza, "*Per substantiam intelligo id, quod in se est et per se concipitur*—By 'substance' I mean that which is in itself, and is conceived through itself" (*Ethica I*, def. 3), without inquiring into the legitimacy of matching the thought of substance with its Being for itself, which exactly *ontologia* radically dissociates.

will prefer to speak, in this case, of a body, but to better insist on its subsistence: "[*corpus*] ... propter independentiam autem a nostra cogitatione *subsistens per se;* et propterea quod extra nos subsistit, *existens*—body ... because it depends not upon our thought, we say is *a thing subsisting of itself;* and as also *existing*, because subsisting outside of us."[18] In other words, *substantia* only unfolds properly as *subsistence*; and, as subsistence implies subsistence *per se,* substance comes to be only if it is *causa sui.* Spinoza, quite logically, begins with this requirement.[19]

What do the passages from a being to substance and from substance to subsistence show us? Subsistence only subsists by persisting. Spinoza imposes the privilege of the one substance, because only it can be *in se*; that is, remain in its being, without even passing or seeing it pass; but all other figures of a being, the mode or even the *res* (a term he leaves indeterminate, but which allows him to find a name for *ens* in general) are only inasmuch as, and to the degree (weak, moreover) that they persist in being. To be means to persist, and thus to persevere in being. At least in the sense of *metaphysica*, to be means to persist, perdure, persevere: "Unaquaeque res, quantum in se est, in suo esse persevare conatur—everything, in so far as it is in itself, endeavors to persist in its own being."[20] In other words, for a being to be, it is not enough for it to be in time, one time, and for a time; that, the accident and the *ens rationis*, can achieve, like the *ens creatum*, without truly being, since such a mode of being only remains conditionally, under a time-limited contract, but Being demands to remain there for itself, to remain in the presence and full strength of perseverance. To be is to remain; it is to be able to claim that I am there, that I remain there.

This perseverance in being, by which the substance owes it to itself to subsist, we call persistence in presence. Heidegger taught us that, right from the beginning, the Greeks themselves interpreted οὐσία first, if not only, as παρουσία, as if presence alone constituted the proper basis (the first meaning of οὐσία) of the nature of the thing, as if having a basis implied possessing it as a good in the sun; or, conversely, as if alone this proper basis succeeded in dis-enclosing itself in presence, itself present only insofar as it becomes insistent and persevering. But, still following Heidegger, we must go further: the self-interpretation of presence as perseverance, such as it is radicalized in the *conatus in suo esse perseverandi*, implies above all that Being can only be thought as it eventuates—according to time. The discovery of essence, *Anwesenheit*, makes itself available temporally by reducing itself to persistence and to insistence in presence. Essence, from οὐσία, becomes insistent in presence, παρουσία. Kant called this indiscreet insistence *Beharrlichkeit*, a presence that insists in order to last as long as

---

[18] Hobbes, *De Corpore*, VIII, 1, *Opera philosophica latine* (ed. Molesworth; London: Aalen: Scientia, 1839). sq., t.1, p. 91.

[19] Spinoza: "Per causam sui, intelligo id, cujus essentiam involvit existentiam; sive id, cujus natura non potest concipi nisi existens—By 'that which is self-caused,' I mean that of which the essence involves existence, or that of which the nature is not to be conceivable except as existing" (*Ethica I*, def.1). Besides finding the concept of spirit juxtaposed, once again without justification, with the Being of the thing, we note that the *causa sui* goes back to the argument Descartes termed the "ontological" in his *Meditation V*.

[20] Spinoza, *Ethica III*, §6. Or: "Conatus, quo quaeque res in suo esse perseverare conatur, nihil est praeter ipius rei actualem essentiam—The endeavor, wherewith everything endeavors to persist in its own being, is nothing but the actual essence of the thing in question" (§7).

possible (*conatus perseverandi*). To be truly (*ontologically*, ὄντως εἶναι) in presence, it is not enough to appear there; one must ever and always stay there and settle there; occupy presence for oneself and eventually *against* other pretenders to its light: *Gegenwart* says nothing else. It is a matter of standing guard around *one's* own presence *against* those who wish to come and occupy it in turn. Against whom? First, of course, against other beings laying claim to, even demanding, present existence. But above all (and to explain this first resistance) against the process of apparition itself, against the *rise* into presence of another present yet to come. Once the edifice of its presence is completed, once its present is assured to the present, each being withdraws the ladder and the scaffolding that got it there, not only to prohibit access to the beings coming after it, but to claim itself to be without beginning, without genealogy, without other modalities, ever, than the effective presence, the only truly persistent precedence because without past possibilities, without origin—in short, *causa sui* finally and again. We must make no mistake about what the multiform demand *causa sui* as the liberty of the finite being itself signifies: Sartre could only, with this contradictory requirement, attribute the divine *causa sui* to man, as the perspicacious announcer of the deliria of his time of an unconditional autonomy of the supposedly autarchic individual. But, behind (and sustaining) this ideological agitation, we must read a more radical ontological stake: the interpretation of presence as persistence, of persistence as perseverance, of perseverance as possession of presence in the present, indicates the refusal of the coming (and going) of the presence itself in the process of phenomenalization. With the delirious impulses of the *causa sui*, it is a matter of refusing the very phenomenality of presence, a matter of the denial of the dimensions of its process of appearing, a matter of presence's own censure of the deployment of the rise of a phenomenon into presence. As if presence, clinging desperately to its own insistence, burned its ships in order to forget its journey toward itself and to force itself to remain on the land now conquered. As if it could recover the opening of its discovery by covering through the uncovered itself the coming to be of its ancient uncovering. As if the present, acquired, possessed, and claimed could safeguard itself without the process of its uncovering and in order to re-cover it.

Yet, *metaphysica*, or at least what in it resists this, namely, philosophy itself in its critical mode, has demonstrated that the present pure and simple, presence reduced to the gains of the possession of the present, contradicts and dissolves itself. Aristotle and St. Augustine established this; Hegel, Nietzsche (and Bergson) confirmed it: presence can be understood as a taking possession of the present only by dissolving the present itself. For, if being amounts to temporalizing oneself, and if temporalizing oneself amounts to possessing what can be possessed in and of time, namely, presence reduced to a single present time, then this present (and thus the present Being which therein temporalizes) "either is quite simply not, or barely and obscurely is—[ἢ ὅλως οὐ ἔστιν ἢ μόλις καὶ ἀμυδρῶς]."[21] Time, reduced to the possession of the present, and thus finally to the instant, has properly only to not be, and this only in the mode of not-being: "ut scilicet non vere dicamus tempus est, nisi

---

[21] Aristotle, *Physics* IV (ed. and trans. Philip H. Wicksteed and Francis Macdonald Cornford. Loeb Classical Library. Cambridge, MA: Harvard University Press, 1934), 10,217b32-33.

quia tendit in non esse—we cannot truly say that time is, because it is tending not to be," comments St. Augustine.[22] In effect, how to persevere in time, if time reduced to the strict present does not last: for the present is not measured in a year but is composed of months; and it is not measured in a month if a month is divided into weeks; but the week only lasts days, which themselves only last hours; and hours, minutes; and minutes, seconds; seconds, instants; and the instant tends toward the limit, which tends toward nothing. As soon as it is here the instant (the ultimate form of the possession of presence in the present) is no longer there. St. Augustine develops this aporia and fixes it briefly: "the present" not only "has no space—... praesens nullum habet spatium," but neither does it have duration: " ... nulla morula extendatur."[23] The present has no *mora*; hence what I have called "the *im-morality* of the present excludes it from presence, thus from παρουσία, thus from οὐσία."[24] Time does not precisely give time to time, nor presence to the present. Or, conversely, time has not the means to ensure presence, still less to assure itself of presence, because it does not persevere in it. Time, understood in the sense of the possession of the present, thus turns out to be incapable of ensuring presence, of either receiving it or retaining it. The present, in the metaphysical sense of that in which the *conatus* would persevere, cannot give Being.

Presence cannot possess itself, because the present does not offer anything to possess, since it dissolves itself as soon as it appears. The present passes through loss and without profit. It passes indirectly, "under the radar." We must not consider the presence of Being as that which we might possess in the present, in order not to consider the being of the present as something to possess—[οὐχ ἁρπαγμὸν ἡγήσατο τὸ εἶναι] (Philippians 2.6).

IV

Before claiming to respond to this question, already so strange that one wonders about its very formulation, it is advisable to go back over what has led us to it.

The aporia of the presence of a being, reduced to the possession of presence, comes to us from metaphysical thought (by *metaphysica* in the strictly historical sense, the only operative one). But it appears crucial only to a non-metaphysical reflection of philosophy. How far can we clarify this reflection? In order to keep to the essentials, we will pay attention once more, but against certain bad habits, to a decisive analysis of Heidegger in his reading of *The Words of Anaximander*. Commenting on the first line, which was doubtlessly added to the fragment by Simplicius, who cites it—"For beings, wherever genesis is from, it is from these same [things] that destruction is

---

[22] St. Augustine, *Confessions* (Paris: Institut d'Etudes Augustinennes, 1992) (accent aigu over the E in Etudes), XI, 14, 17, BA 14, p. 300.

[23] Ibid., XI, 15, 20, BA 14, p. 304. It is not clear that Bergson escapes this aporia simply in passing from time to duration—if duration itself does not endure, neither does it hold itself back. The passage from the one word to the other, doubtless, does not suffice to think the passage of the passing present itself.

[24] *Au lieu de soi. L'approche de saint Augustin* (Paris: PUF, 2008), p. 282.

born, according to necessity"—[25] Heidegger notes not so much the reciprocity between genesis and corruption (Aristotelian, in fact), but the fact that ὄντα "do each other justice and reparation of their mutual injustice according to the allocation of time."[26] In what sense can an "injustice" arise between beings, and, especially, in what sense does this "injustice" have to do with time? Obviously, because a being manifests itself and makes itself seen in presence by entering into the present and occupying it, and because this occupation, by seeking to install itself and persevere in the possession of the present, commits an injustice against other beings, who remain in waiting to attain presence in turn, and find themselves delayed precisely by the first occupant who perseveres in the present. The *That* that presents itself in the present remains equivocal and ambivalent: "Das Anwesende bleibt zweideutig." ("The present remains ambivalent.")[27] Ambivalent, but in what sense? In the sense that "τὰ ἐόντα *nennt zweideutig sowohl das gegenwärtig Anwesende, als auch das ungegenwärtig Anwesende, das, von jenem her verstanden, das Abwesende ist*" ("calls *ambivalent* the present presence as also the unpresent presence, which, understood from this, is the absent").[28] We no longer understand this ambivalence, decisive for Anaximander, marked as we remain by *metaphysica*. For us, nothing shows itself in presence but the beings which occupy and persist in the present, while the beings not yet present or no longer present do not belong to presence at all. But for thought that is not yet or no longer metaphysical, the ambivalence of presence essentially broadens it beyond and within the simple present. "Beings" *here* name not only that which presents itself in the present by occupying and persevering in it, but especially and just as much that which no longer or not yet presents itself in the present, but which, just because we do not understand only from the present, is not simply absent, but always present in the mode of the past or the passing. For that which what presents itself (*das Anwesende*) presents, at once and indissolubly as present and facing us, and, in perfect ambivalence, as also non-present facing us, *das gegenwärtig und das ungegenwärtig Wesende*. "*Auch das Abwesende ist Anwesendes und, als Abwesendes aus ihr, in die Unverborgenheit anwesend. Auch das Vergangene und das Zukünftige sind* ἐόντα. *Demnach bedeutet* ἐόν: *anwesend in die Unverborgenheit*" ("Likewise the absent is present, and as absent from it presencing in unconcealment. Similarly the past and the future are ἐόντα. Hence ἐόν signifies: presencing in unconcealment.")[29]

As injustice consists, for a being manifesting itself in presence in the metaphysical mode, of only persevering in the occupation of the present; justice and reparation

---

[25] Anaximander, in H. Diels and W. Kranz, eds., *Die Fragmente der Vorsokratiker*, Bd. I 12th ed., 3 vols. (Dublin/Zürich: Weidmann, 1966), 12 B 1, p. 89 (which they here translate: "Woraus aber das Werden ist den seienden Dingen, in das hinein geschieht auch ihr Vergehen nach der Schuldigkeit"). See the philological discussion summarized by M. Conche (whose translation we here correct), which lays out the current status of the debate among the editors and interpreters concerning the beginning of the quote of this same fragment of Anaximander, *Anaximandre. Fragments et Témoignages* (Paris: PUF, 1991), p. 161.
[26] Ibid., see M. Conche, p. 174 et seq., whose translation we here follow.
[27] M. Heidegger, *Der Spruch des Anaximander* (ed. Ingeborg Schussler, Frankfurt: Vittorio Klostermann, 2010), GA 5, p. 347.
[28] Ibid., GA 5, p. 349.
[29] Ibid., GA 5, p. 347. Further along, it is a question of a *zweifaches Abwesen* (ibid., p. 361).

consist in not stretching or spreading oneself in presence (*sich spreizen*), in not stiffening (*sich versteifen*), in brief, in not remaining there in full force, not persisting there (*beharren*).[30] Justice between beings, which pass in the present without taking root there, thus consists of renouncing precisely what Kant understood by the name of presence, renouncing *Beharrlichkeit*, the Kantian word for presence, for παρουσία, as the ultimate meaning of οὐσία: "Far from our being able to derive these properties [those of *fortdauern*, persevering] from the simple concept of a substance, we should sooner derive the perseverance of a given object from the foundation of experience, when we wish to apply to it the usable concept of a substance."[31] For Kant, we cannot admit any presence without an equal obstinacy in presence, without a persistence in the present, however contradictory this presence may prove—for finally external experience does not supply a more immovable persistence than does internal experience: in the end, everything in the world *passes*, no matter how long the wait. In response, Nietzsche made a perfect critique of this: "faith in the persistence of the substance, that is to say in the Same's staying-*similar* to itself (*Glaube an das Beharrende der Substanz d.h. an das* Gleich*bleiben Desselben mit sich*)" by highlighting the evidence: "But *Being* (*l'être*), the only thing granted to us, is *changing, not identical to itself* (*das* Sein *also, welches uns einzig verbürgt is, ist* wechselnd, nicht-mit-sich-identisch)."[32] De facto and de jure, the reduction of the coming-into-presence of a being to the perseverant occupation of the present does not justify itself by itself and confirms, to the contrary, an injustice toward presence itself.

For we can find an injustice of the present moment toward presence itself. In effect, to manifest itself in presence (*Anwesenheit*), each being must also make present that which the present moment—in which it claims to persevere—denies and forgets: the moment of the not-yet-present becoming (the future), and the moment of the accomplished and already-past becoming (the past). For lack of these two non-present moments of presence, the process of entry into and passage through presence, the process of the *discovery* in and through presence obscures and covers itself: the atomistic and in fact untenable present covers not only the opening of the being, but especially the process of its *discovery* in presence. To do justice to the being in its presence supposes much more than its positioning in the present, where *metaphysica* obstinately wishes to fix and attach it. To do justice to the being in its presence also and firstly implies following its path from its presence not-yet-present to the coming into its presence no-longer-present in the past, through present presence, thus and for the first time fully visible and accomplished. The discovery of the being is only accomplished if its uncovering—that which makes it come out from being covered and returns it there again—discovers itself, instead of covering

---

[30] M. Heidegger, *Der Spruch des Anaximander*, GA 5, pp. 355 and 356 (see 257).

[31] I. Kant: "Es fehlt so viel, daß man diese Eigenschaften aus der bloßen reinen Kategorie einer Substanz schließen könnten, das wir vielmehr die *Beharrlichkeit* eines gegebenen Gegenstandes aus der Erfahrung zum Grunde legen müssen, wenn wir auf ihn den brauchbaren Begriff von einer *Substanz* anwenden wollen—So much is lacking for us to be able to infer these properties solely from the pure category of substance, that we must rather ground the persistence of a given object on experience if we would apply to that object the empirically usable concept of a substance" (*Kritik der reinen Vernunft*, A 349).

[32] Nietzsche, *Nachgelassene Fragmente*, 11 [330], Colli-Montinari, Bd. V, 2, p. 468.

itself up and dissimulating, that is to say amputating itself of its two non-present dimensions. Without these dimensions, the present conceals presence, of which it denies the process of discovery and recovery. Presence must be understood not only as the being discovered in the present, but as the passage of the being in *discovery,* namely, the coming out from under cover of the not-yet-present and the non-present covering-over of the passing. A being does not merit its present moment and does not truly appear there unless it brings its emergence out from under concealment; and it does not truly accomplish its moment in the present unless it assumes its covering—the covering in the surpassed allows the being to recover all presence, even and including its final closure, since it does not recover the brightness of its present except in conquering it by its exit from the first covering. A being only becomes present if it comes into presence; it only comes into presence if it enters into Being inasmuch as Being comes into being itself in the aforementioned three-part process of *discovery.* A being must renounce possessing the unique atom of the present as prey, so as not to cover up the *discovery,* where the passage of coming to presence is accomplished; this, in such a way that the being bears witness in its present moment, that it happens according to even the moments not-yet- or no-longer-present to presence, according to the event in which presence is given (and gives presence to itself).

Can we formulate this requirement further, or, frankly, can we expose it without playing too much with words but by describing recognizable phenomena? In fact, we have just sketched it, without perceiving it: by pronouncing two decisive words in a phrase: "according to the *event* in which presence *gives* itself."

Let us begin with the *gift*. To think of Being otherwise than as a being's persevering taking-possession of the present moment; otherwise, then, than *metaphysica* thinks it, the phenomenon of the gift already asks for this and imposes it on us, often without our noticing it. The gift, in fact, provokes, in our inattentive everydayness, its own disappearance, its own covering. In effect, in the process of the gift, the gift given (the present, the favor, the thing, etc.) enters into presence as a subsistent being, which occupies the present moment; on the scene of the present moment, the gift eclipses all other actors, confiscates space, and concentrates all the beneficiary's attention. The beneficiary, the recipient, gladly lets himself be fascinated by *what* the gift gives, in order to take hold of it and enjoy it, to the point where the gift immediately loses its gratuity to become (again) a possession which has simply changed owner, the recipient replacing the giver (and is this not the very function of the gift?). From that point on, the gift, having been accomplished according to the exchange of possessors, nullifies itself as gift. Thus, in the taking possession of presence by the gift, which seizes it with its perseverant subsistence in the present moment, the very process of the gift—the advent of the giver, depriving itself of a present, to make it present to another, thereby discovering its own benevolence—disappears in its result: the gift must escape the giver, certainly; otherwise there would not truly be a gift given; but, this way, the gift, from now on glorified in the moment of its present, exclusive of all else on the scene of presence, masks the giver, excludes him from presence, covers him, and makes him disappear. Ingratitude constitutes nothing but the reverse and the moral effect of ontic disappearance, which crosses out the giver by crossing out the gift given. The giver, and thus the process of the gift, disappears precisely because the gift, as a given thing, appears. Must we conclude from this that the conditions of the possibility of the gift are one and the same with the conditions of its impossibility (Derrida)? We must suspect, to the contrary, that the gift only appears as the entire process of its advent, according to a presence, in which are discovered as much the actors and the non-present moments as the presence to the present of the given present. To receive the gift demands much more and a totally different thing than seizing possession of the given; to receive the gift consists in seeing the given *as* given, *as* happening to the giver who is from now on necessarily absent, but nevertheless not only its (bygone) origin, but also absent to its recipient in return—recipient in the sense in which destiny sends (*Geschick*) and provokes a process of coming, without which the gift would only appear as a brute fact, a simple lucky find, a chance meeting, without meaning or intention, incapable of allowing not only acknowledgment but also refusal, contempt, even the taking-possession itself. Without the shadow of the absent giver, the gift disappears into a pure insignificant contingency, a fact that raises no attention. It is not a matter here of an acknowledgment of gratitude toward a giver who would like a reward, if only symbolic, for a gift given in fact reluctantly, almost abandoned; it is rightly a matter of a brute fact to be found apprehended *as* having to be received (or refused), *as* coming from elsewhere, *as* charged, even distorted, by alterity, waiting for the hermeneutic that makes it a gift. What we call sacrifice, namely, the renunciation of keeping possession of the gift, says nothing other than this—the gift, to be received (or refused) *as* a gift, requires that the giver crosses it out and effect its reduction or its homage, to redirect it to the receiver, who, appearing anew, *re*gives the gift and thus qualifies it, and it alone, *as* a gift. This means that the gift does not appear without being discovered in a presence that greatly exceeds the present moment where its perseverant possession can confine it. The gift is only discovered in the *dis*covery of an accomplished presence and especially in what fulfills the present.[33]

The event comes next. The gift is only discovered if the present does not tense up in its present moment, but takes place (lets come, lets pass, and, finally, lets itself be surpassed) in its advent (from the giver to the recipient) and sanctions it by acknowledging this advent (sacrifice). The gift happens thus. The event thus defines the *dis*covery. How? According to *metaphysica*, as has been shown,[34] the event remains unintelligible, thus invisible. In effect, the event (as, moreover, classical French understood it) signifies the final result (positive or negative) of a process, a result that (against Hegel or at least the vulgate of his French translators) does not rebound toward its origin, but, on the contrary, sinks itself into its facticity and persists there as much as it can maintain its *epoch*, which holds the advent in the present moment. The result is that the arrival (what Heidegger calls *Ankunft*) covers, and covers in a persistent and perseverant being, sole and imperious proprietor of

---

[33] For the details of this analysis, see *Etant donné. Essai d'une phénoménologie de la donation* (Paris: PUF, 1997, 2nd ed., corrected, 1998), "Quadrige" 2005, Livre II, and *Certitudes Négatives* (Paris: Grasset, 2010), Chapter IV.

[34] C. Romano, *L'événement et le temps* (Paris: PUF, 1999). Except that Heidegger had made possible a decisive breakthrough, no doubt the first—not, to be sure, in 1927, in *Sein und Zeit*, but in 1957, in "The Onto-theological Constitution of Metaphysics" (see *Identität und Differenz*, GA 11 [Frankfurt: Vittorio Klostermann, 2006]) and in 1962, in *Sein und Zeit*, GA 14 (Berlin: Akademie Verlag, 2007).

his present moment, the advent (what Heidegger calls *Überkommnis*) of the entire process of *dis*covery. The arrival, completed journey, voyage without incident, successful transfer, settles into the reduced presence of its final experience, the station where the whole world descends, the present moment reached, possessed, conserved as much as possible. As a consequence, the *pro*cess, the *trans*port, the *dis*placement, the passing-over (*traversée*), in brief, the advent itself disappear, excluded from the present moment: *in fine*, the *dis*covery finds itself thus covered over. In the best cases, an investigation, for example historical or technical, will be able to reconstitute the causes, conditions, and antecedents of the result, but it will conceal that much more the ontological process of the advent under ontic hypotheses, explaining, moreover by simple probabilities, Being by a being, itself reduced to its obstinacy in the present (*Beharrlichkeit, Vorhandenheit*). In order to think the event as a *dis*covery, it would be necessary to think the event precisely from the discovery. It would be necessary that the arrival (*Ankunft*) remain visible in the process of the advent that supervenes (*Überkommnis*) and that holds them in contact, Heidegger says a contract, a compromise, an agreement (*Austrag*), in whose terms the displacement of the event would cover, would open, and would remain open ever and again in its final outcome, such that in return the outcome so to speak continues to tremble and vibrate from the movement which made it possible. It would be necessary that the process of advent, presence without present, nevertheless remains the truth, the *dis*covery discovering that the result of the arrival itself comes again. Here, what the French translates, no doubt unfortunately, as *il y a* (there is), but which the German happily calls the *es gibt*, takes all its force. We say, the *cela donne* [that gives] (as in the popular expression "What is the point?" [lit. "What does that give?"]) What that gives, what the point is, the final *cela* (that), most of the time, is sufficient unto itself: the thing is *that* that it is, we know it as *that*, and we are interested in it: it, in order to ensure its perseverance in the present; we, in order to maintain our knowledge and thus our mastery of all that remains in the state, so much and for as long as possible. Let's hope that it lasts!— which must be understood thus: let's hope that the *that* has nothing to do with what it *gives*. But, in the case where this would have the status of an event, that is to say would not have any other *stature* than to happen, than to arise into presence by an advent, then we would no longer be able to forgo what imparts and discovers the *that*, to forgo the donation in it. The "marvel of marvels (*Wunder aller Wunder*)" is no longer attached to a being (as in the metaphysical question par excellence, which asks only "*Why* is there something rather than nothing?," without being surprised *that* there is something), but to the fact *that* the being might be. *That* the being might be at all has nothing ontic to it; it does not arise from a being, but from Being. Provided at least that we understand Being in its ambivalence—otherwise than as the persistence *in se* and *per se* of an essence in *its* Being, *in suo esse*. For Being no more belongs to a being than it restricts itself to the present moment. Being, if we must admit such a thing, *comes as given, dis*covered in the presence beyond the present.

Present? But what present are we speaking of? The ambivalence of the present bursts in here in full light. Is it about the present moment in the sense of [to nun], *nunc stans, jetzt, now* of *metaphysica*, or about the present of *es gibt*, the present *given* by presence and the gift *passing* through it from *not yet* to *no more*, spreading there as well? But then how does presence give itself when it gives the present in this sense? Does not the ambivalence of Being prolong itself and culminate in the ambivalence of the *present*? For *metaphysica*, the present indicates the restriction of presence to the present moment, thus supposing (in vain, moreover, since nothing lasts) that a being can and must persevere in *its Being*, precisely because it sees or believes itself authorized to consider Being as its own, to make Being ontic, as it were, and thus to confirm a forgetting so deep that it forgets its forgetting (a being, in *metaphysica*, would thus be defined as *that which forgets itself*, in every sense of the word). In light of a different thought about Being, the present means what is not restrained (at the moment of its inception), but overflows and surpasses itself; that which comes like the effect of a gift, given not only at the moment of its sending into the present, but intrinsically given, including when presence no longer or not yet shines in a present moment. In its truth (its *discovery*), a being, or whatever one chooses to call it, lasts only as long as and inasmuch as it is given. It thus remains given (its only perseverance resides in this redundancy) at each instant of its presence, including absence. It is not given once for all and then abandoned to itself, but given for the whole length of its advent, given so as to be received, to be experienced as transpierced and held by the integral donation from the upsurge at the beginning, according to the rhythm of the *discovery*.

Philosophy can hope to describe this being, even to anticipate it. And it must, because only it can. But can it accomplish what it has described thus? *Who* can show us how this gives, for example, Being, such that we access Being otherwise than Being, otherwise than according to *metaphysica*?

V

Who can do and wholly accomplish (εἰς τέλος, Jn 13.1) what philosophy tries to glimpse, if not the one who has been able to say in truth that all has been accomplished (τετέλεσται, Jn 19.30)? Hereby we glimpse an audacious, risky hypothesis, but for all that, perhaps reasonably qualified: that of sketching another understanding and another implementation of the manner of being of a being, from the manner in which Christ, passing and residing among us, undertook to be. It is not a matter of looking for a "theologal ontology," even less a "christic" one, but of seeking to glimpse how Christ *is* and *was* in another mode than Being such as *metaphysics* (ontology, then) understands it.

The mode of being that *metaphysica* designates is defined, we have seen, by the persistence of each being in its Being, by the measure in which it takes and keeps possession of its presence. Yet, strangely enough, Christ's mode of being, his mode of implementation of what we call "Being," finds him also described, in the brief and rather enigmatic indications in the New Testament, but with such a precision that we find there certain concepts which will support the metaphysical history of Being. To notice this, one needs only a connecting thread, provided by a verse already mentioned, which opens the liturgical hymn Paul cites in the Letter to the Philippians: "ὃς ἐν μορφῇ θεοῦ ὑπάρχων, οὐκ ἁρπαγμὸν ἡγήσατο τὸ εἶναι ἴσα θεῷ—

He, being in the form of God, did not consider as a possession-to-keep-for-himself [*rapina*, a theft] to be equal to God" (Phil. 2.6). Strange formulation. First because it concentrates into two lines a number of technical terms in what will become the lexicon of *metaphysica* (μορφή, θεός, ὑπάρχειν, τὸ εἶναι, ἴσον); next because it uses a very rare (even unknown) formula in the New Testament (the infinitive τὸ εἶναι, "to be") complementing a term (ἁρπαγμός) itself rare in the Greek world and unique in the New Testament. But it is an especially remarkable formulation in the rigor of its argumentation: the Christ is (ὑπάρχειν, to be in principle, at the beginning, to be from himself, by rights) in the position and form (μορφή, thus, εἶδος, essence, even substance) of God; in terms of and according to the manner of Being of *metaphysica*, he could and even should thus take possession of this essence and substance, keep it for himself; in short, persist in it as in *his* Being. One cannot but think here that it would be more exactly in the mode of the younger son in the parable of the prodigal son, which Luke recounts: this son demands of his father his portion, the taking possession by rights of his οὐσία (essence and substance): "δός μοι τὸ ἐπιβάλλον μέρος τῆς οὐσίας—Give me the part of οὐσία that is due me" (Lk. 15.12). In so doing, he merely follows the *conatus in suo esse perseverandi*, the effort to persist in possessed presence (having to be possessed).

Yet—and the whole intention of the hymn is found here—Christ, unlike the younger son (and unlike us all, who are spontaneously metaphysicians), does not justly consider his οὐσία (his μορφή) as a good to possess (ἁρπαγμός). But what οὐσία does this concern? It concerns an essence that consists precisely in equality to God (ἴσα θεῷ); yet, because he *is already* in the divine form and essence that *already* defines him, there is nothing for him to claim, nor any part to demand. This equality with God signifies, for him, his equality with himself (τὸ ἴσον): it is the implementation of the principle of identity, A=A, a thing is what it is and not another thing.[35] This metaphysical sense of οὐσία means all the more clearly that if the term is lacking, it is replaced by another, ever so slightly rarer, but also infinitely stronger, τὸ εἶναι [ἴσα θεῷ]: we must therefore understand that Christ did not consider himself—de facto and de jure—to be *properly* what he nevertheless was (i.e., equal to God, even God). In short, he did not consider τὸ εἶναι in general (*überhaupt, schlechthin*) as a possession, but that he foreswore it even to the point of emptying himself (ἐκένωσεν, Phil. 2.7), even to the point of voluntarily taking on another οὐσία, the μορφή δούλου, that which the prodigal son undergoes involuntarily (μίσθιος, employee, *Knecht*, servant, Lk.15.9).

Why this inversion of roles? Why does not he who is lord ("You call me master and lord, and with good reason, for I am that," Jn 13.13) keep this οὐσία as his possession? Because he knows that it is a present given by his father, because he knows both the Father who gives and the gift that comes ("If you knew the gift of God and that which you speak," Jn 4.10), and thus that this μορφή and this οὐσία can only be received, but never possessed, since that of which they consist comes to them from elsewhere

---

[35] It is this equality to God, incidentally, with which the Jews reproach Jesus, because they do not see in it only a claim of possession by himself of equality (with himself), ἴσον ἑαυτὸν ποιῶν τῷ θεῷ (Jn 5.18).

(from the gift, thus from the giver), not from themselves (*per se et in se*). Christ knows what the prodigal son is (and we are) ignorant of: the prodigal thinks that in acknowledging himself a slave and a workman, he loses his rank (his essence) as son, because he does not believe that the Father loves as a Father. However, Christ knows that in abjuring possession of divinity he will continue precisely to receive it from his Father—"and that is why God exalted him and gave him the name which is above every name" (Phil. 3.9). Paradoxically (and against any metaphysical interpretation of Being), only the loss of or the voluntary renunciation of perseverance in essence and presence (in his οὐσία) allows one to receive "a hundredfold." What persists in τὸ εἶναι as in a possession loses it; who loses τὸ εἶναι in order to acknowledge it as a gift of the Father, receives and thus saves it.

But how and why this paradox? What is at best revealed therein—at best—for beings in general, for the human being in particular, and—at its highest worth—for God above all? It is clearly a matter—and we see this already—of Christ's implementation (who else could do it before or without him?) of the principle proposed in advance to the disciples, who themselves were incapable of it, but "Whoever seeks his soul will lose it, and whoever will lose it for love of me will keep it—ὁ ἐθρὼν τὴν ψυχὴ αὐτοῦ ἀπολέσει αὐτήν, καὶ ὁ ἀπολέσας τὴν ψυχὴν αὐτοῦ ἕνεκεν ἐμοῦ εὑρήσει αὐτήν" (Mt. 10.39, see Mk 8.35 or Lk. 9.24). But once again, this response only displaces the question: for finally, from the point of view of a comprehension of Being (and not from the theological point of view of a comprehension of the mystery of Christ) why is it necessary to renounce the calm (however provisional) possession of self, the transcendentality of the ego?

A first response comes from the story of the agony at Gethsemane, when Jesus definitively inscribes himself into the figure of Christ, in other words when he perfectly assumes his status as the Son of the Father—namely, when he exchanges his human will for the Father's will, thus manifesting it as such and manifesting himself therefore as the Son, in a reciprocal glorification (Jn 13.1, 32; 17.1-5). This is accomplished with the decision upon which everything pivots: "Not my will but may yours come to pass— μὴ τὸ θέλημά μου ἀλλὰ τὸ σὸν γινέσθω" (Lk. 22.42, see Mt. 26.39 and Mk 14.36). This decision, which inverts the will, converts it in the precise sense of itself into another, the will of the Father. It opens in all its breadth and depth, its height and length, the trinitarian scene of the final act of Christ, in brief, theology. But it also takes on a crucial significance for philosophy: the *conatus in suo esse perseverandi*, namely, the will to possess one's οὐσία as far as possible and at any cost ends up, at the end of *metaphysica*, with the will that wants itself and wants nothing other than its own affirmation, in other words the will willing with all its power its rise in power—in short, the *Wille zur Macht*. The great *amen*, by which Nietzsche imitates and blasphemes he "in whom the *Yes* is found" (2 Cor. 1.27 referring to Mt.11.26), is distinguished by the fact that Zarathustra only says *yes* to what *his* own will can want and endure, while Christ says *yes to all* that the Father wants and "bears all things" (1 Cor. 13.7). Thus if the will to power defines nihilism, if nihilism itself confirms the end of *metaphysica*, it is therefore necessary to go so far as to suspect that to want the will of the Father, that is of an other par excellence, that to want what *I* do not want and do not want to want, constitutes the only and the definitive response to nihilism and the final imposition of an alternative interpretation of the Being of beings. The ambivalence of Being thus will play between its sense according to *metaphysica* (Being as *conatus in* suo *esse perseverandi*, will to *its* own power) and its Trinitarian sense according to the *admirabile commercium* of the exchange of wills of the Son with the Father.

But does there then remain a mode of *Being* of a *being*? No doubt, if the Being of a being arises, as such, from creation, instead of preceding it, as *metaphysica* claims without rhyme or reason. Under what expression could this Being be said, viewed from God's point of view, the point of view of God, and of God as revealed in the Trinity? According to the principle that "Every good gift and every complete gift (every presented present) comes from above—πᾶσα δόσις ἀγαθὴ καὶ πᾶν δώρημα τέλειον ἀνοθέν ἐστιν" (Jas 1.17). Even and especially for Christ, but also for us through adoption, nothing is except that it is received, and nothing is received except that it is given, so that to Be consists of receiving oneself, when one still has nothing and *is* nothing, and to return the gift received by *surrendering oneself*. This trinitarian mode of Being according to givenness, we read expressly: "Son, you are always with me, and all that *is* mine *is* yours—τέκνον, σὺ πάντοτε μετ' ἐμοῦ εἶ, καὶ πάντα τὰ ἐμα σὰ ἐστιν" (Lk. 15.31). Or: "All of my things *are* yours and all of yours [*are*] mine—τὰ ἐμὰ πάντα σὰ ἐστιν καὶ τὰ σὰ ἐμά" (Jn 17.10). Put differently, the Trinitarian communion of the wills of the Father and the Son, exchanged as gifts given and giving, which are re-given infinitely from one to the other in the Spirit, precedes and determines the mode of *Being* of the things that are.

Thus we begin to make out a glimmer of light in our initial question: before asking what the good hypothesis is between God *without* being and god *with* being, thus before subjecting God (unknown) to Being (supposedly well-known), in short, before asking what happens to God under the hypothesis of Being, we must understand another question: What happens to the question of Being according to the hypothesis of God, in the perspective opened up by God, from the point of view of God already accepted? What does the question of Being become when it is posed from the point of view of God? (*Was geschiet in der Seinsfrage wenn man über Sein vom Gott aus fragt?*). Thus, by *Being* we understand (or rather we most often pass our time *not* understanding) its ambivalence: either Being as something to be possessed like a property, or else Being as something to be received and given as a gift. With *this* question, Christian thought, provided that it truly becomes such, could return to the question of Being—turn toward it, or rather return it toward God.

4

Being, God, Nihilism, Love: On Marion's "Ambiguity of Being"

Hugh Miller

I

In "God and the Ambivalence of Being," Jean-Luc Marion returns to a topic which has been a central concern of his thinking at least since the appearance of *God without Being*: namely, the question of the relationship of God to beings, to the Being of beings, and to our thinking of that relationship.[1] As a tribute to the late Dominique Dubarle, OP, who had attempted to establish what he termed a "Christic" ontology, Marion takes up anew the issue of what might be called the proper orientation for raising and answering the question of God and Being: must God be thought of in terms of Being, or must Being be interpreted according to the terms of revelation, especially the revelation who is Christ?

In what follows I will first try to give a reading of Marion's argument for that orientation (or re-orientation) of thinking about God and Being. In the later sections I will address Marion's argument with critiques which are not negative, but that I think call for more reflection on the issues at stake. I will be especially concerned with the topics of nihilism, love, and the gift.

In *God without Being*, as Marion notes, he had argued for "a God radically outside of being, in the name of *agape*." Using as his primary foil Heidegger's fundamental ontology, he there argues that thinking of God as a being, or even as the Being of beings, is to deploy what he terms a "conceptual idol": an idea which fills and dazzles thinking, but which, in reality, is no more than a reflection of thinking back upon itself.[2] To this "idolatry" Marion opposes what he terms "iconic" thought. Such thinking, he claims, differs fundamentally from that of the idolatrous kind, both in its termini and in its effects. While the movement of idolatrous thinking originates in the (human) subject and returns to it, the movement of the iconic gaze is one which, originating from without, arrives at the subject and bears it back out of itself, toward the origin. Iconic thinking thus has the effect of "crossing" (and thus disturbing and disrupting)

---

[1] Jean-Luc Marion, *God without Being* (trans. Thomas Carlson; Chicago, IL: University of Chicago Press, 1991).
[2] Ibid., pp. 11–14.

conceptual idolatry like that of Heidegger's thought of Being, and of the ontological difference. Iconic thinking represents the theo-logical perspective par excellence.[3] This distinction between idolatrous and iconic thought is the *topos,* in *God without Being,* for the two orientations in thinking of being and God: ontology as conceptual idolatry subjects God to the demands and requirements of Being; iconic thought theo-logically disrupts ontology and absolves God of the necessity to be, and to be thought of according to the categories of Being.

In his later works, however—especially in his central trilogy, *Reduction and Givenness, Being Given,* and *In Excess,* he thoroughly modifies and supplements this account with a far-reaching reformulation of phenomenology in its entirety. Laying out his approach in terms of the performance of the phenomenological reduction, Marion claims to move beyond both Husserl's reduction to categorial intuition and Heidegger's reduction to Being and the ontological difference, to disclose a third (and ultimate) reduction: the reduction to givenness. "As much reduction, as much givenness," is his proposed new "last principle" of phenomenology.[4] "Givenness" in these texts does not connote only what shows itself in phenomena (Husserl),[5] or what is unconcealed in the perdurance of the overwhelming arrival of Being and beings (Heidegger),[6] but an initiative that lies beyond both. Everything that shows itself does so on the basis of its first giving itself; but not everything that gives itself shows itself,[7] and everything that is, is because it first gives itself—but not everything that gives itself *is.*[8]

At the heart of Marion's account of givenness is the threefold deployment of the gift (*le don*) in *Being Given.* In a gift three moments are articulated: the giver; what is given, and the receiver or "givee." Access to these moments is secured by way of a "triple *epokhē.*" The "bracketing" of the transcendence of each moment is necessary for a phenomenology of givenness to be accomplished. The transcendence of the *giver* must be bracketed, lest the gratuity of the gift be read as an effect of a cause; that of the givee must, in order that the gratuity of the gift not be interpreted as desert; and, finally, that of the gift itself must, lest it provoke repayment or reciprocity and thus annul itself as gift.[9]

But the bracketing of these transcendences does not, indeed cannot, make givenness as such show itself, or be. Instead, the bracketing points phenomenology toward certain phenomena, which Marion calls "saturated" phenomena or paradoxes, and which are characterized by an excess of intuition over formal conceptual determination. Using

---

[3] Ibid., pp. 20–24.
[4] Jean-Luc Marion, *In Excess* (trans. Robyn Horner and Vincent Berraud; New York: Fordham University Press, 2002), pp. 17, 25–26; Jean-Luc Marion, *Being Given* (trans. Jeffrey L. Kosky; Stanford, CA: Stanford University Press, 2002), pp. 14–19.
[5] Edmund Husserl, *The Idea of Phenomenology* (trans. William P. Alston and George Nakhnikian; Boston, MA: Kluwer, 1990), p. 24; Marion, *In Excess,* p. 21.
[6] Martin Heidegger, "The Onto-theological Constitution of Metaphysics," in *Identity and Difference* (trans. Joan Stambaugh; New York: Harper & Row, 1969), p. 65.
[7] *In Excess,* pp. 30–31, 50.
[8] *In Excess,* pp. 22–23. Marion here cites Meinong's claim that objects whose definitions are self-contradictory ("goat-stag" "square circle," and the like) are "outside of being" yet still, for all that, objects, and thus *given* to knowledge. See also Husserl, *Idea,* p. 59.
[9] Marion, *Being Given,* pp. 83–118.

Kant's table of the categories in the *Critique of Pure Reason* (quantity, quality, relation, and modality), Marion argues that, respectively, events, the idol (e.g., painting), the flesh, and the icon (the face of the Other) evidence precisely by the limitless superabundance of intuitive content over conceptual form the excess of givenness over phenomenal manifestation.[10] Moreover, the one who undergoes these phenomena—whom Husserl called noesis, the transcendental "I," and Heidegger "Dasein"—is designated *"l'adonné"* by Marion, to indicate that it (I) is (am) only the *terminus ad quem* of the arrival of givenness. "I," *l'adonné*, have my origin as the stopping point, the resistance offered to the overwhelming flux of givenness; I come into being and take my being from the fact that, upon me, givenness spreads out and rises to manifestation, like a photographic image on a projector screen does when the screen backscatters light.[11]

It is against the backdrop of this reconfiguration and radicalization of the horizon of phenomenology that Marion takes up again the problem of the orientation in thinking regarding Being and God. And it is to this renovated phenomenology of givenness that he returns, in his conclusion, to try to resolve what he takes to be the "decisive" question: "When it comes to God, must not even the question of being, or, to put it bluntly, of ontology, receive a new qualification?"

II

What does Being have to do with (the Christian) God, or God with Being? A very great deal, of course, as both Christian *traditio* and the history of philosophy, especially metaphysics, make clear to us. Tellingly, however, Marion does not engage ancient or Scholastic sources to discuss the manifold senses of Being and beings, or to argue, as he does in several other places, against univocity of predication between creatures and God.[12] Nor, as in his treatment of Augustine in *In the Self's Place*, does he outline a counter-tradition to metaphysics, a thinking of God and being orthogonal to it.[13] Instead, he turns to modern metaphysics, the *metaphysica generalis et specialis* developed out of Suarez by way of thinkers like Clauberg, Wolff, and Baumgarten, on the grounds that this is metaphysics "in the strictly historical sense, the only operative one." It is against this *metaphysica* that Marion deploys his careful but polemical analysis, to show that ontology need not have the final or exclusive word when it comes to God.

His analysis proceeds in three stages. First, he shows how *metaphysica* places the Being of beings upon the Procrustean bed of the modern concept of *substantia*. Modern *substantia*, the "*ens reale* par excellence," is being which subsists by persisting in its own being, as (in Spinoza's formulation) *causa sui*. The meaning of Being is

---

[10] Marion, *In Excess*, pp. 112–113. Revelation, a fifth type of saturated phenomenon, Marion asserts, incorporates an excess with regard to all four tables of the categories at once; cf. *In Excess*, pp. 158–162.
[11] Marion, *In Excess*, pp. 48–53.
[12] Cf. Christina Gschwandtner, *Degrees of Givenness* (Bloomington: Indiana University Press, 2014), p. 152.
[13] Jean-Luc Marion, *In the Self's Place: The Approach of St. Augustine* (trans. Jeffrey L. Kosky; Stanford, CA: Stanford University Press, 2012).

conatus in suo esse perseverandi, "the will to persist in one's own being." The argument is as follows. In thinking the *ens in quantum ens* thought must form only the least determinate of concepts, in order to express, not particular beings, but that which all have in common. But this leads thought to a formal representation of a being in terms of what it is *not*, i.e., as this determinate being. From this, Clauberg (via Goclenius and Timpler) concludes that *ens* is "everything that is in any manner possible, [everything that] can be thought and said": being is unthinkable except as that which can think itself, or at least represent itself to itself. Spinoza then reaches beyond mere representation to think the real essence of *ens in quantum ens* by defining it as *substantia*, the *ens reale*: "that which is in itself and which conceives by itself." But for a substance to be "in itself" means for it to subsist *per se*—that is, to *persist* in its being. To persist means to persevere, to perdure in being, and for *substantia* which subsists *per se*, this means for an indefinite time. Such a substance is God, precisely thought as *causa sui*, self-caused.[14]

The second stage of Marion's analysis takes its cue from Heidegger's essay "The Anaximander Fragment."[15] Heidegger makes clear how substance's perseverance is accomplished temporally, as an "occupation" by persistence in presence. Heidegger, Marion says, has taught us that, since early Greek philosophy, *ousia*, the basis of the nature of beings, has been read as presence (*parousia*). To be in presence, to be present, involves more than simply showing up in the present moment: it means to occupy, indeed to colonize, the present. It is to install oneself in the present and to keep watch against (*Gegenwart*) all other possible contenders for that privileged position in being—what Kant terms *Beharrlichkeit*. Here is to be found the "injustice" of insistent persistence that Heidegger draws out of his reading of the Anaximander fragment: "Whence things have their origin, there they must also pass away according to necessity; for they must pay penalty and be judged for their injustice, according to the ordinance of time."[16] In order to secure its claim to the present, substance must contest, by power and force, the claims of all other pretender beings, past, present, or to come. It does so by covering up its own having come into being and its possible future passing away, as well as by concealing the very frailty of the temporal present—i.e., the inability of the present, continually itself dissolving in every instant, to provide a foundation for the persistent subsistence that the *conatus perseverandi* posits. What such a doctrine of perseverance covers up, however, Heidegger insists, is the "ambivalence" (*Zweideutigkeit*) of presence: concealed in the present presence is the absent—namely,

---

[14] The most substantial study of Marion's reading of Spinoza is Stéphane Vinolo, "Le don de Spinoza à la phénoménologie de Jean-Luc Marion," *Laval théologique et philosophique* 72, no. 2 (2016), pp. 299–317. While Vinolo reads Marion as opposing a Spinozist metaphysics, he goes on to claim that Spinoza actually affords an exit from metaphysics, and does so under the aegis of the gift. He quotes *Ethics* I, Axiom 3 to this effect: "A determinate cause being given, an effect necessarily follows; and, on the other hand, if there is no determinate cause, it is impossible that an effect can follow." Vinolo makes, I think, too much depend upon the "being given" in the axiom. While perhaps an argument could be made that, on some readings, Spinoza might be said to escape the charge of metaphysics, it is not an argument that Marion would likely follow.

[15] "The Anaximander Fragment," in *Early Greek Thinking* (trans. David Krell and Frank Capuzzi; New York: Harper & Row, 1975), pp. 13–58.

[16] Ibid., p. 13.

the past and the future. This absent is also present, but in the mode of *Unverborgenheit*, "unconcealment." In order, therefore, to make redress for the "injustice" of persistent, insistent occupation of the present, and therefore, truly to enter into presence, a being must give up the possession of the present. If it does so, it will be able to apprehend not only the present moment, but the moments of future and past, the not yet present and the no longer present, which now can disclose themselves in presence.

Rather than follow Heidegger further, though, Marion now offers his own departure from *metaphysica*, in order to venture a new "qualification" of the question of Being and God, and to afford us another possible way of thinking them, otherwise than as modern *substantia*. The departure involves consideration of the gift, of the event, and of Christ as the One who kenotically lays down and offers up His own being to the Father.

We saw above that, for a gift to be grasped as it shows itself as a gift requires a phenomenological reduction, carried out in three parts. But what can be said about the gift outside of such a reduction? What befalls a gift when it is not attended to with the care and insight of the phenomenological gaze? In part due to our "everyday inattentiveness," which is carried out within the "enframing" (to use a Heideggerean term) of *metaphysica*, but also in part due to the very requirement of the gift, a thing given insistently, persistently fills the present of the recipient. In accordance with the demands of perseverance, it covers over its giver, and thus its status as a gift. Its past (its having-been-given by a giver) is concealed—so much so, in fact, that the recipient is barely, if at all, aware of its having arrived. If they conceive of a past to the thing before them, it is as nothing but an already accomplished transfer of ownership of a piece of property from one self to another. And it is a transfer that can, indeed, be "accounted for"—on the basis of desert, debt repayment, etc. Any sense of gratitude, to say nothing of a desire to reciprocate the (non-)gift, to give it away to another, to destroy it, etc., is averted.[17]

How can the self escape this prison of ingratitude—an ingratitude, moreover, to which it is wholly oblivious? To do so the self would somehow have to accede to an awareness of the moments of giving: of a giver, anonymous and untraceable; of the movement from the giver toward the self, now to be understood as a givee; and of the thing given, as a gift, demanding that it be passed on as a gift in turn.[18] On what basis could this accession be possible? It could only be through recognition of the event-character of the giving. While Marion treats events as special kinds of saturated phenomena in *In Excess*,[19] here he is rather concerned with their temporal structure. In experiences and in thinking viewed through the lens of *metaphysica*, "events" are conceived of as effects of prior causes, belonging to a nexus of determinations which are in principle rationally comprehensible and controllable. In this scheme, wholly ontic, the ontological character of events is covered over and concealed. The self in the

---

[17] The *locus classicus* for the anthropological description of gift-giving and -reception is Marcel Mauss's *The Gift: The Form and Reason for Exchange in Archaic Societies* (trans. W.D. Halls; London: Routledge, 2002). See also Jacques Derrida, *Given Time I: Counterfeit Money* (trans. Peggy Kamuf; Chicago, IL: University of Chicago Press, 1992), pp. 34–70.
[18] Marion, *Being Given*, pp. 86–88.
[19] Marion, *In Excess*, pp. 30–53.

grip of *metaphysica* cannot grasp the process of transition, of arrival of the gift in the giving by the giver. Nor can it truly realize the adventitious and gratuitous character of the initiative of the giver. To grasp the gift, the whole process of giving must be discovered. And this can only take place if the self somehow manages not to "stiffen" itself, to give up its rigor of insistence and perdurance in presence in its own being.

The paradigmatic example, in Marion's view, for this kind of surrender or sacrifice of rigor is Christ. As St. Paul says, "He, being in the form of God, did not consider as a possession-to-keep-for-himself to be equal to God, but emptied himself (*ekenosen*)" (Phil. 2.6-7). Christ is already God; and yet he sacrifices his divine *ousia* in an act of kenosis. He does this because he comes to understand—if only in the garden of Gethsemane—that that *ousia* is a gift which comes to him from a giver (the Father). And, as a gift, it must be given away again, in a re-gifting to a new givee. For sacrifice takes the form of surrender, by Christ, of his will: in that dreadful garden he inverts his will and redirects it back to the Father: "Not my will but may yours come to pass" (Lk 22.42). Unlike Nietzsche's Zarathustra, as Marion points out, whose "great Yes" is addressed only to his own will, Christ's affirmation of his father's will sacrifices His own. "If," therefore, he writes:

> The will to power defines nihilism, if nihilism itself confirms the end of *metaphysica*, it is therefore necessary to go so far as to suspect that to want the will of the Father, that is of an other par excellence, to want what *I* do not want and do not want to want, constitutes the only and the definitive response to nihilism and the final imposition of an alternative interpretation of the Being of beings.

In so far as nihilism, as Heidegger claims, is necessarily the destiny of the unconcealedness of Being, "the Trinitarian sense of the *admirabile commercium* of the exchange of the wills of the son and the father" provides us with a response to nihilism.

III

The word "nihilism," which, by way of Heidegger's cited presence in Marion's chapter, seems to haunt the entire piece, makes its first appearance only in the concluding paragraphs. There it is invoked twice: first, in connection with "will to power" (Nietzsche), and then in connection with "the end of *metaphysica*" (Heidegger). In his essay, "The Word of Nietzsche: 'God Is Dead,'" Heidegger writes:

> Metaphysics is an epoch of the history of Being itself. But in its essence metaphysics is nihilism. The essence of nihilism belongs to that history as which Being itself comes to presence ... The word 'nihilism' indicates that *nihil* (Nothing) *is*, and is essentially, in that which it names. Nihilism means: Nothing is befalling everything and in every respect. 'Everything' means whatever is, in its entirety. And whatever is stands there in every respect proper to it when it is experienced as that which is. Hence nihilism means that Nothing is befalling whatever is as such, in its entirety. But whatever is, is what it is and how it is from out of Being. Assuming that every

'is' lies in being, the essence of nihilism consists in the fact that Nothing is befalling Being itself ... Thus nihilism would be in its essence a history that runs its course along with Being itself. It would lie in Being's own essence, then, that Being remain unthought because it withdraws.[20]

Importantly, Marion does not share Heidegger's view of nihilism as the destiny of the thinking of Being, in its entirety and without exception. In *God without Being* he argues, forcefully, that Heidegger's charge can only justifiably be lodged against metaphysics when it subjects all thought of God to the prior conditions and requirements of the thought of Being—a situation he terms "the double idolatry."[21] Modern *metaphysica*, in his present essay, with its insistence on understanding the essence of Being as *conatus in suo esse perseverandi*, certainly fills the bill. Indeed, in Marion's view *metaphysica* inevitably terminates in the Nietzschean will to power. But modern metaphysics, and even the critique of it by thinkers like Nietzsche and Heidegger, are not all there is to the thinking of being. Marion's effort in his book on St. Augustine is in great part an effort to present a reading of the saint not as a philosopher—certainly not as a metaphysician— but rather as an anti- or post-metaphysician, but one for whom the language of being is inescapable, even though the supreme desideratum is love.[22] And in the previous chapter of the current volume, the effort is not directed at a destruction (or deconstruction) of the thought of Being in the name of the thought of God, but at a reorientation which liberates the thinking of God from any prior restraint imposed by the thinking of Being, and which would lead to a new way of thinking of Being, in the Name.[23]

If, then, the thought of being and the thought of God are always in some sense entangled with one another; and if the thinking of being called metaphysics (or even *metaphysica*) is an ineluctable part of the history of the thinking of being; and if nihilism is the destiny of metaphysics, how are we to understand nihilism? If nihilism is the meaning and destiny (*Geschick*) of the unfolding of the truth of the essence of Being (*phusis, logos, hen, idea, energeia*, substantiality, objectivity, subjectivity, the will, the will to power, the will to will[24]), and if, in the present moment of the enframing of technology,[25] we have come to a point of closure for that destiny, then thinking both requires a new inception and is liberated to seek it. And to the extent that the question concerning God is entangled and indicated with the question concerning Being, does that not mean as well that theology demands a new inception, and is free to seek it? The answer to both of these questions, it seems to me, is "yes"—and not just to me, but to Marion as well.

Although Marion's approach to nihilism is polemical, other recent thinkers concerned with its role in philosophy and theology have attempted a more positive reading. Jean-

---

[20] Martin Heidegger, "The Word of Nietzsche: 'God Is Dead,'" in *The Question Concerning Technology and Other Essays* (trans. William Lovitt; New York: Harper & Row, 1977), pp. 110–111.
[21] Marion, *God without Being*, pp. 16–17, 25–52.
[22] Marion, *In the Self's Place*, pp. 4–9.
[23] See Jean-Luc Marion, "A Logic of Manifestation: The Trinity," in *Givenness and Revelation* (trans. Stephen E. Lewis; New York: Oxford University Press, 2016), pp. 89–115.
[24] Heidegger, "Onto-theological Constitution," p. 66.
[25] Martin Heidegger, *The Question Concerning Technology*, pp. 18–35.

Luc Nancy, for example, has argued that Christianity is "self-deconstructive," and thus itself nihilistic. First, in the figure of Christ and his renunciation of divine power, this renunciation becomes the proper deed of God, an emptying out without remainder which undoes theism itself. Second, Christian monotheism demythologizes religion, erasing all distinctively religious significations. Third, Christianity presents itself historically as a composite: it has a prominence in, and yet detachment from, Judaism, Islam, and Greco-Roman philosophy. It thus is something other than "a religion *stricto sensu*": it carries within itself always the option of developing and interpreting itself in more than one register. And the mysteries which Christianity preaches—above all, that concerning the incarnation of Christ—present themselves as problems for the intellect, and not merely a narrative and an evangel. Fourth, Christianity appears to be less a body of doctrine than a depiction of a self disquietedly in search of itself, lacking, but yearning for, an identity. Fifth, and finally, Christianity as self-deconstruction takes the form of a perpetual process of self-rectification and self-surpassing. Christianity seems to have developed, at the same time, both as an affirmation of power and domination (the Roman Empire) and as a destitution and abandonment of self, "whose vanishing point is the evaporation of self." Both dialectical surpassing and nihilistic decomposition, in Christianity monotheism delivers itself over to humanism.[26] Far from proclaiming that nihilism blasphemes Christianity by imposing a prior philosophical hermeneutic upon all possible theology, Nancy argues that really existing historical Christianity bears within itself a nihilistic and secularizing tendency. In fact, Christianity has always already been "dis-enclosed" (*déclosé*), and the kenosis that enacts this dis-enclosure leads it, in the end, to what Nancy terms an "*éclosure*" the word for the emergence of a butterfly from its chrysalis.

Thus, the kenosis Marion remarks upon at the conclusion of this paper, Christ's emptying himself of his will and of his divine *ousia*, is for Nancy destinally linked to nihilism and to secularization in the form of humanism. But another thinker perhaps more useful for reading nihilism and kenosis and their relation to philosophy and theology is Gianni Vattimo.

Perhaps the power and significance of Nietzsche's and Heidegger's readings of nihilism are not *opposed to*, but rather draw their significance and power from, the Christianity that forms the "substratum" of the world from which they come, Vattimo asks.[27] According to Heidegger, "nihilism" is not just the "history of human errors," but the history of being itself: "Being has a nihilistic vocation and ... diminishing, withdrawal and weakening are the traits that Being assigns to itself in the epoch of the end of metaphysics and of the becoming problematic of objectivity." For Vattimo, the key was seeing that the "idea that the history of Being has as a guiding thread the weakening of strong structures" was "nothing but the transcription of the Christian doctrine of the incarnation of the Son of God."[28]

---

[26] Jean-Luc Nancy, "Deconstruction and Monotheism," in *Dis-enclosure: The Deconstruction of Christianity* (trans. Bettina Bergo, Gabriel Malenfant, and Michael B. Smith; New York: Fordham University Press, 2008), pp. 35–39.

[27] Gianni Vattimo, *Belief* (trans. Luca D'Isanto and David Webb; Stanford, CA: Stanford University Press, 1999), pp. 33–34.

[28] Ibid., pp. 35–36.

Therefore the weakening of the natural religions by the Christian *evangelium* is coordinate with the weakening of metaphysics discovered by Heidegger. This double weakening he calls "secularization": "the process of 'drifting' that removed modern lay civilization from its sacral origin." Vattimo thinks the Incarnation, "God's abasement to the level of humanity," can be interpreted with the help of a post-metaphysical philosophy of weakening into a theology of finitude, immanence, and nonviolence.[29]

"Weakening" is going on within religion, and within that part of Christianity which assimilated itself to the older (violent, sacrificial) religious forms. Secularization views two modern phenomena condemned by the traditional Church—"the loss of temporal authority and human reason's increasing autonomy from its dependence upon an absolute God"—as "precisely a positive effect of Jesus' teaching, and not a way of moving away from it."[30] Secularization does not proclaim itself as an objective "teaching" or "doctrine"—this would make it a metaphysical idea or school and negate its meaning. It is, instead, an event, finite, fragile, tentative, corrigible, open, discursive. It is based in part on the biblical saying, "I no longer call you servants, but friends" (Jn 15.15). "The rigor of post-metaphysical discourse consists in the effort to cultivate an attitude of persuasion without proclaiming a 'universal' viewpoint, which is no viewpoint at all, an attitude that is aware of coming from and addressing someone belonging to the same process, of which it has no neutral vision but risks an interpretation."[31]

The weakening of strong structures thus presents not a danger but a promise. Nihilism, properly conceived, is not a transitional period before a repositing of a new (and equally metaphysical) set of "highest values," or a "fully realized nothingness."[32] It is instead an "infinite history," an "indefinite drift" of the play of interpretations "limited only by the principle of charity." The drift must be infinite or indefinite, since only the violence of a finality from which there could be no appeal could end it.[33]

Vattimo thus affords us yet another passage from kenosis and nihilism to secularization, and on to an infinite and indefinite hermeneutic, one limited only by charity—after all, the supreme theological virtue. Moreover, in so doing he presents us with a schematism for such a hermeneutics, one which is largely absent from Marion's oeuvre, as Christina Gschwandtner, among others, has pointed out.[34] Far from being a threat to philosophy, nihilism would announce a new instauration. And far from being a threat to theology and to faith, "secularization" would mark theology's new openness to the future of interpretation and action which would not so much destroy tradition as make it possible to add something decisively new to it—and perhaps, as Vattimo claims, to accede at last to a new limit principle of charity in the "indefinite drift" away from the sacral origins of the West. Such a charity or *agape*—and, as Marion remarks,

---

[29] Ibid., p. 39.
[30] Ibid., p. 40.
[31] Ibid., p. 46.
[32] Ibid., p. 63.
[33] Ibid., pp. 65–66.
[34] Gschwandtner, *Degrees of Givenness*, pp. 34–47. See also Richard Kearney, *Debates in Continental Philosophy: Conversations with Contemporary Thinkers* (New York: Fordham University Press, 2004), pp. 15–32.

God is "without Being in the name of agape"—would not and could not be a "limit" in the violent form of a finality. As Vattimo writes:

> The interpretation which [Jesus Christ] is, reveals its true and only meaning: God's love for his creatures. However, this 'ultimate' meaning precisely by virtue of its being caritas, is not really ultimate and does not possess the peremptoriness of the metaphysical principle, which cannot be transcended, and before which all questioning ceases. Perhaps the reason why nihilism is an infinite, never-ending process lies in the fact that love, as the 'ultimate' meaning of revelation, is not truly ultimate. Moreover, the reason why philosophy at the end of the metaphysical epoch finds it can no longer believe in foundations, in the first cause which is given objectively before the mind's eye, may be that it has become aware (in so far as it has been educated also, if not only, by the Christian tradition) of the implicit violence of every finality, of every principle that would silence all questioning.[35]

The question, then, would be: Is the relation between nihilism and Christ a necessarily polemical one? Is there room in a phenomenology of the gift for a "charity" of the kind Vattimo describes? Especially since, in its form as *metaphysica*, metaphysics calls for and deserves its own weakening?

IV

The word "love" appears only fleetingly in the text of Marion's paper; but it is, as we know, a major theme of his work, and indeed the subject of an entire text, *The Erotic Phenomenon*.[36] Indeed, traces of the argument of that book can be spotted in this paper.[37] It is especially clear in the concluding section, in the remarks on the *admirabile commercium* of the Father and the Son of the Trinity, Jesus's sacrifice of his own will and acceptance of the Father's, knowing that in precisely that sacrifice he will receive the loving gift of equality with God. But this argument, I think, needs to be more closely connected to the analysis of giver, gift, and gifted which comes at the very end of *Being Given*.[38] There, after having announced that the phenomenology of givenness is finished with the "subject" and all its recent avatars, Marion raises almost immediately the question of access to the Other—the central question of Emmanuel Levinas's oeuvre, who determines that access in his own works in purely ethical terms. If the gifted (the "givee") is she who receives the given, and receives herself from the given, then she can receive, according to no horizon, *a priori* principle, or constitution, the face of the Other. But the gifted, too, Marion claims, is inscribed within the phenomenality of givenness, and thus can give herself, too, and in a "privileged way." "Above all," he writes:

---

[35] Vattimo, *Belief*, pp. 64–65.
[36] Jean-Luc Marion, *The Erotic Phenomenon* (trans. Stephen E. Lewis' Chicago, IL: University of Chicago Press, 2007).
[37] Ibid., pp. 221–222.
[38] Marion, *Being Given*, pp. 323–324.

The gifted can glimpse the possibility of giving itself to an exceptional given—
the given that would show itself in the mode of the gifted, it too accustomed to
receiving itself from what gives itself to it. When the other shows itself, it is a case
of one gifted giving itself to another gifted: first as a common given (a phenomenon
given), next as a gifted (to whom givens are given). The difficulty no longer
consists therefore in deciding if the other can appear ... But in grasping how the
other shows himself by giving himself to the gifted that I remain ... This would
no longer concern intersubjectivity or interobjectivity, but intergivenness—less an
exception to ordinary phenomenality than one of its most advanced developments
and, perhaps, its completion.[39]

And yet Marion immediately insists that his account not only authorizes a revisiting of ethics in order to confirm its legitimacy on the basis of a phenomenology of givenness, but can surpass it by arriving at "what ethics cannot attain": the definitive individualization of the Other, achieved in love alone.

Christina Gschwandtner argues[40] that Marion's aim, particularly in the section of *In Excess* entitled "In the Name," devoted to the saturated phenomenon of revelation, is to push phenomenology to its utmost limits, to a kind of purity and radicality of language and expression. This is accomplished particularly in the description of prayer, in which the icon supplants the face: "It is not only the other of ethics (Levinas), but more radically the icon which imposes its appeal."[41] At its purest level, therefore, intergivenness is the *commercium* between the anonymous giver and the gifted who decides to give herself over to the given. And it is precisely Jesus's prayer in the garden of Gethsemane which is the paradigmatic instance of this prayer. The ethical relation, therefore, cannot be more than a particular, subsidiary instance of this more general and fundamental phenomenon of intergivenness.

My question is: Must the relation between ethics, as Levinas conceives it, and this final horizon of intergivenness in love be thought this way? Gschwandtner finds fault with Marion's characterization of prayer as too individual, as lacking a kind of social, corporate, collective dimension (pp. 174–175). But my point is different: for Levinas, the phenomenality of the relation between God and the ethical subject is marked by what he calls "illeity." What does this neologism designate, for Levinas? Levinas says, in an interview with Philippe Nemo in 1982:

> I am going to tell you a peculiar feature of Jewish mysticism. In certain very old prayers, fixed by ancient authorities, the faithful one begins by saying to God "Thou" and finishes the proposition thus begun by saying "He", as if, in the course of this approach of the "Thou" its transcendence into "He" supervened. It is what in my descriptions I have called the "illeity" of the Infinite. Thus, in the "Here I am!" of the approach of the Other, the Infinite does not show itself. How then does

---

[39] Marion, *Being Given*, p. 324.
[40] Christina Gschwandtner, "Prayer—Pure and Personal? Jean-Luc Marion's Phenomenologies of Prayer," in *The Phenomenology of Prayer* (ed. Bruce Ellis Benson and Norman Wirzba; New York: Fordham University Press, 2005), pp. 176–181.
[41] Marion, *In Excess*, p. 118.

it take on meaning? I will say that the subject who says "Here I am!" testifies to the Infinite. It is through this testimony, whose truth is not the truth of representation or perception, that the revelation of the Infinite occurs. It is through this testimony that the very glory of the infinite glorifies itself.[42]

"He-ness" (*illéité*) expresses the manner in which, when the face of the Other is manifested, the Absent has already withdrawn from all revelation and dissimulation, into an absolute past. It is this disruption in withdrawal which is the absolutely Absent from out of which the face of the other person emerges in visitation. The Other stands in the trace; "He," that is to say, God, in withdrawal produces the nudity of the face of the Stranger, who stands in the trace left by His withdrawal.

In this context, Levinas begins explicitly to employ the name "God" in connection with the trace of the departure of God: the Absent is "God" who has passed, and left in being the trace in which the face of the Other arises. For Levinas, divine illeity represents a third component in the relationship of desire between myself and the absolutely other person. Levinas characterizes the relationship now as an *"intrigue à trois"*: "The I approaches the infinite by going generously toward the you, who is still my contemporary, but, in the trace of illeity, presents himself out of a depth of the past, faces, and approaches me."[43] The face of the other person is thus the site of ethical responsibility because the face arises within the trace left through divine illeity's utterly exceptional and unique manner of signifying. This manner is at one and the same time both perfectly discreet and the most disruptive of conscious intentionality: it is refusable, all too refusable, by the triumphalist ratio of self-identification, but if attended to, it promises to shake the very foundations of ratio in the name of ethical responsibility. The divine illeity, God's having always-already-passed, produces the "radical irrectitude" characteristic of the trace, and thereby the dimension of moral height and command from which the Other approaches and addresses me.

Such a "God" cannot be the term (*fin*) of any possible movement on my part; rather, illeity ceaselessly directs and redirects me to the concern with the welfare of my indigent neighbor. There can be no "participative" religion or cult of such a God; for there is participation only where there is disclosure of Being, and the divine illeity has departed the scene, as it were, in advance of all such possible disclosure. In illeity, therefore, all attempts to direct one's gaze upon the trace of the passing of God succeed only in disclosing the (finite, human) Other—naked, destitute, appealing for help. For Levinas this marks the limit of any possible engagement with God, in prayer, service, or worship. God does not solicit my individual prayers; God solicits my redoubled dedication to the service of my neighbor—my finite, temporal, human-all-too-human neighbor.

There seems to be, in Marion's phenomenology of the intergiven, of love, no place for such a notion. And yet, I would argue that it is a most important one, one that

---

[42] Emmanuel Levinas, *Ethics and Infinity* (trans. Richard A. Cohen; Pittsburgh, PA: Duquesne University Press, 1985), pp. 106–107.
[43] Emmanuel Levinas, "Phenomenon and Enigma," in *Collected Philosophical Papers* (trans. Alphonso Lingis; Boston, MA: Martinus Nijhoff, 1987), p. 72.

actually makes *caritas* or *agape* the limit condition of which Vattimo writes. The true term of *agape* is not God, who needs no counter-gift. It is our fellow human beings, who need all we can give them. Charity does not only not begin at home, it was never at home to begin with, since the home was always and ever expropriated land. *Caritas* is the going forth of the subject, hitherto sufficient unto himself in perseverant being, into the pragmatic service of the desperate needs of the widow, the orphan, and the stranger. Illeity, as, to use Marion's phrase, "the process, the transport, the displacement, the passing-over (*traversée*), in brief, the advent itself," seems to me the foundation, at the level of the "one and only givenness,"[44] of genuine *agape*.

And so my second question—or, rather, hypothesis—is this: perhaps prayer, and the pure and radical scene Marion sets for it in the *admirabile commercium* between the Son and the Father in Gethsemane, is not the limit. Perhaps, instead, devotion is best devoted to the Other, in the intergivenness of ethics, after all. The real ambiguity of Being (or, in Levinas's language, Being's "otherwise"), then, is its play between the Absent God and devotion to the human Other, *terminus a quo* and *ad quem*, of our own privileged giving, as *l'adonné*.

---

[44] Marion, *Being Given*, p. 323.

5

A Phenomenology of Revelation: Contemporary Encounters with Saint Ignatius Loyola

Robyn Horner

The enduring legacy of Saint Ignatius Loyola is that he experienced the passing of God in his everyday life, and showed the way for others to discern this passage and live accordingly. This extraordinary understanding of the possibility of a truly personal relationship with God is a beacon of hope for the ordinary person who, not drawn to a contemplative commitment, still longs to be caught up in the love that is promised as the meaning and dynamism of Christian existence. Moreover, it affirms unequivocally the value of the secular, not as that to be defined negatively against what is apparently sacred, but as the locus of God's care and concern, and the sphere of God's activity. In 1956, Karl Rahner argued that the *Spiritual Exercises* were deserving of greater theological consideration, and it is my view that this is still the case, not least in terms of the theological recontextualization of revelation for today.[1]

Even if it is not so for theologians (although arguably this could be the case), the question of revelation has largely become incoherent in the contemporary world. As the decisive point where belief essentially outstrips any supposedly neutral approach to "religion" (it is tolerable, for example, to study the Bible as literature, but not to take seriously its claims on the reader or believing communities), the whole notion of revelation is troublesome in detraditionalized, demythologized, pluralized, and individualized societies.[2] In an academic context, to speak of revelation is frequently to exclude oneself immediately from the possibility of serious philosophical or other conversation. And in many Western cultural contexts, the idea of belief in God on the basis of revelation is often greeted with sheer incredulity. It is my view that the sense that revelation is an incoherent or outmoded concept relates in some ways to the perceived gap between revelation and experience. The attractiveness in some quarters of activities or perspectives that are claimed to be "spiritual" but not "religious" is suggestive of the priority of (a certain type of) experience in contemporary life—one that does not especially resonate with the notion of a transcendent God typically called

---

[1] Karl Rahner, "The Logic of Concrete Individual Knowledge in Ignatius Loyola," in *The Dynamic Element in the Church* (London: Burns and Oates, 1964), pp. 84–86.
[2] See Lieven Boeve, *God Interrupts History: Theology in a Time of Upheaval* (trans. Brian Doyle; New York and London: Continuum, 2007).

upon by organized religions. Theologically, the gulf between narratives of religious experience and the articulation of an understanding of revelation simply repeats and reinforces this issue.

What is needed, then, is a way of thinking about revelation that permits some kind of credible dialogue about it to take place within contemporary thought and culture, particularly in the context of personal experience. My argument is that recent developments within French phenomenology allow for this kind of dialogue, and that Ignatius's *Spiritual Exercises* are a useful lens through which this can be both illustrated and explored further in the experience of everyday life.[3] In the present chapter, I propose to outline major features of this argument, in advance of a more lengthy and detailed examination.

Revelation and religious experience

There are good reasons to reinforce the distinction between religious experience and revelation—after all, as Jean-Yves Lacoste observes: "experience ... is not self-evidently a theological datum," and we are wise to be cautious in our readings of religious experience.[4] Moreover, when in the Christian Church it is understood that all revelation has its apex in the incarnation of God's Word in the person of Jesus Christ, the Word that speaks everything of God, so that everything before or since is understood to be the unfolding of what has already been spoken, we commit ourselves to the echoing or recognition of that Word in our experience rather than to the possibility of a novel experience of revelation as such.[5]

Nevertheless, if we are to take *Dei verbum* seriously, and to believe that revelation is always God's self-revelation, then we must understand revelation in relational terms, and relationships depend on personal experience. We might consider much of the contemporary emphasis on personal experience to be misplaced, but we will have missed something essential to Christian faith if we do not appreciate that unless God speaks to us in the depths of experience, we will not have tasted God's love, and if we do not taste this love, there will be no reason at all to pursue it. It is not enough that I hear God's Word spoken in general terms; I must hear it addressed to me directly, and that requires not only the repetition of the *kerygma* but also and especially that Word speaking in the specific circumstances and shape of my own life—God speaking to me.

---

[3] Ignatius Loyola, *The Spiritual Exercises of St. Ignatius: Based on Studies in the Language of the Autograph* (ed. and trans. Louis J. Puhl; Chicago, IL: Loyola University Press, 1968).

[4] Jean-Yves Lacoste, *La Phénoménalité De Dieu: Neuf Etudes* (Paris: Cerf, 2008). Study III. Nevertheless, as Dermot Lane noted some years ago: "A religious experience ... may be described as a revelatory experience of God." Dermot Lane, *The Experience of God: An Invitation to Do Theology* (New York: Paulist, 1981), p. 41.

[5] "Revelation is a mode of religious experience, while our experiences of the holy as judging, assisting, addressing, and the like, all have a revelatory element. One cannot therefore draw a hard and fast line between experience and revelation, but in practice it is desirable to keep these two formative factors distinct in our theological thinking. We do not normally dignify our day-to-day experiences of the holy by the name of 'revelation', and no theology properly so called could be founded on private revelations, for, as has been stressed already, theology expresses the faith of a community." John Macquarrie, *Principles of Christian Theology* (repr. 2003; London: SCM, rev. edn, 1977), p. 8.

One of the difficulties we encounter when we try to speak about revelation is to think through its actual character. While Christians believe that God wants to communicate with humanity and has so communicated, particularly in the history of the Jewish and Christian traditions, the disjunction between the divine and the human poses particular difficulties for the whole notion of something like revelation. It is easy to repeat the biblical injunction that "for God, all things are possible," even if they are not possible for human beings (Mk 10.27 NRSVCE), yet this can mean that we do not take as sufficiently serious our human context and the fact that God does not appear *as such* within it. From a philosophical perspective, Michael Andrews sums up the difficulty with precision: "How can an experience of absolute transcendence be constituted by human consciousness without violating the very principle of givenness that makes the field of transcendental experience and its universal structures possible in the first place?"[6] From a theological point of view, Avery Dulles's now-classic systematization of revelatory models and his exploration of revelation as symbolic mediation are helpful to some extent.[7] Nevertheless, his expressed anxieties about conceiving revelation as the possibility of "ecstatic encounter with God that has no explicitly doctrinal content" actually go to the heart of the issues I seek to explore here.[8] If revelation is thought along the lines of personal encounter, it would be odd to conceive it as the impartation of a set of concepts, and yet that is the point to which it seems that we are returned repeatedly.[9] Lieven Boeve observes of the contemporary theological landscape: "Time and again, it would appear that the dialogical principle at the heart of the concept of revelation developed at Vatican II is truncated and conceived as unilateral and asymmetrical. The potentially renewing—or interrupting—impact of such dialogue is thus restrained because of the possible risk of a too far-reaching adaptation or renewal and a loss of continuity."[10]

In short, it is extremely difficult to link revelation and experience: philosophically, because we simply cannot think God according to the manner of beings or even of being itself, and theologically, because it is often considered that there is ultimately too much at stake in doctrine for revelation to be considered as a genuinely personal encounter. It is for this reason that the work of Jean-Luc Marion is so important:

---

[6] Michael F. Andrews, "How (Not) to Find God in All Things: Derrida, Levinas and St Ignatius of Loyola on Learning How to Pray for the Impossible," in *The Phenomenology of Prayer* (ed. Bruce Ellis Benson and Norman Wirzba; New York: Fordham University Press, 2005), p. 195.

[7] Avery Dulles, *Models of Revelation* (Maryknoll, NY: Orbis, 1992).

[8] "Some prominent theologians, whose numbers are apparently growing, identify revelation as an ecstatic encounter with God that has no doctrinal content." Avery Dulles, *Catholic Doctrine: Between Revelation and Theology, Proceedings of the Catholic Theological Society of America* (1999), p. 83.

[9] So Marion observes, following a discussion of Thomas Aquinas and what follows up to Vatican II and *Dei Verbum*: "The non-epistemological intention of revelation aims to manifest God in person." Jean-Luc Marion, *Givenness and Revelation* (trans. Stephen Lewis; Oxford: Oxford University Press, 2016), pp. 26–27.

[10] Lieven Boeve, "Revelation, Scripture and Tradition: Lessons from Vatican II's Constitution Dei Verbum for Contemporary Theology," *International Journal of Systematic Theology* 13, no. 4 (2011), pp. 416–433 (431), http://dx.doi.org/doi:10.1111/j.1468-2400.2011.00598.x.

by seeking to give a phenomenological account of revelation, he highlights—both theologically and philosophically—the nature of experience, and opens a way forward for thinking revelation that is neither solipsistic nor excluded in principle from academic discourse.

Some insights from recent French philosophy

Marion observes that philosophy typically depends on the principle of sufficient reason to determine in advance the possibility (and impossibility) of the phenomena it may consider. Revelatory phenomena are thereby excluded from philosophy by definition. Following Heidegger's insight that phenomenology may concern itself with the inapparent, Marion expands the scope of the phenomenological reduction beyond objectivity, and even beyond being, to include potentially whatever gives itself to consciousness. Phenomenology can thus be open in principle to the possibility that revelation may take place, although it cannot rule definitively on the question of its actuality, which is the task of theology.[11]

Over some thirty years, Marion has developed this idea through his use of the concept of the "saturated phenomenon," where what is given to consciousness is so excessive that any attempt to meet it with a corresponding intention can only fail, or at best, signify very incompletely. Revelation is a special type of saturated phenomenon, because it incorporates each of four other types Marion identifies: the event, which saturates by its quality (being unforeseeable and unrepeatable); the idol, which saturates by its quantity (its excessive visibility); flesh, which saturates by relation (it is absolute); and the icon, which saturates by modality (it is resistant to all constitution).[12] Commentators have questioned the extent to which it is really possible to distinguish absolutely between these types, and it is true that there is some slippage between them. It may be that we are best served by using the overarching category of the event.[13] However, when it comes to revelation, it is clear that we are contemplating what most intensely resists our capacity for constitution: revelation is the ultimate "counter-

---

[11] Jean-Luc Marion, "The Possible and Revelation," in *The Visible and the Revealed* (New York: Fordham University Press, 2008).

[12] In its classic formulation, see Jean-Luc Marion, *Being Given: Toward a Phenomenology of Givenness* (trans. Jeffrey L. Kosky; Stanford, CA: Stanford University Press, 2002), §21, pp. 199–212.

[13] Christina M. Gschwandtner argues that the event could and does often describe all types of saturation as an overall type. Christina M. Gschwandtner, *Degrees of Givenness: On Saturation in Jean-Luc Marion* (Bloomington: Indiana University Press, 2014), pp. 25–26. Mason Brock observes: "While the experience of God may be more glorious, infinite, or incomprehensible than the experience of the other, this doesn't give us any concrete phenomenological distinctions between the two. Again it comes down to the fact that Marion has not provided a phenomenological way to differentiate between the experience of God and the experience of the human other, except that one is grander or more infinite than the other. Apart from that broad gloss, the phenomenological approaches both to revelation and to the icon seem essentially the same"; "perhaps the inability to substantially differentiate between the icon and revelation says a lot more about God than it does the shortcomings of phenomenology." Mason M. Brock, "Saturated Phenomena, the Icon, and Revelation: A Critique of Marion's Account of Revelation and the 'Redoubling' of Saturation," *Aporia* 24, no. 1 (2014), pp. 25–38 (36, 37).

experience."[14] As Marion writes, "what is experienced in revelation can be summed up as the powerlessness to experience whatever it might be that one experiences."[15] In his more recent work, he will speak of this powerlessness as productive of a type of "negative certainty," where what is best known about a phenomenon is that it will and must remain unknown.[16]

Let us try to give an example of such a phenomenon from a biblical text: the story of the Woman with the Hemorrhage, which I take from Luke's Gospel (Lk 8.43-48).

> Now there was a woman who had been suffering from haemorrhages for twelve years; and though she had spent all she had on physicians, no one could cure her. She came up behind him and touched the fringe of his clothes, and immediately her haemorrhage stopped. Then Jesus asked, "Who touched me?" When all denied it, Peter said, "Master, the crowds surround you and press in on you." But Jesus said, "Someone touched me; for I noticed that power had gone out from me." When the woman saw that she could not remain hidden, she came trembling; and falling down before him, she declared in the presence of all the people why she had touched him, and how she had been immediately healed. He said to her, "Daughter, your faith has made you well; go in peace."[17]

When we contemplate this scene, what is given to us?

First, we see a woman, but we see her only as she tries to remain hidden. Nameless throughout the narrative, the woman's illness makes her repellent. Even if we cannot yet see the inevitable stain of her disease on her clothes, we are given its characteristic smell, and the stigma of her uncleanliness hangs like a pall around her. While she apparently believes that Jesus can heal her, she evidently feels she can only approach him anonymously. Jostling in the crowd, her stench undoubtedly competes with all the surrounding smells of an ancient town, and she stands a chance of momentarily disguising her approach. Her healing reportedly takes place as soon as she touches the fringe of Jesus's clothes.

The Jesus we are given in this narrative is characterized by strangeness. The description of his feeling power having gone out from him is just plain odd to the modern ear, and appears even stranger as his evident powerfulness contrasts with his apparent lack of awareness of who has touched him. If we have been educated to any degree about Jesus's context in ancient Palestine, we might see him in terms of a

---

[14] "If, for the saturated phenomenon, there is no experience of an object, it remains for us to imagine that there might be a counter-experience of a non-object. Counter-experience is not equivalent to a non-experience, but to the experience of a phenomenon that is neither regardable, nor guarded according to objectness, one which therefore resists the conditions of objectification. Counter-experience offers the experience of what irreducibly contradicts the conditions for the experience of objects." Marion, *Being Given*, p. 215.

[15] Marion, "The Possible and Revelation," p. 9.

[16] Jean-Luc Marion, *Negative Certainties* (trans. Stephen E. Lewis; Chicago, IL: University of Chicago Press, 2015).

[17] The version at Mark 5.24-34 has only slightly less detail. While it would be preferable to take the pericope as a whole (i.e., to include the story of the healing of Jairus's daughter), this is not possible here.

culture where wonder-workers are relatively commonplace. His complete otherness to the contemporary mind makes him resistant to the gaze.

Jesus's question, however, brings him sharply into personal focus. *Who touched me?* Not only the woman and others in the crowd, but also we, the hearers of the narrative, are brought into the sphere of his address. Peter's response is logical but dismissive; Jesus's insistence on the point ("someone touched me ... ") begins to draw he and the woman together in a different way. Her givenness in the narrative is altered at this stage: the woman comes into full view, and her selfhood erupts in her testimony: *she came trembling; and falling down before him, she declared in the presence of all the people why she had touched him, and how she had been immediately healed.* In responding to Jesus, she herself becomes visible—as one who confesses (and thus brings to manifestation) Jesus's power to heal. At this point, we also see Jesus himself more clearly as a person, as he addresses her, not only with authority, but also with tenderness and compassion: *Daughter, your faith has made you well.* Yet with these words, Jesus declines the identity of a healer or wonder-worker; he ascribes the healing to her faith, and in doing so, invites our further questioning about his identity. In almost the same moment, however, both she and we are gently dismissed from him: *go in peace.*

We can use Marion's categories—themselves inversions of Kant's categories with regard to the possibility of experience—to analyze the narrative. Doubtlessly, it takes place as an event. We are unable to give an adequate account of its quantity or dimensions: it is "unforeseeable," "not exhaustively comprehensible," and "not reproducible."[18] In terms of quality, the scene functions technically as an idol: there is too much to see, which means that what we see of it is always too little. In terms of relation, we are not able to determine a reason for what has happened to the woman and Jesus's part in it; we cannot explain it in terms of causality. And in terms of modality, the given is invisible: while the woman witnesses to Jesus, we see neither the healing nor his divinity *as such*. We are left with a question, then, which is whether or not to trust this woman, to believe her. And we may then ask: Is this a revelatory text? Am I addressed by it, now?

In proposing an example of a saturated phenomenon, I selected something biblical to make my way forward a little simpler. By asking about the personal resonances of the text, I sought to link it with contemporary experience. But I drew from the canon, which is considered to be revelatory, and any personal resonances there were, or are, could be considered revelatory in a secondary or derivative sense.[19] It is, indeed, possible to encounter Jesus in a prayerful reading of a text, but what I mean

---

[18] Marion, *Being Given*, p. 207. I am thankful to Shane Mackinlay for drawing my attention to precisely these elements of Marion's description, in Shane Mackinlay, *Interpreting Excess: Jean-Luc Marion, Saturated Phenomena, and Hermeneutics, Perspectives in Continental Philosophy* (New York: Fordham University Press, 2010), p. 132.

[19] It is in this way that I understand John Macquarrie when he writes: "A revelation that has the power to found a community of faith becomes fruitful in that community, and is, so to speak, repeated or re-enacted in the experience of the community, thus becoming normative for the experience of the community. Yet only because the primordial revelation is continually renewed in present experience can it be revelation for us, and not just a fossilized revelation." Macquarrie, *Principles*, pp. 8–9.

to get at is a thinking of revelation that enables this aspect of personal encounter to be interrogated more fully.

Marion gives us very powerful descriptions of how the saturated phenomenon gives itself to experience. When I refer to "experience," of course, I do not mean that the saturated phenomenon is reducible to the Husserlian *Erlebnis*, or "lived experience" of consciousness. Instead, the recipient or "gifted one" (*l'adonné*) receives what runs counter to experience, and this gifted one "resists" it in such a way that he or she brings the saturated phenomenon to light. Marion explains: "the receiver, in and through the receptivity of 'feeling', transforms givenness into manifestation."[20] The given impresses itself on the receiver without appearing as an object to be theoretically constituted; it is the *effect* (or feeling) of the given that is primary.[21] He specifies that "'feeling' does not result from the 'thing' as its effect, [or] double it as its appearance, but ... shows it as its one and only possible apparition." In other words, the effect *is* the appearance. Yet this apparition or manifestation is at once "hidden from the gaze," that is, from object constitution.[22] To quote Marion again: "This presentation implies reception in 'feeling', and it aims precisely at showing for thought, manifesting for a consciousness, forming for vision what, otherwise, would give itself to the blind."[23] Not only does *l'adonné* make the given visible in this transmutation, but the very act of transmutation makes *l'adonné* him or herself visible. This provokes a double visibility, which happens in the response made by *l'adonné* to the given (or "the call," in the sense of "call and response"), and the making visible of *l'adonné* in the process.[24] Marion allows that receipt of the (divine) given also provokes a double response (*mysterium tremendum et fascinans*): to the one open to God, it might provoke a sense of paralysis or terror, or perhaps lead to an "obsession with evoking [and] discussing"; to the one not open in this way, it might lead to even "denying that of which we all admit that we have no concept."[25]

---

[20] Marion, *Being Given*, p. 264.
[21] When it comes to the givenness of a saturated phenomenon, Marion specifies that this will impact upon the receiver as a call. Marion, *Being Given*, p. 266.
[22] Marion, *Being Given*, p. 264.
[23] Ibid., p. 265.
[24] "The given, as a lived experience, remains a stimulus, an excitation, scarcely a piece of information; *l'adonné* receives it, without its showing itself ... I will risk saying that the given, unseen but received, is projected on *l'adonné* (or consciousness, if one prefers) as on a screen; all the power of this given comes from crashing down on this screen, provoking a double visibility." Jean-Luc Marion, *In Excess: Studies of Saturated Phenomena* (trans. Robyn Horner and Vincent Berraud; New York: Fordham University Press, 2002), pp. 49–50.
[25] "Access to the divine phenomenality is not forbidden to us; in contrast, it is precisely when we become entirely open to it that we find ourselves forbidden from it—frozen, submerged, we are by ourselves forbidden from advancing and likewise from resting. In the mode of interdiction, terror attests the insistent and unbearable excess of the intuition of God. Next, it could also be that the excess of intuition is marked—strangely enough—by our obsession with evoking, discussing, and even denying that of which we all admit that we have no concept. For how could the question of God dwell within us so deeply—as much in our endeavoring to close it as in our daring to open it—if, having no concept that could help us reach it, an intuition did not fascinate us?" Marion, *In Excess*, pp. 161–162.

I turn now to examine briefly an important contribution to this discussion that can be drawn from the work of Lacoste. In *La Phénoménalité de Dieu*, Lacoste observes that if we are to know God, it will be in the domain of affection: "God can appear," he writes, "not in theophany but in the modest form of a presence felt." By presence, Lacoste cannot mean the coincidence of meaning and being, since he has just described phenomenologically the experience of a knowing that is always dependent on the memory or the anticipation of what is not present. Moreover, he is at pains to point out that an affective knowledge does not imply an understanding that grasps the totality, but instead, is knowledge by means of acquaintance or recognition.

> The fact that the heart can sense God's absence and presence at the same time is the cornerstone of all interpretation of so called "religious" experiences. God is not felt more than he is unfelt. To know that he eludes the always possible domination of feeling is to respect his transcendence. Anticipations of his eschatological presence, that is to say, of his parousia, can certainly be conceded to privileged witnesses. But in the everyday context to which our experience of God, or quasi-experience, belongs we should be satisfied with a radically non-eschatological presence.[26]

That God is known by means of the affect makes sense of the belief that God is known as love; as Lacoste tells us: "Only if we perceive God as loveable can we perceive God at all."[27]

While Lacoste allows the possibility that God is felt as event in experience and so draws us in love, in much of his work, and more commonly, we find ourselves dealing with the situation where God does not seem present to the believer at all. This is exemplified in his discussion of the Eucharist. One might naïvely expect that the Eucharist, as the "source and summit" of Christian life (*Lumen gentium*, 11), is the site par excellence where one might encounter God in feeling, and yet this is frequently not the case. As many of the mystics have observed, a commitment of faith that apparently begins rewardingly in the affect gradually seems to yield less over time, so that the Eucharist—as with prayer more generally—might also become a place or time of great aridity. Here, as elsewhere, the price of love is death. Lacoste describes this in far more restrained terms as a "wound of experience"—the feeling that I do not feel. However, he argues that not feeling can be a way of feeling, or at least a way of feeling by lack, the felt recognition that I do not feel what I should or could feel, an experience of non-experience.[28] Joeri Schrijvers explains the double nature of this non-experience:

> On the one hand, I experience my non-experience through experiencing a certain lack, and on the other, I experience *that which is lacking* from this non-experience.

---

[26] Lacoste, *La Phénoménalité De Dieu*, p. 51.
[27] Ibid., pp. 92–93.
[28] Jean-Yves Lacoste, *Être En Danger* (Paris: Cerf, 2011), pp. 110–112.

I experience a lack of experience and that which is lacking from experience. In other words, I experience simultaneously that God does not come to experience and I experience that what I am experiencing is not God.[29]

In the celebration of the Eucharist, the spoken words authoritatively name what is given—the Eucharistic gift, yet this is not a phenomenon that is perceived with the senses, even if reference is made to it in the phenomena of the sacramental things. The lack that is felt, then, is more precisely the gap between the phenomenon of the given things (*sacramentum*) and the phenomenon of the sacramental gift (*res*), an experience of non-experience, that we can distinguish from Marion's counter-experience. Whereas the givenness of counter-experience provokes a resistance of some sort, a response to a call that brings the phenomenon to appearance in some way—be it positive or negative, an experience of non-experience can appeal only to the authority of the words accompanying the gift to confirm its givenness.

According to either account of divine phenomenality, believer and non-believer alike could actually share something of the same experience, although their contextualized interpretations will yield different results. In the case of a positive experience (a saturated phenomenon, an experience of counter-experience), it could signify either in awe, or in denial. In the case of a negative experience (the experience of non-experience, the experience of lack or of nothing given), it could signify in a desert(-ification) that is the experience of faith, or equally, the experience of unbelief.[30]

To sum up the contributions of Marion and Lacoste to a thinking of revelation: both allow that God gives Godself to be felt in experience. For Marion, that felt givenness can be transmuted into a showing by means of the recipient, although it will never be expressed exhaustively. For Lacoste, while it may be that God is felt as present, for most believers, this will be what he calls a "radically non-eschatological presence" rather than an anticipation of "eschatological presence." More often than not, we will experience the non-experience of God, and will be left to discern whether this is an experience of the holy or whether we are deceived instead by the sacred— the sacred being what Emmanuel Lévinas calls the "bubbles of Nothing in nothing," as Lacoste reminds us.[31]

---

[29] Joeri Schrijvers, *An Introduction to Jean-Yves Lacoste* (Farnham, UK: Ashgate, 2012), p. 155. Cp. "Prayer may be defined as the experience of a non-presence. Such a 'nonpresence,' however, must either be something or nothing. If prayer is the experience of something, then nonpresence *is* and can be manifest to consciousness either thematically or nonthematically. But if prayer is the experience of nothing, then nonpresence is merely nothing and therefore not experienceable; prayer cannot experience a 'nonpresence' that is nothing. This distinction, I submit, is vital to understanding the play of presence that lies at the heart of phenomenological analysis: 'Lord, I believe; help my unbelief'." Andrews, "How (Not) to Find God in All Things," pp. 204–205.
[30] See Emmanuel Falque, "Khôra or 'the Great Bifurcation': Discussion with Derrida," *Louvain Studies* 39, no. 4 (2016), pp. 337–363.
[31] Lacoste, *Être En Danger*, p. 119. Emmanuel Levinas, *Nine Talmudic Readings* (trans. Annette Aronowicz; Bloomington: Indiana University Press, 1990), p. 141.

Ignatius and the spiritual exercises

We turn now to consider the possible contribution of the *Spiritual Exercises* to a rethinking of revelation along these lines. Ignatius is a great believer in the value of examining experience, particularly as feelings emerge in the course of that experience. In this process of examination, he believes not only that it is possible to know God's will, but also that what we come to know in discerning God's will is God. However, if we are to undertake the discernment process authentically, we must put our own interests completely aside, with the development of a personal quality that Ignatius describes as "indifference."[32] He looks carefully at what is given, in its very givenness, without any pre-commitment as to its origins or meaning. Any judgment about its divine quality is delayed until what appears in feeling has been examined, especially in light of context, earlier factors or later responses. From this perspective, we might consider Ignatius a proto-phenomenologist.

Two sections of the *Exercises* are immediately relevant to the question of how God communicates with us: the three ways of "making a choice of a way of life," commonly known as the election (numbers 169–177), and the "Rules for the Discernment of Spirits" (especially numbers 316–317, 330, and 336).

To summarize the three modes of election: the first experience of election occurs "when God our Lord so moves and attracts the will that a devout soul without hesitation, or the possibility of hesitation, follows what has been manifested to it." In the second mode, the choice is arrived at because "much light and understanding are derived through experience of desolations and consolations and discernment of diverse spirits." Finally, when the soul is in a state of "tranquility," other means of arriving at a determination are needed, such as weighing up the pros and cons of the situation. While all three modes are relevant, it is the first mode that is of special interest to us now.

What does Ignatius mean by the first mode? As many have noted, the text is unhelpfully brief and in many ways equivocal. It is not clear, for example, whether what has been made manifest is the "Lord so mov[ing] and attract[ing] the will," or some further revelation specific to the course of action. Rahner and other commentators, such as Jules Toner, agree that it is a matter of the communication of God's will within the will of the person as he or she is drawn to something specific.[33] Many commentators make much of the self-authenticating nature of this mode of election; however, Toner believes that it must be subject to further critical examination in order

---

[32] Hence, in the "First Principle and Foundation" (number 23) of the *Spiritual Exercises* we read: "Therefore, we must make ourselves indifferent to all created things, as far as we are allowed free choice and are not under any prohibition. Consequently, as far as we are concerned, we should not prefer health to sickness, riches to poverty, honor to dishonor, a long life to a short life. The same holds for all other things." The need for indifference is noted throughout the *Exercises*.

[33] Rahner, "The Logic of Concrete Individual Knowledge in Ignatius Loyola," p. 94. Jules J. Toner S.J., *What Is Your Will, O God? A Casebook for Studying Discernment of God's Will, 4: Original Studies Composed in English* (St Louis, MO: Institute of Jesuit Sources, 1995), p. 11.

to be confirmed.[34] In this way, Toner views the three modes of election as one. Rahner also sees the three modes as inherently connected, but unlike Toner, sees the first mode as the basis for the other two, providing the ultimate standard for all discernment.[35] He also views the first mode as "a divine revelation … whether it belongs to public revelation or is a 'private revelation.'"[36] In contrast, Dulles claims that it is private revelation, underscoring its rarity with reference to its occurrence in the lives of the great saints.[37] This reminds us that, for Dulles, experience of God as the ineffable is really the prerogative of the mystics and not of the everyday believer.

While it is revelatory in character, the first mode of election is not beatific. The working of God that Ignatius describes is in the will, although Rahner maintains that this, too, is a type of knowledge.[38] Now, Toner distinguishes firmly between the will and the affect, defining this aspect of the first mode as "a volitional tendency towards something to be done, a conative act of will," while in parenthesis emphasizing that it is "not a feeling of consolation in the affective sensibility" and stressing that "not a word is said about spiritual consolation."[39] This is written in an attempt to make clear his disagreement with Rahner, who reads the whole notion of election in light of the Rules for the Discernment of Spirits, and so interprets the first mode in terms of the experience of God's intimacy offered in the Consolation without Previous Cause, or CSCP, against which it can be tested in terms of its consolatory quality, origins, and indubitability.[40]

---

[34] "The first-time experience, even with its spontaneous certainty of what God wills, is only data for a discernment by critical reflection on it. By such reflection, the person who has the experience can arrive at a critically validated reflective certainty or a critically justified doubt about the unreflective certainty." Jules J. Toner S.J., *Spirit of Light or Darkness?, 3: Original Studies Composed in English* (St Louis, MO: Institute of Jesuit Sources, 1995), p. 11.

[35] "The first method is the ideal higher limiting case of the second method and the latter itself includes the rationality of the third as one of its own intrinsic elements." Rahner, "The Logic of Concrete Individual Knowledge in Ignatius Loyola," p. 106.

[36] Rahner, "The Logic of Concrete Individual Knowledge in Ignatius Loyola," p. 107.

[37] Avery Dulles, "Finding God's Will," *Woodstock Letters* 94 (1965), p. 142.

[38] "In the Exercises Ignatius candidly assumes that a man has to reckon, as a practical possibility of experience, that God may communicate his will to him. And the content of this will is not simply what can be known by the rational reflection of a believing mind employing general maxims of reason and faith on the one hand and their application to a definite situation that has also been analyzed in a similar discursively rational way, on the other." In the footnote, Rahner continues to explain: "That does not mean that the contrary of this kind of knowledge which, according to our interpretation of the Exercises, is not in every case sufficient for knowing God's will, is 'feeling', 'instinct' or something similar, contrary to or apart from the intellect. It is, rather, a thoroughly intellectual operation of the 'intellect', in the metaphysical, scholastic sense of the word, in which it is capable of apprehending values. Only it is not cognition of the rationally discursive and conceptually expressible kind but an intellectual knowledge which is ultimately grounded in the simple presence to itself of the intrinsically intelligible subject which in the very accomplishment of its act has knowledge of itself, without that contrast of knower and known which holds when it is a question of those objects that are known by adverting to a context of sensory perception and imagery." Rahner, "The Logic of Concrete Individual Knowledge in Ignatius Loyola," p. 94, 94-5n.

[39] Toner S.J., *What Is Your Will?* p. 11.

[40] "K. Rahner highlights the Exercises as a method for making a supernatural, existential decision based upon an experienced concord or discord which occurs when a person's choice is savored in the presence of his central, God-evoked religious stance which becomes thematic as CSCP." Harvey Egan, *The Spiritual Exercises and the Ignatian Mystical Horizon, Series Iv: Study Aids on Jesuit Topics* (St Louis, MO: Institute of Jesuit Resources, 1976), pp. 16–17. CSCP is the acronym for *"consolación sin causa precedente."*

Ignatius describes the CSCP in paragraph 330:

> God alone can give consolation to the soul without any previous cause. It belongs solely to the Creator to come into a soul, to leave it, to act upon it, to draw it wholly into the love of His Divine Majesty. I said without previous cause, that is, without any preceding perception or knowledge by which a soul might be led to such a consolation through his own acts of intellect and will.[41]

Yet to understand what is meant by the CSCP, we must first gain some appreciation of what Ignatius means by "consolation." In paragraph 316, he states: "I name it consolation when *some inner motion is prompted in the person* of such a kind that he begins to be aflame with love of his creator and Lord and, consequently, when he cannot love any created thing on the face of the earth in itself but only in the creator of them all." He specifies further: consolation can come in love that moves to the expression of tears over sin, or Christ's passion, or something else ordered to the praise and service of God; it is also "every increase of hope, faith, or charity," and "every inward gladness …."[42] What we have with spiritual consolation is a wide range of affective responses. It can come from God, or from elsewhere. When consolation is God-given, it is distinguished by the intense love felt at its base and by having God as its sole aim.[43] Spiritual desolation, in contrast, which never comes from God, is understood by Ignatius as a feeling of being "separated, as it were, from its Creator and Lord."[44]

Without entering more fully into the debate between Rahner and Toner, we might ask whether it is nevertheless possible that feelings of consolation might pertain to the first mode of election. While Toner is right that Ignatius does not mention consolation in this instance, in the immediacy of God's movement and attraction in the will, it is hard to imagine that this could be undergone otherwise than as a moment of consolation. For the soul that is open and drawn to the love of God, God's nearness would necessarily be felt as welcome. This enables us to reconcile—more fully than Toner is able to do—both first time election and CSCP by means of the oft-quoted passage from the letter to Teresa Rejadell:

> It often happens that our Lord moves and forces us interiorly to one action or another by opening up our mind and heart, that is, speaking inside us without

---

[41] Loyola, *Spiritual Exercises*, p. 330. On "tears" as characteristic of sixteenth-century Spanish thinking on authentic prayer, see Elena Carrera, "The Emotions in Sixteenth-Century Spanish Spirituality," *Journal of Religious History* 31, no. 3 (2007), pp. 235–252.

[42] Loyola, *Spiritual Exercises*, p. 316. Emphasis added.

[43] Toner emphasizes the need to understand consolation as strictly spiritual. Toner S.J., *Spirit of Light*, p. 17.

[44] Loyola, *Spiritual Exercises*, 317. This is not because God inflicts desolation or ever moves away from us; although the felt distance from God that Ignatius describes constitutes real lack to those who genuinely desire God.

any noise of voices, raising us entirely to His divine love, without our being able to resist His purpose, even if we wanted.[45]

In this letter, we find a fuller description by Ignatius of the nature of the experience of God's self-revelation in personal intimacy—opening up mind and heart; speaking without noise; raising into love; communicating an irresistible purpose.

Extremely difficult to determine is what Ignatius means by "without previous cause." Harvey Egan suggests that the phrase should be placed in the context of the whole exercises, to mean that it relates to grace "*not previously* asked for."[46] However, if it is to be argued that spiritual discernment is not an activity strictly limited to exercitants—in other words, that it is possible to "find God in all things," and not to limit God's self-giving in grace to those choosing a way of life—then it is hard to maintain that the CSCP should only be seen as occurring within the meditations, prayers, and disciplines of the *Spiritual Exercises*.[47] Moreover, it seems strange that an exercitant should have set a limit on what he or she expects from any given meditation. I am thus inclined to take Ignatius's words at face value here, to suggest that "previous cause" refers to the capacity of the person to have produced the intense consolation that is given in this situation. We could agree with Egan that without previous cause means "out of all proportion" with what has gone before (without limiting that to a specific request).[48] And I agree with Rahner and others that the disjunction between the capacity of the person to "be led to such a consolation through his own acts of intellect and will" and the experience of the consolation can be read in terms of an experience that has content but no conceptual object.[49] Rahner theorizes that in the CSCP, an object of consciousness fades to reveal the ground of subjectivity, present to consciousness in a way similar to that in which consciousness is present to itself, which is to say, at once revealed as imageless or as

---

[45] Letter to Teresa Rejadell, letter 4 in Joseph A. Munitiz and Philip Endean, eds., *Saint Ignatius of Loyola: Personal Writings* (Harmondsworth, UK: Penguin, 1996), pp. 133–134; Jules J. Toner S.J., *A Commentary on Saint Ignatius's Rules for the Discernment of Spirits, Series III: Original Studies Composed in English* (St Louis, MO: Institute of Jesuit Sources, 1982), p. 313.

[46] "If a consolation is given in such a way that it was *not previously* asked for, that is out of proportion to 'what I want and desire', that it transcends the grace *expected* from the meditation at hand and draws the exercitant wholly into God's love, then we have the consolation without previous cause. We agree ... that the consolation cannot be causeless, ... that it is an uncreated cause, and ... that it is 'without conceptual object.'" Egan, *Spiritual Exercises and Ignatian Mystical Horizon*, p. 35.

[47] In the Foreword to Egan's book, Rahner writes: "One should certainly not evaluate this 'consolation without previous cause' as a singular mystical phenomenon open only to a select few, but as the foundation and highpoint of 'normal' Christian life." Rahner in Egan, *Spiritual Exercises and Ignatian Mystical Horizon*, p. xv. In this regard, I also note Dulles's gloss of Rahner: "The method of discernment of spirits is thus closely related to what Rahner calls the 'fundamental formula of Ignatian spirituality'—the finding God in all things. This, in Rahner's view, is simply 'the persistent putting into practice of that supernatural concrete logic of discovering the will of God through the experimental test of consolation'. The affective logic of the second-time election, therefore, is inseparably connected with the characteristically Ignatian synthesis of contemplation and action which has always been a mark of Jesuit spirituality." Dulles, "Finding God's Will," p. 149.

[48] Ignatius does not say "uncaused," (as Egan does) and I wonder whether we are over-interpreting him to read this passage in terms of Aristotelean causality.

[49] Rahner, "The Logic of Concrete Individual Knowledge in Ignatius Loyola," p. 135.

mystery. Philip Endean draws our attention to the fact that in considering such an experience of God, Rahner echoes the words of Bonaventure: "and then, in truth, they feel rather than know."[50] It is in their exploration of this feeling rather than knowing that Marion and Lacoste offer a rich way of thinking through the Ignatian experience.[51]

Recapitulation and further questions

To rephrase my key question, if revelation is authentically described in Christian tradition as the action of "the invisible God," who, "out of the abundance of … love speaks to [us] as friends," then how does this communication take place?[52] It seems to me that God's givenness to the individual, as Ignatius describes it, can readily be framed in terms of the saturated phenomenon, particularly insofar as it is experienced as a felt pressure, the communication of which transmutes an altogether excessive intuition into an intentional showing. We can describe this using the various typologies of saturation: revelation happens as an event (quite literally, "without previous cause"); metaphorically, as an idol (in this circumstance, it is not so much that there is literally too much to see, but that any concept ascribed to it will be inadequate; as flesh (it happens internally to me, and while there remains in principle a distinction between self and God, such a distinction cannot be felt, since I am feeling the felt without any

---

[50] See Philip Endean, *Karl Rahner and Ignatian Spirituality* (Oxford: Oxford Scholarship Online, 2011). In chapter 2, "Immediate Experience of God," Endean quotes Rahner's 1978 writing "Ignatius of Loyola Speaks to a Modern Jesuit" (pp. 18–19): "There has to be here an encounter with God which '*versatur in pure intellectualibus*'. Now, it must be said also that this is an awkward and easily misunderstood expression of Nadal's: today it can easily be misinterpreted along the lines of an Enlightenment intellectualism or rationalism. But all it refers to is how this experience of God was imageless." At the same time, Rahner observes in the same text: "Ignatius is, in a very singular way, on the most familiar of terms with God. For he has gone beyond all visions, whether real (such as seeing Christ or the Virgin etc. as present) or based on images and likenesses, and he is now taken up with what is purely intellectual, with the unity of God." Endean also notes Rahner's quoting from Bonaventure (p. 25): "In their regarding there is no image formed of a creature. And then, in truth, they feel rather than know." See also p. 28: "'If God touches this deepest point of the soul from within, informing it as it were', Rahner concludes, 'the *apex affectus* will be able to have an awareness of this immediate union of love, without the intellect thereby becoming active'. At the deepest level of the self, deeper than intellect or will, there is God." Note Bernard Lonergan's comment: "Have you read Rahner on St. Ignatius and consolation without a cause? Well. That sort of thing I would call *an experience of God.*" Quoted in Gordon Rixon, "Bernard Lonergan and Mysticism," *Theological Studies* 62, no. 3 (2001), pp. 479–497 (pp. 489–490). Rixon also quotes Lonergan at p. 494n57: "*Has consolation got a content?* Yes. It has a content but it hasn't got an object; this is Rahner's way of putting it."

[51] And here we break from Rahner (and Lonergan) explicitly. As Andrews comments, "If prayer constitutes the condition of possibility of the appearing of a 'nonappearance', then, in terms of the givenness of pure transcendence, the goal of the *Exercises* might best be described *not* in terms of a traditional metaphysics of presence." Andrews, "How (Not) to Find God in All Things," p. 201. Andrews refers to the analysis of the *Spiritual Exercises* by Roland Barthes, and especially the way in which the exercitant "is cut off from the perfection of language, which is assertive closure … " (pp. 203–204). Andrews continues: "Such a nonphenomenal experience of a (non)presence corresponds significantly to what Jacques Derrida describes in terms of the phenomenology of the gift" (p. 204).

[52] *Dei Verbum, Dogmatic Constitution on Divine Revelation*, http://www.vatican.va/archive/hist_councils/ii_vatican_council/documents/vat-ii_const_19651118_dei-verbum_en.html.

sense of its being exterior to me—it is absolute); and as icon (there is nothing to see—I am present to God, rather than God present to me beatifically). Needless to say, in the transmutation of the saturated phenomenon into words and other symbols of revelation, we recognize a hermeneutic act that takes place in the context of a specific religious tradition and is tested by the community of that tradition.[53] As Marion underscores: "Without the hermeneutic decision there is nothing to see, nothing to believe, and nothing revealed."[54]

If we use Lacoste's language instead of Marion's, we could describe the Ignatian experience in terms of non-eschatological presence, a felt presence that is a kind of knowledge in terms of acquaintance or recognition rather than a concept. We can see here a helpful way of thinking about the tension between revelation as once-and-for-all, already given, and revelation as meaningful self-revelation to the individual: in revelation as it unfolds personally, I recognize the God who approaches me as the God of the tradition, while coming to know that God in a uniquely interpersonal way.

A number of questions remain in this preliminary consideration of the articulation of Ignatian experience in phenomenological terms. For instance, it might be helpful momentarily to consider what relationship, if any, Lacoste's "experience of non-experience" bears to the Ignatian understanding of desolation. Ignatius is clear that desolation itself does not come from God, but from the evil spirit. Nevertheless,

> when one is left in desolation, he should be mindful that God has left him to his natural powers to resist the different agitations and temptations of the enemy in order to try him. He can resist with the help of God, which always remains, though he may not clearly perceive it. For though God has taken from him the abundance of fervor and overflowing love and the intensity of His favors, nevertheless, he has sufficient grace for eternal salvation.[55]

It is possible, then, that the experience of non-experience might in some ways resemble the experience of desolation, since there is a felt lack of God's presence (while God in fact remains, the person "may not clearly perceive it").

Further, it will be important to consider the process of Ignatian discernment with respect to establishing the authenticity of any consolatory experience, and especially the CSCP. Besides those criteria already mentioned (the experience is distinguished by the intense love felt at its base and by having God as its sole aim), there is that of the requirement for the exercitant to distinguish carefully between the experience of consolation and those resolutions and plans that may arise from it:

---

[53] On the need for hermeneutics, see Jean-Luc Marion, *Givenness and Hermeneutics* (trans. Jean-Pierre Lafouge; Milwaukee, WI: Marquette University Press, 2012), p. 55: "Hermeneutics manages the gap between what gives itself and what shows itself by interpreting the call (or intuition) by the response (concept or meaning)."

[54] Marion, *Givenness and Revelation*, p. 41. We note, nevertheless, the statement soon after: "Revelation happens to me through hermeneutics, that is to say, through the *conversion* of one intentionality to another." This will require further exploration.

[55] Loyola, *Spiritual Exercises*, p. 320.

But a spiritual person who has received such a consolation must consider it very attentively, and must cautiously distinguish the actual time of the consolation from the period which follows it. ... In this second period the soul frequently forms various resolutions and plans which are not granted directly by God our Lord. They may come from our own reasoning on the relations of our concepts and on the consequences of our judgments, or they may come from the good or evil spirit.[56]

In the context of making the *Spiritual Exercises*, the close examination of the consolatory experience takes place in dialogue with a spiritual director. For Ignatius himself, becoming precisely attuned to the phenomena involves a lifetime of experience, and requires in each case the practice of what we could call the phenomenological *epoche*, the bracketing of self-interest or the practice of indifference. So, in our attempts to discern the possibility of a genuinely revelatory encounter, the bar is set high. We can draw a line to exclude what is merely emotional self-indulgence, sentimentality, kitsch, wishful thinking, and so on.

This insight leads us to consider any legitimate role of the imagination in meditation on scripture or the experience of prayer. Ignatius sets tasks for the exercitant that are based around the engagement of imagination, which might at first seem to be contrary to the phenomenological impulse. Yet, to the extent that such exercises involve the immersion in a scriptural scene, for example, they may heighten attentiveness to what is given rather than involving flights of fancy. As we saw in our meditation on the story of the woman with the hemorrhage, the engagement of the imagination did not take us away from the scene but placed us more fully in it. Ignatius's own use of imagination— as, for example, when he reflects on the lives of the saints during the period of his recovery from his injury—reveals that it is an important tool for phenomenological discernment. We are clear about what is imaginary—in this instance, what Ignatius dreams he will do to emulate the lives of the saints (and better them). However, the imaginary functions to show—through attentiveness to the related experiences of consolation and desolation—authentic resonances and impulses. The use of the imagination allows the exercitant to find where God passes in experience. In this sense, it becomes a type of "reduction."

Finally, while we have begun to translate the Ignatian experience of God's self-revelation into terms we might use within the academy, we have not yet considered if there is more that we can say in relation to meaningful dialogue within contemporary culture. The Ignatian search for God "in all things" has an ongoing relevance with regard to the recent cultural emphasis on the importance of personal experience, as well as to what Boeve calls "individualization" (as distinct from "individualism"), which is relevant to the construction of individual identity.[57] Learning to be attentive to the subtle internal movements that influence decision-making is more important now

---

[56] Ibid., p. 336.
[57] Boeve notes of the contemporary context: "Against a background of detraditionalization and pluralization, identity construction also occurs ... in an individualized manner. This means that identity construction is structurally more reflexive, because the awareness is growing that identity is not obvious, and everything could have been different" (p. 45).

than ever, in terms of promoting authentic identity development. Individuals must be sensitized in a critical and reflective manner to the ways in which feelings move them to decisions and actions. This provides an opportunity for the consideration of the possibility that God is internally operative, that God actually reveals Godself in human experience.

At the same time, such sensitization and the opportunity it provides for the discernment of God's prompting to relationship is made more complex by the question of the extent to which we take seriously that our context today is not one where Christian faith can simply be projected onto a range of human experiences, in an attempt to preempt their fullest meaning. A great challenge, in other words, will be to live out the Ignatian search in genuine dialogue with people who begin their searching from a different place.[58] The sensitization to a critical awareness of feelings, using a language of excess (Marion), always supplemented by the language of lack (Lacoste), expressed in terms of the multiple possibilities opened in experience, tempered by the recognition that experience is shaped inevitably by hermeneutic contexts, and offered in respectful witness as part of a genuine dialogue—this is one way to approach the question of revelation in contemporary culture.

---

[58] See, for example, Lieven Boeve, *Theology at the Crossroads of University, Church and Society: Dialogue, Difference and Catholic Identity* (London: Bloomsbury T & T Clark, 2016), pp. 44–45. D. Pollefeyt & J. Bouwens, "Dialogue as the Future. A Catholic Answer to the 'Colourisation' of the Educational Landscape," available at http://web.cecv.catholic.edu.au/projects/identity/ISS_Pollefeyt_articles_book.pdf. English translation of the Dutch article: Didier Pollefeyt and Jan Bouwens, *Identity in Dialogue: Assessing and Enhancing Catholic School Identity. Research Methodology and Research Results in Catholic Schools in Victoria, Australia* (Berlin: Lit Verlag, 2014).

6

"Consolation without Previous Cause"? Consolation, Controversy, and Devotional Agency

J. Michelle Molina

Robyn Horner takes up Ignatius of Loyola's Spiritual Exercises and particularly the notion of "consolation without previous cause" as an example of how Jean-Luc Marion's concept of the "saturated phenomenon" can offer workable, translatable ideas about revelation. She is frustrated by the ways in which discussion of revelation is often reduced to a catalog of categories and finds in Marion's work a way to link revelation to its experience. At stake is a chance to engage in difficult dialogue, according to the compelling challenge which Horner poses as a question: What is it to "live out the Ignatian search in genuine dialogue with people *who begin their searching from a different place*?" In spite of Horner's clear interest in "contemporary" encounters with Ignatian spirituality, my response emphasizes the Spiritual Exercises in historical context. In my critique of Horner's chapter, I use this history to amplify her observations about the way in which modes of "revelation" mattered when seeking "genuine dialogue" and how both could stumble upon the roadblock of the problematic category of "religious experience."

Horner notes that, like all religious experience, revelation is mediated by the hermeneutic act that entails "the transmutation of the saturated phenomenon into words and other symbols of revelation, [and these are expressed] within the context of tradition, they are tested by community." In many ways this is where she finds an affinity with the Ignatian Spiritual Exercises. The process of making the Exercises is governed by processes of spiritual discernment, which can be thought of as the process of figuring out and putting into language what was "really real" about a felt experience. "However," Horner writes, "when it comes to revelation, it is clear that we are contemplating what most intensely resists our capacity for constitution: revelation is the ultimate 'counter-experience.'" This is the saturated phenomenon that she locates in the experience of "consolation without previous cause" and it occupies a privileged place in her argument because, in that mode, there is no hermeneutic necessity. Consolation without previous cause—which Christian theologians deem a mode of "infused contemplation"—is mentioned briefly in the Ignatian Exercises, yet it is not only, in my view, perhaps the least important aspect of the Spiritual Exercises, but further, in emphasizing its importance, Horner undercuts her claimed payoff. If the aim is to make possible greater dialog among people who may disagree, why privilege a form of Christian revelation that exempts itself from human interpretation?

In this chapter, I want to take Horner's concerns seriously, but to do so, I take us back to the drawing board with the Spiritual Exercises, because Horner is correct in that this series of meditations offers a mode of practice that *is conducive to dialogue*, she is just looking in the wrong place. But I shift the emphasis from Ignatius's *words* to the practice of making the Exercises. And in so doing, I point out that our shared object of study—the Ignatian Spiritual Exercises—is a recalcitrant object. Whether searching for a better understanding of the revelation of the Christian God (Horner's scholarship), or how the human quest to find God via the meditative practices in the Exercises motivated global Catholicism (my scholarship[1]), we both seek to understand something that the text itself makes difficult to know because the Exercises provide only an outline, a series of directives, and, as such, does not offer many of the answers to the questions that we initially set for ourselves about religious experience. To remain with the text is to embrace a roadblock.

This is nothing new in the study of the Exercises. In an oft-stated analogy, it would be folly to study the blueprint for building a train if one seeks to understand the experience of *riding* a train. Accordingly, one cannot know the Exercises until one inquires what it is to take them for a spin, as Ignatius and his followers exhorted people to do. Loyola's legacy was an outline of a theory of practice.[2] Rather than a singular "master plan," the Exercises were conceived as an ongoing project, the taking up of Catholic philosophy (to "know thyself") as a way of life that would compel one to take up ministry to others, both near and distant.

My own approach is to work with and against the text, to approach *making* the Exercises *not merely* as an encounter with a set of instructions, but as a material engagement with a series of historically shaped embodied practices. Because the Exercises are, indeed, "unhelpfully brief" and "in many ways equivocal," as Horner describes them, then to understand a mobilizing religious experience (my aim), I cannot rest with this brief and flexible set of instructions written for the director who is assisting such a wide variety of exercitants. Instead, I reach for sources that help me situate Jesuit devotional practices in a lived historical context. Some of these sources include the guides for directors giving the Exercises,[3] commentaries on the Exercises,[4] devotional guides based upon the Exercises or written to instruct specific "classes" of person (nuns, school-aged boys, etc.), the spiritual diaries, and/or letters written by those who had made the Exercises or part of them, sometimes

---

[1] J. Michelle Molina, *To Overcome Oneself: The Jesuit Ethic and the Spirit of Global Expansion* (Berkeley: University of California Press, 2013).

[2] True enough, one version was declared "an autograph" and there was a "formalization" which consisted of creating a Latin translation at the time of the foundation of Society of Jesus.

[3] This was a small industry in the early modern Jesuit world. See Martin E. Palmer, *On Giving the Spiritual Exercises: The Early Jesuit Manuscript Directories and the Official Directory of 1599* (Jesuit Primary Sources, Series I, In English Translation, no. 14; St. Louis: Institute of Jesuit Sources, 1996); Ignacio Iparraguirre, *Comentarios De Los Ejercicios Ignacianos (siglos XVI–XVIII) Repertorio Critico* (Subsidia Ad Historiam S.I., Bibliothecae Instituti Historici S.I. Series Minor, 6; Rome: Institutum Historicum S.I., 1967).

[4] See Ibid.

detailing what one had discerned of God's will while undertaking the Exercises, and of course, Inquisition records pertaining to those whose practice of the Exercises fell athwart Catholic Reformation norms. What I want to discuss in this chapter are the discussions among the Jesuits themselves as to the proper modes of prayer and meditation for an order of religious men with an avowedly worldly mission.[5] Accordingly, this chapter opens with a historical view of early modern Catholic traditions and contexts in which the Ignatian Spiritual Exercises were forged, honed, and tested by the first generations of Jesuits.

Mine is a historical exploration of the nature of *making* the Exercises in the early modern period. The early Jesuits used the term "consolation" to indicate an embodied way of knowing, as Horner is correct to note, that required one to hone methods of discernment. Was this God's will? Was it my own? But the Spiritual Exercises also asked exercitants to engage in *practices* of embodied attention in order to attune themselves to catching glimmers of consolation.[6] Scholars have dubbed these "practices of belief"[7] or "practices of grace,"[8] phrases that ironically link the agentive embodied notion of "practice" to "belief" (which is often conceptualized as mental or cognitive), or to "grace" (which is theorized as agentless). This is an excellent way to frame the Ignatian Exercises, wherein spiritual consolation was understood to rely upon a causal scaffolding of embodied practices that put one in the position of attaining consolation. It is worth noting that Jesuit writers did not often use the term "revelation." In some letters, Ignatius uses this term in discussions about how to discipline members who, via infused contemplation, made prophecies about the state of the Catholic Church. Here, the terms were most often conjoined, as in "prophecies, or revelations."[9] But what is more necessary to point out here is that, in the case of the early modern Jesuits, "consolation without previous cause"—a form of infused contemplation—became the source of controversy sufficient to compel the first Jesuits to distance themselves from any prayer that was not "ordinary." I close by suggesting that if at stake in Horner's argument is a desire to set the stage for greater dialogue about various forms of revelation, then the *ordinariness* of the Spiritual Exercises is what makes them an *extraordinary* means of reaching people where they live.

Controversial

The Exercises resulted from Ignatius of Loyola's own hermeneutic acts, that is, what he had discerned to be helpful in his own spiritual struggles to find and name God's

---

[5] Molina, *To Overcome Oneself*.
[6] Molina, especially Chapter Three: "Consolation Philosophy," in *To Overcome Oneself*.
[7] Moshe Sluhovsky, *Becoming a New Self: Practices of Belief in Early Modern Catholicism* (Chicago, IL: University of Chicago, 2017).
[8] David Marno, *Death Be Not Proud: The Art of Holy Attention* (Chicago, IL: University of Chicago, 2016).
[9] See his letters collected in the subheading "On Prophecies and Revelations," in *Saint Ignatius of Loyola: Personal Writings* (ed. and trans. Joseph Munitz and Philip Endean; London: Penguin, 1997).

will in his life, and what he learned through practical experimentation with a variety of early followers about what could be useful to others.[10] Ignatius implored people to undertake the Spiritual Exercises.

> Still, let me repeat once and twice and as many more times as I am able: I implore you, out of a desire to serve God Our Lord, to do what I have said to you up to now. May his Divine Majesty never ask me one day why I did not ask you as strongly as I possibly could! The Spiritual Exercises are all the best that I have been able to think out, experience and understand in this life, both for helping somebody to make the most of themselves, and for being able to bring advantage, help and profit to many others. So even if you don't feel the need for the first, you will see that they are much more helpful than you might have imagined for the second.[11]

This emphasis on bringing advantage, help, and profit to others is part how the Jesuits distinguished themselves from their mendicant counterparts. While Ignatius of Loyola may have composed his Spiritual Exercises in an early sixteenth-century Spanish devotional milieu in which a Franciscan mysticism encouraged the practice of *recogimiento*, or withdrawal,[12] the first Jesuits felt compelled to move quickly to distance themselves and the Spiritual Exercises from this contemplative legacy that would have estranged them from the human interaction that was central to their worldly sense of ministry. "The world is our home," the Jesuit Jeronimo Nadal famously pronounced. As Moshe Sluhovsky has summarized the issue, what the Jesuits were compelled to iron out was how to "combine its mission to sanctify the world with its members' personal goal of sanctifying themselves."[13]

These concerns were influenced by the prior *alumbrado* crisis of the 1520s and 1530s, after which Ignatius had several run-ins with Spanish inquisitors who were very skeptical about his Spiritual Exercises. The *alumbrados* were a group of Spanish lay-persons who had pursued a quiet relationship with the God and sought to be *alumbrado*—illumined—from within, for which they were promptly condemned for "Lutheranism." Notably, the *alumbrados* eschewed both clerical intermediaries and external or bodily expressions of divine ecstasy. In light of that controversy, the Spanish Inquisition regarded Ignatius and his Exercises with suspicion, which in part explains why Ignatius found it expedient to leave Spain and take up his studies in Paris. Throughout the early modern period, the availability of this set of meditations—written in the vernacular and available to the laity—caused flare ups of vocal opposition on the part of Jesuit critics (usually the Dominicans).[14]

But even after the Jesuits had been firmly established in Rome (1542) with a corporate identity founded upon worldly activism, they had to negotiate among themselves their own conflicting ideas about the value of contemplative withdrawal.

---

[10] John O'Malley, *The First Jesuits* (Cambridge, MA: Harvard University Press, 1993), 1992 (131).
[11] Ignatius to Fr Miona, November 16, 1536. *Saint Ignatius of Loyola: Personal Writings*.
[12] Andrés Martín Melquiades, *Recogidos: Nueva visión de la mística española, 1500–1700* (Madrid: Seminario Suárez de la Fundación Universitaria Española, 1975).
[13] Sluhovsky, *Becoming a New Self*, p. 73.
[14] Ibid., p. 73.

At the leadership level, the Society had distanced itself from Spanish mysticism. Yet a group of Spanish Jesuits had vociferously advocated *recogimiento* in order to facilitate infused contemplation. This was worrisome to the Jesuit Provincial of Aragon, Diego de Avellaneda, who warned in a series of letters to the Jesuit General Everard Mercurian that this trend could pose a serious threat to the Spiritual Exercises and thus to the very foundation of Jesuit devotional life. Mercurian moved to quash what came to be seen as an internal rebellion, especially when Jesuits intent on seclusion formed a spiritual circle in the new Jesuit college in Gandía.[15]

Jesuit leadership came to the conclusion that it was necessary to transform the prayer habits of early Jesuits to be more in keeping with what was offered in the Spiritual Exercises. The Jesuit Baltasar Álvarez provides a case in point. Álvarez spent sixteen years praying and meditating according to the methods in the Spiritual Exercises, but then reached a state of infused contemplation, after which he became a strong proponent of this style of prayer. Chastized by Jesuit leadership, he wrote a responded using language that precisely summarized the way in which the Society of Jesus was making decisive moves to sever itself from the devotional roots that had initially inspired Ignatius. His letter argued quite logically that to restrict the spiritual life of the Society of Jesus to the mode of prayer taught in the Spiritual Exercises would be to reject one of the other fruitful paths that Ignatius himself had also followed. He valued the meditations in the Spiritual Exercises, Álvarez wrote, "but there is another position, different and higher ... that is the way of silence."[16] Jesuit leadership replied firmly that men of the Order should use no method that differed from the Spiritual Exercises. Another Spanish Jesuit, Diego Alvarez de Paz (1560–1620), was described as following a mode that was "more hermetic and *frailero* [akin to a friar]" and decidedly not in keeping with the Jesuit way of proceeding. In his capacity as visitor, Miguel de Torres described Alvarez de Paz offered an even more definitive statement: his prayer life posed an obstacle to the Jesuit way of proceeding:

> He is a good friend to the solitary life and quite enveloped in prayer which he communicates with the Fathers and Brothers, [but as such he is] not attempting to conform himself to the Exercises that the Compañía uses. In my humble judgment, it seems that this prayer attempts to unite the soul with God, which although this is very good, peaceful, and delightful to those who know to give over to her [saben dar a ella], but it does not extend itself very well to those exercises of the active life, it is not appropriate to the Company, whose end is this [the active life], nor does such prayer allow one to reach the purity and perfection of obedience, she is such a substantial column; and to think that only with this prayer one can reach the proper mortification of the passions does not apply very well to the action of the ministries of the virtuous active life; finally, this prayer has, in my view, many occasions for illusions and deceptions.

---

[15] Elizabeth Rapley, *The Lord as Their Portion: The Story of the Religious Orders and How They Shaped Our World* (Grand Rapids, MI: Eerdmans, 2011).
[16] Ibid.

The Jesuits at Coimbra in Portugal remained defiant *recogidos*, defining themselves as *claustrales* (cloistered) in contrast to *los de allá*—"those other Jesuits". The Society's leadership disciplined the Coimbra men, too. Gil Gonzales Dávila explained that prayer is a gift from God that comes in two forms: one is an ordinary gift; the other extraordinary. He stated firmly that the Society teaches ordinary prayer "accommodated to human nature."

In sum, while the sixteenth-century Jesuits had been born into this milieu and raised on a Franciscan-inspired diet of *recogimiento* and mystical contemplation, the Society of Jesus nonetheless had to wean some of its members from infused contemplation and push them in the direction of the Order's worldly mission, to which the Spiritual Exercises ordinary prayers and meditations were better suited. This restructured notion of contemplation as attainable not only through ordinary prayer but also through worldly action extended beyond the Iberian peninsula to the overseas branches of the Society in Goa Province (India) and Japan under the leadership of Francis Xavier, and later in the sixteenth century to the American provinces under Spanish rule.[17]

A causal scaffolding or devotional agency

Whether dubbed "practices of belief" or "the art of holy attention," scholars have taken a new look at the manner in which making the Spiritual Exercises offered a means of crafting thoughts about God. Such mediations were understood as theological *practice*, that is, as studied, ritualized, embodied leanings toward knowing God.[18] Most recently, David Marno has described such exercises, including the Spiritual Exercises, as an experimental "set of techniques whose goal is, paradoxically, to allow the unpredictable to happen."[19] As Marno points out, the objective of *undistracted attention*—named forthright as an impossible goal—underwrites practices of what he calls "holy attention." This regulative ideal is the structure that teaches one to adopt a state of attentiveness.[20] Marno's discussion of grace is illuminating. While grace is described as inaccessible via human action, it nonetheless shapes "practices of grace," that is, the modes of cultivating and creating a "hollow spot." The space itself, he contends, cannot be reduced to the binary absence/presence, but, rather, holy attention marks out a space of possibility. Marno offers the analogy of sleep: one cannot *will* falling asleep, but one can assume a position that invites sleep.[21] This is the nature of Ignatian prayer

---

[17] Molina, *To Overcome Oneself*.
[18] In religious studies, this literature can be thought of a series of Russian dolls in which Saba Mahmood's ideas about submission as a form of agency depend upon Talal Asad's insights into the disciplinary aspects of ritual practice that are key to the genealogy of religion that are, in part, dependent upon Michel Foucault's work on techniques of self formation, which in turn were inspired by Pierre Hadot's notion of ancient philosophy as spiritual exercise. In a separate vein, scholars (usually of European devotional history) depend upon these, but also the brilliant insights about monastic memory practices found in Mary Carruther's *The Craft of Thought: Meditation, Rhetoric, and the Making of Images, 400-1200* (Cambridge Studies in Medieval Literature, 34; New York: Cambridge University Press, 1998).
[19] Marno, *Death Be Not Proud*, p. 27.
[20] Ibid., pp. 10–11.
[21] Ibid., p. 19.

and meditation, yet I would push his observations about the Spiritual Exercises further, because the attempt to "bring on" sleep is not mere analogy. Rather, the comparison is quite literal. Just as positioning oneself for sleep is to adopt an anticipatory embodied posture, so too is positioning oneself to attain consolation. The Spiritual Exercises entail a series of embodied exercises that, to reiterate Horner's point, were ingeniously designed to "meet people where they live."

Let us take a closer look at the Exercises to make this clear. The text of the Spiritual Exercises themselves, as we have said, is opaque. Yet this is the beauty of the Exercises: they are a process, one knows them by making them, not by reading them. The path entailed a continuous tweaking, on the part of the Director, who had to determine anew what served each person best, and, for the exercitant, who had to understand his own needs at this particular moment in time. As Horner notes, the Exercises are structured as a preparatory guide toward the central task of making and maintaining a decision to follow Christ. The meditations therein offer different ways of praying, from meditating upon a single word, to rhythmically breathing between words. Drawing upon centuries of monastic tradition, this scissors-and-paste working guide, as John O'Malley has dubbed them, was itself the product of Ignatius's ongoing note-taking about his experiments with crafting thoughts about God. This patched-together process for finding consolation, both during the retreat, and in attending to God in all things, in everyday life, beyond the walls of the retreat house, was key to setting "contemplation in action" as the bedrock of the Society's global mission to reach people from all walks of life, both near and distant.

Let us return to discernment. To know God, you must overcome your self. But to overcome self, *you must know self*, must forge a self that was not quite there in the first place. Recall Ignatius's words as to why one ought to make the Exercises: to make the most of oneself, and to be helpful to others. Ignatius's brilliance was that he knew well the nature of the problem he was dealing with, namely, human beings. Even though he assumed a shared Catholic tradition among those who would take up his Exercises, he recognized that they began their searching from different places. Accordingly, the *Directories* (printed accounts of the methods and ideas that spiritual directors found helpful when directing those undertaking the Spiritual Exercises) accounted for these different walks of life. There would be no "revelation" in the singular. Rather, preparations to find consolation were adapted to the differing life experiences of Jesuit novices, professed Jesuits, businessmen, boys in school, women, nuns, soldiers, etc. This does not begin to account for those who began their searching from places quite remote from Ignatius's Catholic worlds of Spain, France, and Italy. He codified his Exercises in the era of early modern global expansion and, although this was not on Ignatius's mind when he began to scribble notes about his own methods for finding spiritual consolation, by the time that St. Francis Xavier traveled to Asia, the Exercises were clearly a crucial part of his tool-kit as he (and Jesuits after him) aimed to accommodate Catholicism to people who began from different life-worlds.

The Exercises were adapted to meet people not only in various life stages, but also to accommodate their changing dispositions. There are a lot of "or's" in the Exercises. Do this—or—that. The options were many. Ignatius jotted down notes for the sick or physically incapacitated, but also advised: "Even if robust and in the right dispositions, change the timetable … in order better to find what one desires" (Second Week, Note [133]). Or, if one is not finding any consolation in a particular series of Exercises, skip the midnight meditation. Sleep well, eat properly. Know precisely what one requires to eat. Spend longer on this week of the Exercises. Or, shorter. Experimentation was the point. What could work for an individual at a certain moment in life was the key. Ignatius had an intense faith in God, but he also had conviction about engaging in a process, a process that was adaptable, a process that continued to be mysterious, unfixed. Even if one had made the Exercises many, many times, one was always compelled to begin again. Thus, in approaching the singular "consolation out of all proportion to what has gone before" we must pause to account for the fact that, in making the Ignatian Spiritual Exercises, *so much* would have gone before an exercitant experienced those fleeting moments of consolation.

How exactly did this communication take place? Ignatius had an answer and he paid less attention to God than he did to humans with bodies. These bodies were anchored in a now, with their pasts newly constructed in a present, in the series of individual "nows" of each meditation, even in each *break* between meditation. All of this, then, was the process of making oneself attentive. Examples abound: The Exercises contain notes about posture—sitting, kneeling, prostrate upon the ground. Figure it out for yourself, is the Ignatian advice. Avoid anxiety, but find what works, and settle in. And then at the end of an exercise, take a break, release the body: "I shall either sit down or walk around for a quarter of an hour while I consider how the contemplation or meditation has gone" (First Week, Addition 5, [77]). In an effort to embody the proper attitude, pay attention to light and dark, that is, in the First Week, when single-mindedness on the sinning self might cause one to close the shutters, to darken the room, to avoid laughter, to cover one's eyes. But in the Fourth Week, to better attain joy, one might open the shutters, take in the light and feel the cooling breeze, or, the heat of a fire—whatever best allows one to rejoice at the Resurrection. This was conceived as a program of affect management; the aim may have been spiritual indifference to whatever God (and the Jesuit superior) demanded, but Ignatius was in no way indifferent to the nature of embodied experience. The exercitants, through imaginative exercises called *composition of place*, engaged in a fully embodied, sensorial experience of the life of Christ. Again, at every step, one was required to evaluate. What offered glimmers of consolation? Where was one lost in moments of desolation? In the process, one was cautioned not to negate the body but to labor to better incorporate it, to listen to it.

Roland Barthes offered one of the most astute observations about the interplay between the known and the unknown critical to making the Spiritual Exercises that highlights the human drama entailed in the desire to understand God's will. "The retreatant cannot (and must not) know in advance anything about the series of experiments which are gradually being recommended to him." This is why, at least initially, the practitioner does not *read* the text of the Spiritual Exercises. "He is in the situation of a reader of a narrative who is kept in suspense, a suspense which vitally concerns him, since he is also an actor in the story whose elements are gradually being given him." Accordingly, the focus on banal activity also functioned to "combat the vague and the empty," organizing all the "insignificant details of his daily life" and contributing to the development of a rhythmic language internal to the Exercises.

> Thus the temporal needs from which he cannot escape, light, the weather outside, food, dress, which must be made "profitable" in order that they may be turned into image objects ("During meals, consider Christ our Lord as though one saw Him eating with His Disciples, His way of drinking, of looking, of speaking; and try to imitate Him"), following a kind of totalitarian economy in which everything, from the accidental to the futile and trivial, must be utilized: like the novelist, the exercitant is "someone for whom nothing is lost." (Henry James)

This sensorially rich, yet blind approach to the divine could provoke intense anxiety. Yet, we must shake it off, says Ignatius, take a walk, avoid the cliff of unproductive anxiety, take a few notes, and begin again. Given Jesuit insistence on making oneself entirely indifferent to what might occur, combined with Jesuit attention to how changing contexts could inform one's spiritual life, even exercitants repeating the Spiritual Exercises would be instructed to adopt an attitude of blind anticipation, perhaps even more attuned to what might be discerned *this time*.

Ignatius intended the Spiritual Exercises to be accessible to the average person, to facilitate spiritual progress, and to find consolation. "Para todo género y estado"—for every type and state—or "para todo género de persona"—for all types of people—these were common endings to Jesuit guides to meditation that began to proliferate in the seventeenth century. From its inception, the Jesuits quickly moved to make the Spiritual Exercises palatable for a larger public by making available a shortened experience. This shortened retreat generally lasted eight to ten days and emphasized the First Week, which was the "purgative" week, in which one contemplated his sinful nature. But this truncated version also excerpted exercises from other weeks of the full retreat. In the modified version, less emphasis was placed on vocation. Instead, retreat participants were instructed in methods of prayer and contemplation. By the eighteenth century, there were publications demonstrating how one could make the Spiritual Exercises alone in one's home, in the middle of a busy schedule, without the guidance of a director. These guides emphasized techniques of attunement so that an exercitant could embody the shape of waiting, a position of active attention that honed one's ordinary means of knowing more about—as the Jesuit motto goes—a "God in All Things."

Conclusion

Horner uses these Exercises to ask, how do we gain access to a saturated phenomenon of revelation that is prior to the symbols and traditions that shape individual and communal judgment about revelation's veracity, validity, etc.? The answer is not to be found. "Religious experience" is a vexing category. Scholars never have access to the ineffable. What is more interesting, in my view, is how the texts we study were born of a seeker's hermeneutic acts, sometimes difficult struggles, to make sense of the ineffable for themselves, or to explain the experience to others, or to provide notes to serve as breadcrumbs that might make a re-seeking possible.[22] To approximate the experiences of historical actors who have described moments of spiritual consolation, the historian has to find ways *to account for the accounts* of being touched, gifted, consoled, or confused by God. My response here has relied upon historical method, that is, I have placed Ignatius of Loyola's ideas about consolation in a sixteenth-century context. In doing so, I have made clear that "consolation without previous cause" was, in fact, the cause of innumerable problems for the first Jesuits who moved to distance themselves (as well as defend the Ignatian Exercises) from any accusations that the techniques were "extraordinary." The Spiritual Exercises, they argued instead, were comprised of "ordinary" prayers, meditations, and spiritual experiments that early modern Catholics understood as quite effective in bringing about consolatory moments to the widest range of persons.

Horner's concern to find the saturated phenomenon has limited her reading of the Exercises such that she has zeroed in on a single "extraordinary" form of consolation mentioned in the Exercises, while ignoring the larger implication that "consolation" was vague, inchoate and therefore could be attained in a variety of ways by an even wider variety of people. Ignatius lived in a Catholic Reformation moment wherein many grassroots religious movements were born of efforts to re-center lay people as important participants in religious life, as well as to reach (in methods both coercive and persuasive) people who were not Christian. A focus on the *ordinary prayer* that subtended the Spiritual Exercises would better support Horner's stated desire to have more open dialogue among Christians and non-Christians, academics and non-academics, alike. The opacity and elasticity of the term "consolation" points toward the possibility of meeting humans where they stand, humans who may, indeed, begin their searching from different places, but are often more willing to engage on ground of the shared need for some kind of consolation rather than upon more exclusive ideas that subtend Christian revelation.

Clearly I approach the Ignatian Spiritual Exercises from a different place than Horner. In part, I follow Bruce Lincoln's insistence that "history" and "religion" are concepts that often stand in a tense relationship to one another:

> Religion, I submit, is that discourse whose defining characteristic is its desire to speak of things eternal and transcendent with an authority equally transcendent and eternal. History, in the sharpest possible contrast, is that discourse which speaks of things temporal and terrestrial in a human and fallible voice, while staking its claim to authority on rigorous critical practice.[23]

But I also want to incorporate Robert Orsi's insistence that we interrogate "the gods really present" because his small "g" and the use of the plural offer a mode of conversing

---

[22] Molina, "Technologies of the Self: The Letters of Eighteenth-Century Mexican Jesuit Spiritual Daughters," *History of Religions* 47, no. 4 (2008), pp. 282–303.

[23] Bruce Lincoln, "Theses on Method," *Method & Theory in the Study of Religion* 8, no. 3 (1996), pp. 225–227.

about worlds in which diverse cultural scaffoldings shaped various modes of devotional attention, as well as varied experiences of presences—whether consolatory, awe-inspiring, or revelatory—in modes extraordinary and mundane.[24] Human and fallible voices speak, but humans also express themselves as embodied actors, shaped—sometimes contorted—into those attentive postures. What, if anything, Orsi contends, is the experience of the gods based upon, other than a human struggle to comprehend oneself, to explain to another, or to hope (or fear) that a presence might make itself known again? And I insist that those comprehensions, explanations, cannot be taken as *explanatory*. Prayer and meditation follow a poetics of possibility, dependent upon the prior descriptions of religious experience that managed to be captured before they could melt into a half-life, and become re-inscribed as metaphors that in turn shape the mode in which bodies lean attentively toward known/unknown experiences.

---

[24] Robert Orsi's framing of religious studies is that it "is or ought to be the study of what human beings do to, for and against the gods really present—using 'gods' as a synecdoche for all the special suprahuman beings with whom humans have been in relationship in the different times and places—and what the gods really present do with, to, for, and against humans." See *History and Presence* (Cambridge, MA: Harvard University Press, 2017).

7

Tradition and Event: Radicalizing the Catholic Principle

John D. Caputo

A test case

In the summer of 2015, the Philadelphia newspapers headlined the story that a woman named Margie Winters, the director of religious education at a local Catholic academy, had been fired on the grounds that she was openly involved in a lesbian marriage. The word was that this had not been a secret at the academy but that some unhappy parents had complained to the Archdiocese, which forced the hand of the administration. The reaction against the move was swift and strong, as Winters was loved and respected at the school. The most interesting reaction took the form of an "op ed" published in the Philadelphia newspapers signed by a parent, a layman philanthropist, and Sr. Mary Scullion, a well-known Catholic activist in the city and a member of the Religious Sisters of Mercy, who conduct the academy. The signers said that "the Church's truest integrity is at risk when it emphasizes orthodoxy and doctrine without meaningful engagement with human and historic realities." After pointing out that the Church must take responsibility for "its many historic blind spots—persecution of heretics, oppression of indigenous peoples in the name of 'mission', and second-class status for women," they added:

> We are convinced that this is a moment when insistence on doctrinal adherence is clashing with what we believe the Spirit is unfolding in our history—just as it has in the past, with issues like slavery, the rights of women, and the environment. Many Christian denominations have listened to the movement of the Spirit and moved toward both full inclusion and full embrace of the gifts of our gay and lesbian sisters and brothers. The Church is at its best when it listens to the Spirit speaking in our times and through human experiences.[1]

That response—appealing to the promptings of the Spirit in history unfolding in human experience—seems to me exactly right. A very good piece of Catholic theology

---

[1] July 21, 2015, *Philadelphia Inquirer*. http://www.philly.com/philly/blogs/thinktank/On-gay-marriage-let-spirit-guide-the-church.html#puoCsq0wmIGYRQG8.99

had made the local newspapers. Archdiocesan politics aside, this was the right *theological* argument to make. In my view, the Church's position on same-sex love is every bit as wrong as the other historic blind spots to which the letter refers, each one of which eventually succumbed to the pressure of history. Time and again the Church in modernity starts out on the wrong side of history and eventually, several centuries later, catches up with the times and adds a modest apology for standing in the way of science or justice tucked away in an obscure section of *L'Osservatore Romano*. But the framers of this editorial are not speaking of merely being on the wrong side of history, but on the wrong side of the Spirit! They speak of the Spirit "speaking in our times through human experience," of what "the Spirit is unfolding in our history," so that to discern the signs of the times is to discern the promptings of the Spirit.

Their argument presupposes a view of God as the Spirit working in history, and of the Church as the *populus dei*, not as the hierarchy, one of the most important pronouncements of the Vatican II. The argument is theological, pneumatological, and ecclesiological. For the Catholic theologian it is the promptings of the Spirit—not "Pure Reason," or the law of Dialectical Materialism, or the "masses"—that rise up in protest against the violence of history. Against colonialization, say, which the Church provided with a theological cover with its notorious "doctrine of discovery," authorizing the *conquistadores* to engage in their lethal land-grab in the name of God. In this scene the Church as the Spirit immanent in history contests the violence of a "Church" contracted to the official teachings of the hierarchy, which was on the wrong side of both the Spirit and history. Against the deep errancy and fallibility of Church-as-hierarchy, the unfolding of Spirit-in-history is a movement of auto-correction and reinvention. Against the calcification of dogmatic formulae, which results in simple reproduction, the immanence of the Spirit in history unfolds in a productive repetition.

The case is telling. In its defense the Church might rejoin that there is nothing in the scriptures to authorize same-sex love and that Paul appears to have condemned it. Now I would deny that what Paul was condemning back in the first century is what we are talking about today. But the larger point is that in the Catholic tradition it is the tradition that interprets what the scriptures are saying to us at a given moment. The tradition is the *whole* church, not just the uppermost part, the whole body, not just the "head," a figure used by the unknown author of the pseudepigraphic Colossians (1.18-20) which alters the figure introduced by Paul (1 Cor. 12.27) and turns Jesus into a king or emperor. The tradition is the workings of the Spirit in the people of God, and the Spirit often finds itself compelled to take a stand against such a heady Church, the one that Marguerite Porete called the "Little Church," meaning big in power but little in Spirit. *Sola scriptura* is the Protestants' problem, not ours. Unfortunately, the old theological axiom, *ubi spiritus, ibi ecclesia*, has a way of being flipped by the powers that be in the Church: *ubi ecclesia, ibi spiritus*, as if the Spirit has written the Church a blank check and simply does the bidding of Vatican secretaries.

Or the Church might invoke "natural law," which would only make things worse. For one thing, natural law is a Stoic doctrine—to my knowledge Jesus was not a natural law theorist—in which God is thought in terms of nature and nature in terms of necessity; it presupposes a view of God as the necessary immutable order of nature. *Deus sive natura*, as Spinoza said. This completely pagan conception stands opposed to the Jewish and Christian, and in particular prophetic tradition, where God is thought not in terms of nature but of history, and the God of history is thought not in terms of necessity but in terms of making all things new, of the new being, of the future, of the transformability of the future. Stoic natural law was the competing alternative and leading opponent of the Church in antiquity, where the choice was posed between making oneself commensurable with the inevitable, affirming the necessity of things, on the one hand, and affirming the God who will make all things new, on the other. So apart from the fact that natural law has been the argument of choice for justifying the oppression of just about everything, the poor and uneducated, women, children, people of color, animals, and the environment, it is a completely pagan argument—pitted against the God of history and renewal, against the view of God as Spirit.

So what happened in the Margie Winters case? How did the appeal of the Spirit fare before the powers that be downtown at the Archdiocesan offices? We will come back to that, even if I fear my attempt to hold you in suspense is pretty anemic.

The Catholic Principle

The contemporary debate about same-sex love also makes plain that one has a much easier time addressing such problems if one does not have to deal with a doctrine of *sola scriptura*. Even so, the irony is that the Protestant denominations are way ahead of the Catholics in affirming the dignity of women, same-sex love, and the priesthood of the people, but that is only because the Catholic hierarchy is so adept at snatching defeat from the jaws of victory. The underlying theological presuppositions are all on the Catholic side. The old debate between the Protestants and the Catholics is settled even before it gets off the ground. The Protestant notion of *sola scriptura* represents a misunderstanding on every level. It is based on a factual misunderstanding of the history of the composition of the scriptures, as if they represent eyewitness journalistic reports; on a theoretical misunderstanding of the nature of a written text, which is why it has produced the bizarre result of Biblical inerrantism by which, believe it or not, we are still plagued today; and finally on a theological misunderstanding of the Spirit, as if the workings of the Spirit could be contracted to and measured by a book, which is at least as much of a mistake as thinking it is confined to the upper one-tenth of one percent that make up the Catholic hierarchy. The scriptures are not the foundation of the tradition. They are the effect of the tradition. They were produced by the tradition when, at a certain point in time, the Greek-speaking followers of the "way"—we did not yet even have the word "Christianity"—decided they had better start writing things down.

Chronologically, the scriptures are a relatively late formation. The very fact that the various communities chose to write down the sayings and stories that had been orally transmitted—the tradition up to that point—tells us that a great deal of time had been spent waiting for the return of Jesus and the conviction had set in that it might very well prove to be a long wait. Their importance is not chronological—as if they are there at the beginning and reporting back to us latecomers—but kairological. Their composition was the right thing to do at the right time. Right for what? For the *tradition*, for the history of the people of God, in order to allow it to be preserved and transmitted. They serve the life of the tradition; indeed, they are the tradition at work preserving itself. The scriptures are a gift but they are the gift of tradition, of the operations of memory and expectation that define a tradition, and a tradition is an ongoing process of auto-correction. The scriptures do not compete with tradition as an opposing or even as a separate principle, as if there were two. They insert themselves *within* tradition, as a part of the tradition; they are the tradition *in actu exercitu*. They are still more evidence that tradition is first, last and always. If the works of Thomas Aquinas were placed on the high altar at the opening Mass of Vatican I, they would have been well advised to put a good account of tradition, like Gadamer's *Truth and Method*, on the high altar of Vatican II. (It had just come out!)[2]

But do not misunderstand me. While I am pressing the case for tradition, I have not come to engage in a bit of theological braggadocio, to offer a chauvinistic reassurance of the superiority of Catholicism over Protestantism, each of which I think has come up with its own way to give the Spirit in the world a good deal of grief. As we can see from my opening test case, the results of pressing the case for the tradition cause considerable discomfort to the powers that be on both sides of that divide, not only for the hapless defenders of biblical inerrancy but also for the hapless defenders of hierarchical inerrancy, for inerrancy of any sort, the very idea of which drives a Cartesian stake into the heart of any living tradition, Christian or otherwise. Under the pressure of history, that is, of the Spirit in history, I think the fifth volume of the collected works of Hans Küng will eventually prove to be the right response to the idolatrous and patriarchal violence of infallibility.[3]

Hence, in a show of ecumenism, and to prove that I have nothing provincial and merely denominational in mind, I turn now to what Paul Tillich called the "Protestant Principle."[4] By this Tillich did not mean the myopic principles of *sola fide* or *sola scriptura*; no such list of solo performances will do. Any list of *solae* would need to be extended indefinitely and any such solitude would end up being very much disturbed. He meant an axiom which, while inspired by historical Protestantism, makes both a wider sweep and a deeper cut and indeed submits the historical Protestant churches to its judgment. This Principle is a function of a prior distinction Tillich drew between the conditional and unconditional. By the unconditional he meant, on the object-side, some substantive matter—let's say, in German, a *Sache*, a thing that matters—something that lays claim to us unconditionally, without compromise, leaving us no room to negotiate the terms of the deal, no way to talk it down. On the subject-side, the unconditional means what we affirm unconditionally, what matters to us unconditionally. This is a matter for which we are willing to live or die, as a very youthful Kierkegaard said in his

---

[2] The work that David Tracy has done to think contemporary pluralism in terms of the hermeneutics of the tradition, drawing upon Paul Ricoeur and Gadamer, is a case of taking the right approach from my point of view. See David Tracy, *The Analogical Imagination: Christian Theology and the Culture of Pluralism* (New York: Crossroad, 1981).
[3] Hans Kung, "Appeal to Rethink Infallibility," *National Catholic Reporter* 52, no. 12, 1–7 (March 25–April 7, 2016). See Hans Kung, *Infallible? An Unresolved Enquiry* (London and New York: Continuum International Publishing Group, 1994).
[4] Paul Tillich, *Dynamics of Faith* (New York: HarperCollins, 1957), pp. 33, 112–113.

Journals; a matter of ultimate "concern," an English word that would have translated the German *Sorge*, which is the Being of Dasein in *Being and Time*, a book Tillich knew very well. This issues in Tillich's famous description of religion in terms of being seized by a matter of ultimate concern, a definition remarkable for its failure to mention incense, candles, clergy, hierarchy, and dogmas.

Accordingly, the enlarged Protestant Principle is reconfigured as follows. First, *semper reformanda*, which Tillich explains by saying that the church must live in a permanent state of protest, of permanent self-critique, on the grounds that the historical church is a conditioned response to an unconditional demand. Accordingly, the demands placed upon the Church—be it Roman, Protestant, or Orthodox—are never met, structurally, in principle. Secondly, *justus et peccator*: human subjects are always on the short end of the unconditional stick, always falling short of what is demanded of us (*peccator*), so we are put in the accusative, as Levinas says, called out by something for which we are never the match, always falling short, structurally, in principle, guilty, not because of what we did but because of what we are. But we are saved (*justus*) by confessing just how far short we have fallen, saved by this loss, saved not exactly by our faith but by our doubt, by our postmodern incredulity, by our doubt-filled faith (or faith-filled doubt) in something that has seized us unconditionally. Tillich presupposes an idea of God as the unconditional, as something whose least limiting description is the "ground of being." For our purposes, Tillich presupposes the challenge of God in terms of the challenge of the unconditional.

Tillich opposes the Protestant Principle to what he calls the "Catholic substance." By substance he does not mean the *substantia* of Greco-medieval metaphysical theology, which shows up in the Catholic theology of "transubstantiation." He does not mean the natural law tradition, which he too considered pagan and necessitarian. By substance he meant the historical faith that had been handed down through the ages, the Christian legacy. He does not mean *substantia, natura*, or *essentia*—he means history. The inherited historical tradition, the theology and sacraments and liturgies which have been handed down, which stands in need of constant critique. The substance can only be passed down by passing under the principle of protest. There are not two different principles, one Protestant and one Catholic, but one Principle and a substance, a form and a substance. The Catholic substance is the tradition, the historically transmitted faith, upon which the Protestant Principle is the critical reflection.

So it is significant that Tillich does not speak of a Catholic "Principle." It is as if there is a kind of pre-reflective, pre-critical naïveté in the substance, which does not rise to the level of a reflective Principle of protest and criticism. I think Tillich is mistaken about that. The substance is the tradition, and the tradition is *the promptings of the Spirit in history*, and that implies, if not a reflective critical operation, another let us say auto-corrective operation, one embedded *in* history—which we see when we speak of the "force of history," or of being on the "right side of history." That does indeed represent a principle—a principle of historical process. The stirrings of the unconditional always take place under historical conditions. Just as Luther said that the Bible interprets itself, referring to the dialectic between the whole and the part, so does the tradition interpret itself, by the ongoing process of self-correction and reinvention—which being a work of history is far from inerrant. So there is a Catholic Principle, which is the *historical* principle, and this historical principle is the *hermeneutical* principle. Indeed, the neglect of the historical hermeneutical principle is lethal on both sides: it leads Protestantism astray into an ahistorical biblical inerrantism, even as it leads Catholicism astray into an ahistorical doctrine of infallibility which confers unconditional status on a conditional–historical doctrinal formulation. A Pope or a paper Pope! An inerrant book or an inerrant institution! Pick your poison—or your idolatry!

Like Tillich, let us say that while taking its point of departure from historical Catholicism, the Catholic Principle is not restricted to denominational Catholicism, but indeed submits both historical Catholicism and historical Protestantism under its judgment. I want now to propose that the opposite of the Catholic Principle in this wider and deeper sense is not the historical Reformation but more importantly the Gnostic principle.[5] It is the decision made early on in the tradition to insist that Jesus was a man of flesh and blood, a historical agent, datable and locatable. He was a dark-skinned, Aramaic-speaking Jewish Galilean peasant—enough to get him banned from entering the United States by the Christian Right—a healer and an exorcist, who lived in the first century and was crucified during the reign of Tiberius; he was not a phantom or apparition of a pure spirit. The Catholic Principle appropriately broadened and deepened is the principle of *historicality and temporality, materiality, and carnality*. It is wider and deeper than the words of Scriptures or the datable–locatable declarations of the hierarchy; it is polyvalent, polymorphic, and polyglottal. It is the very *Sache* of Christianity, which is Spirit in the world, and—like it or not—the Protestant Principle of protest and critique has been at work in it all along. It has always and already, *semper*, stood in need of being reformed and it has always and already been reforming, reconfiguring—for better and for worse—under the historical–temporal–carnal–material pressure exerted by the Spirit.

Radicalizing the Catholic Principle

Radicalizing the Catholic Principle means both radicalizing the Spirit and radicalizing hermeneutics. Radicalizing the Spirit means that on the Catholic Principle, the world is the *sacramentum mundi*, and the Spirit is entirely sacramental and mundane, not an immaterial being outside the space and time of the world. The Spirit is a thoroughly historical one, not an immaterial substance or what the Scholastics called a *substantia separata*; the Spirit is neither a substance nor separate. The Spirit is not an immaterial being in the sky but a being down on earth, a Spirit-in-the-world, as in "being-in-the-world" (*in-der-Welt-sein*), carrying all the force of the Heideggerian hyphens. The Spirit is the breath of the body of the world, the respiration and inspiration of this body. The Spirit inspires by calling, by forcing air through the lungs of the world and calling for the coming of the Kingdom, for the Kingdom to come.

The Spirit is the people of God so to say that "the Spirit lives" is to say that real people live who are moved by the memory and the promise of Jesus, not that an immaterial

---

[5] John Dominic Crossan, "Our Own Faces in Deep Wells: The Future of Historical Jesus Research," in *God, the Gift and Postmodernism* (ed. John D. Caputo and Michael J. Scanlon; Bloomington: Indiana University Press, 1999), pp. 282–310.

Super-Being in the sky is hovering over them and overseeing the traffic down on earth by means of earthly plenipotentiaries in Vatican offices. What exists are real people, a collective, gathered together by the call that is getting itself called in the memory and the promise of Yeshua, while the distinctions drawn in Christian Neoplatonism between time and eternity, and between material and immaterial substances, are fictions. The living Spirit is the living–breathing Spirit, literally. Make no mistake, I mean breathing, with lungs, with real air. On the Catholic Principle, I am insisting, the challenge of God is to keep the future open, and to count on the past to give us the courage for the future, to have hope in the future because we have hope in the past. Tillich called this the courage to be; let us simply add, the courage for what may be, not *être* but *peut-être*.

The radicalization of hermeneutics means that interpretation goes all the way down, to the roots, *radix*. There are no uninterpreted facts of the matter. Underlying an interpretation is not a pure fact but another interpretation, no less datable and locatable. The hermeneutical principle is a principle because it has critical-reformative force, exciting an ongoing process of reformation, of transformation, of auto-reformation, whether we like it or not. The tradition alters under our feet, whether we resist these changes, like the conservatives, or embrace them, like the progressives. According to the Catholic (historical-hermeneutical) Principle, every historical event is a conditional expression of the unconditional Spirit-in-history. It is in fact disingenuous to speak of "the" tradition or "the" Church because upon closer inspection history discloses to us multiple tradition*s* and many churche*s*, which we cluster together in a kind of grand intellectual shorthand when we speak of them in the singular.

The radical hermeneutical point can be summarized by saying that a tradition does not have a meaning or an essence; it has a history. The substance of the Catholic Principle is not an *essentia*, a *natura*, or a *substantia*; it is hermeneutical and historical. If we ask, "what is the meaning or the essence of the Church?" the answer is that we cannot say. It has not ended yet. We can only speak of the "meaning," "essence," or "definition" of things that were never alive to begin with, like a triangle, or are dead and gone, like a dead language. Then we are free to compile a list of all its usages without fear that someone will come along and coin a new metaphor, or create a new genre, or change the language game, or initiate a paradigm shift—and cause a shift that reverberates throughout the system and alters its course.

The Church, like any tradition, does not *have* a history; it *is* a history. It is the breathing of the Spirit, of the real people who breathe with this Spirit, as it inhales and exhales specific motifs and stories, specific beliefs and practices, through time. As such, it is, just as it likes to say, a "pilgrim church." The church is an historical and conditioned response to something that calls to us unconditionally, which I will characterize as the memory and the promise of Jesus or, as I prefer to say, of Yeshua, using his ancient Aramaic name. This defamiliarization relieves us of some of the baggage of a name that has been freighted, overwrought, and overdetermined with dogma and violence. It serves to remind us of a man of flesh and blood, to remind us of his carnality and materiality, temporality and historicality—dark-skinned, Aramaic-speaking, Jewish—which are the signature marks of the Catholic Principle radically understood.

The worst of all the heresies, the one that is as wrong as wrong can be—in general I do not talk like this, because I think that heresies are innovations of the Spirit that the hierarchy fears—is Docetism. The genuinely damnable idea in this heresy is the one that tries to deny the history, the historicality, the carnality of the Spirit, that claims that Yeshua's material presence in history was an illusion. That is the real sin against the Spirit, the root of all the sins. The one genuinely lethal idea in the tradition is that the body of Jesus is a phantom, that he only appeared to be a man, appeared to suffer, and appeared to die, while in reality he is an immaterial being, which we should all hope to be someday. I am not opposing Gnostic metaphysics with materialistic metaphysics but opposing metaphysics, especially the opposing metaphysics of matter and spirit. In its place I check the guns of metaphysics at the door and think instead in terms of a theopoetics of call and response, of a Spirit calling and people responding. In those terms, the church is a concrete and conditioned response, a historical response, made under the contingent conditions of space and time, to an unconditional call, to something that has seized us unconditionally.

The kingdom of God

The name of Yeshua is not the name of an essence but of an event. Consequently, the challenge of God for anyone who belongs to this tradition, who has confidence in this tradition, is keyed in a special way to Yeshua, to what he said and did, to his life and death, which, to use the language of the unknown author of the Letter to the Colossians (1.15), serves as an icon of God. As we have all learned from Jean-Luc Marion, an icon is to be distinguished from an idol, because an idol traps us with its glitter while an icon yields to an excess, draws us beyond itself and leaves us pointing in the direction of something to which it itself points, while leaving us in the accusative. An icon is something conditional—it exists in space and time, is subject to the constraints of history, of its concrete hermeneutical situation—but it comes about in response to the call of something unconditional, something that calls us, something that *challenges* us. The challenge of God is the challenge God poses to us, that puts us on the spot, puts us in the accusative. The challenge of God is unconditional; it is the challenge of the unconditional—which breaks in on us under contingent, historical conditional circumstances. As an icon, Yeshua is a bit of space and time where the challenge of God breaks in, or breaks out, where the space–time continuum of history is bent or curved by the event that is breaking in or breaking out.

The challenge of God, the materiality of the challenge of God, which is distinctly defined and vividly embodied by Yeshua, can be felt when Mark has Yeshua announce his mission by saying that he comes to bring "the gospel of God," the good news of God, the *evangelion tou theou*. He announces that the *kairos* has been fulfilled, which means the "kingdom of God" (*basileia tou theou*) is near, that we should have a new heart, *metanoia*, and put our trust (*pistis*) in the good news (Mk 1.14). So the gospel of Mark is the "gospel of Yeshua the Anointed" (Mk 1.1), but the gospel of Yeshua is the "gospel of God," which I think we can take as both a subjective and objective genitive. So we have a multilayered icon, a complex, multiplex event: a text coming from a community, later on emblematized under the name of "Mark," transcribing a memory, handed down by an oral tradition about Yeshua, who in turn announces the "kingdom of God," which itself is an icon or emblem of God. Everything that Yeshua says about God is tied to this expression, the "kingdom of God," which means what life would be like if God ruled, not the world; if God ruled, not Caesar. If so, the challenge of God in what Yeshua said was challenging indeed, and first and foremost it was a challenge to Rome. The expression appears to be almost ironic—since Yeshua was and lived among the humblest of people—and the irony did not go unnoticed by the people who run the kingdom, the real one, the *Imperium Romanum*. We can surmise that Yeshua had a silver tongue, which very likely contributed to his demise at the hands of the Romans. It would not have been beyond him to get in the face of the Romans by posing a threatening possibility to them, the threat of an alternative to Caesar, that the day was near at hand when the rule of the God of the Jews would be established.

When Luke has Yeshua announce his ministry, he uses a citation from Isaiah. Yeshua has been anointed—he is the *Christos*—to bring good news to the poor, to announce to the prisoners that they will be released, to the blind that they will recover their sight, to the oppressed that they will go free, and to proclaim the year of the Jubilee, the year that follows seven times seven, in which all debts are forgiven and the people are able to make a new start, a new beginning. That is how it will look when God rules, not Caesar. You will notice the materiality and carnality of this list, the poor, the imprisoned, the blind, the oppressed, which is pretty much the same list we find in Matthew 25. So when we press Yeshua about God, he deflects us to the kingdom of God, and when we press him about the kingdom of God, he deflects our attention again, to things like leaven, dinner parties, and treasures buried in a field. So there is a constant deflection—from God to the kingdom, from the Kingdom to mustard seeds—not metaphysics.

While Matthew has Yeshua speak more often of the kingdom of heaven, probably out of respect for the name of God, the kingdom of God described by Yeshua seems very terrestrial, and while James Joyce speaks of Yeshua as a "heavenman," Yeshua seems to me very much an earthman. That is as it should be according to the Catholic Principle, which is the principle of carnality, materiality, and terrestriality, as opposed to the Gnostic principle, which is very heavenly, immaterialistic, and otherworldly.

Did the kingdom come just as Yeshua said it would? Not at all. The challenging thing is that the opposite happened—Yeshua lost and Rome won. Pilate put down this alternative kingdom, swiftly and violently. Of course, this is quite the opposite of the fantastic way Pilate is portrayed by the author of the fourth gospel, who is trying to make "the Jews" look bad and a bloody Roman procurator look good, who speaks of "the Jews" as if Yeshua were not one of "them." Yeshua would have been appalled by a gospel which, ironically, has earned the nickname of the "gospel of love"! Rome's rule was as firm as ever. So Yeshua's discourse was at best prophetic. Instead of describing a fact of the matter or predicting the future course of events, Yeshua was offering us hope, making us a promise—that is what God means, which means, this is what God means to do. Our challenge is to put our confidence (*pistis*) in that promise, even if it does not happen. The future is better, even when it is not, which is why it is our hope, why we must have confidence in God.

This, I think, is exactly the challenge of God faced by Paul. It all ended in death for Yeshua, and not just death but an execution, and not just execution but a literally excruciating and—in an honor/shame society—a particularly ignominious execution, one that left no doubt about who was ruling. The kingdom was not near, not yet, not now. That was certainly what Paul had concluded, for the longest time. Until he didn't. Until one day, or as is more likely over the course of many months and years, it hit him; he had a breakthrough. In the only first-hand account we have of this event in his own words—not the Romanticized account written many decades later in Acts, no road to Damascus, no voices, no unhorsing, for which we can thank the imagination of the Renaissance painter Tintoretto—he describes an insight (*apocalypsis*, Gal. 1.12), a flash of intuition, that God had—to the utter consternation of the world, of Romans, Greeks, and Jews alike—*revealed himself in the defeat*. The ignominy and the humiliation of the crucifixion bore in fact the mark of God, which is a contradiction of everything that anyone in antiquity had meant by God. The mark of the divine is upon the defeat and the shame. The challenge of God for Paul is to swallow *that*, to accept that unlike gods of the nations, who triumph over their enemies, the divinity of God of Israel is attested in the humiliating defeat of God's Anointed One.

There could hardly be a greater challenge than that, a greater challenge to our expectations about what we think God is to supposed to be. Paul brings his insight to a head in the first chapter of First Corinthians in which the "logic" of this wrenching reversal of our expectations of God is identified in what is, for my money, the most brilliant and explosive account of God, of the challenge posed by God, to be found in the New Testament. There he speaks of the *"logos"* of the cross—of the shame and humiliation, of the death and defeat—which confounded the Greeks, who wanted *sophia*, and the Jews, *us* Jews, including Paul himself, lest we think anachronistically that there were any "Christians" around to oppose to the "Jews," who wanted signs and miracles. Paul puts the challenge of God in the most pointed terms possible. He tells the Christians at Corinth that God has made the wisdom of this world foolish. God's foolishness is wiser than human wisdom, God's weakness is stronger than human strength, and surprisingly, God has chosen them—those at Corinth who put their trust in God's Anointed One—who are not well born, not well educated, not well off. Indeed, he says that God has chosen *ta me onta*, the nothings and nobodies of the world— invoking the very language of being that would have been treasured by the lovers of Greek wisdom at Corinth—to confound the powers that be, the people of substance (*ousia*), who think they are something, who think they are somebody.

If Yeshua is the *ikon* of what we know about God, the challenge of God is to see God in the poor and oppressed, the hungry and the imprisoned, who await the year of the Jubilee (in the Synoptics), to see God in foolishness, weakness, and nothingness, in defeat and humiliation (in Paul). Of course, this is all in keeping with the *promise* posed by Yeshua's announcement of his ministry; it is not an act of Sado-masochistic identification with pain and suffering, and not a simple rejection of every sense of wisdom and strength. So in the second chapter of First Corinthians Paul promises the Corinthians that God's day is coming, that the rulers of this world will come to rue the day that they did not listen to Paul, that God will show their worldly wisdom to be foolish and their worldly strength to be weak, and that the *real* power and wisdom belongs to God. That is the apocalyptic part of Paul's *apocalypsis*. But what happened? The same thing. The Romans also killed Paul, and shortly thereafter leveled the Temple, and the people of God were dispersed. Of course, we might say be tempted to say that three centuries later, God's kingdom was finally established—by Constantine. But for a lot of us—not just Stanley Hauerwas![6]—this was less a matter of the Roman *imperium* converting to Christianity and more a matter of Christianity converting to the Roman *imperium*. This was rather more a betrayal of the kingdom than its fulfillment, and it provided the basis of what we call today the "Roman" church. Can you imagine the effect such a phrase would have had on Yeshua? Could any word have struck more fear in his heart?[7]

So Yeshua was proven wrong, and so was Paul. The establishment of the rule of God was not near. The rule of Rome continued even when "Christians" sat on the throne. And it would be very hard to say that over the centuries anything very much like it ever came about. What Paul called the "powers and the principalities," what we call the evil ones, the greedy, the hateful, the malevolent, continue to do evil and get away with it, and the good continue to do good and to get persecuted for it. As biblical historian James L. Kugel once said, the track record of God in history in intervening on behalf of the good and rectifying evil is so bad we have to wonder why the theologians keep bringing it up.[8]

The challenge of God

As you have no doubt guessed—there was not much suspense about this—Margie Winters did not get her job back. The appeal of the Spirit fell on deaf ears down at the Archdiocesan offices, although President Obama did invite her to the papal reception at the White House in September, 2015. Her firing was a betrayal of the Spirit, a departure from the Catholic Principle, and a failure to rise to the challenge of God. Still, the kingdom comes—in the loss, in the defeat, in the powerlessness. That's the challenge, the same challenge Paul faced. The kingdom comes whenever people like Margie Winters and Sr. Mary Scullion and their colleagues speak out on behalf of what "the Spirit is unfolding in our time," and plead for "listen[ing] to the Spirit speaking in our times and through human experiences," which is a felicitous way to formulate

---

[6] Stanley Hauerwas (1940–) is a pacifist theologian and a critic of Reinhold Niebuhr's Christian realism, who denies the notion of a "just war" and maintains that it is a creation of the post-Constantinian Church. See his *The Peaceable Kingdom: A Primer in Christian Ethics* (Notre Dame, IN: University of Notre Dame Press, 1983)

[7] Indeed, one of the oldest components of the Constantinian Church, "just war" theory, was revisited in a conference held at the Vatican (April 11–13, 2016), the same week as this conference was held, entitled "Nonviolence and Just Peace," co-sponsored by Pax Christi International and the Pontifical Council for Justice and Peace. The final statement is Pax Christi International, "An Appeal to the Catholic Church to re-commit to the centrality of Gospel nonviolence," https://nonviolencejustpeace.net/final-statement-an-appeal-to-the-catholic-church-to-re-commit-to-the-centrality-of-gospel-nonviolence/

[8] James L. Kugel, *The God of Old: Inside the Lost World of the Bible* (New York: Free Press, 2003), pp. 125–136.

the Catholic Principle, indeed, a felicitous way to radicalize it—only to lose. It's an old story. When the people of God speak out, as these women did, they risk being hauled before the *power* of the Church—like Yeshua brought before the power of Pontius Pilate. The comparison is as apt as it is ironic. The people who express the promptings of the Spirit are judged by the powers that be, the long robes, the men of substance (*ousia*) and authority (*exousia*), sitting in big offices. The spirit of the people rises up in dignity against the powers and the principalities—of the Roman Church.

The power of the "Churchmen" is organized, not in the image of Yeshua, who was poor and without power, one of *ta me onta*, but of Diocletian, a Roman emperor who persecuted the Christians and became famous for reorganizing the administrative structure of the *Imperium Romanum*—from the "*Pontifex Maximus*" down to the "*dioecesis*"—the very empire which had put Yeshua to death. In this unhappy scene, as in so many others, captured iconically in "The Legend of the Grand Inquisitor," ask yourself: Who stands in the place of Yeshua and who stands in the place of the Roman Procurator? Who stands on the side of divine weakness and who stands on the side of worldly Roman power? What more tragic farce than thinking that the kingdom of God needs to be bureaucratically administered by imperial Roman rule? A Church more like Rome than Yeshua, which has tragically confused a historically contingent and conditional form of ancient political bureaucracy with the unconditional call for the coming of the kingdom, is exposed for what it is, and exposed by nothing less than the Catholic Principle.

The year of the Jubilee has not arrived. Indeed, this is not a year that is going to have an actual date, one that will go down in history as the year God's rule finally showed up and all things were made new. But if the year of the Jubilee is clearly not a matter of calendar time, what then? There are (at least) two ways to deal with this challenge—the Gnostic way and the Catholic way. The Gnostic way is to say that the year of Jubilee is a heavenly year, that it does not belong to time at all, where time is treated as an ephemeral shadow, but to what the Neoplatonic philosophers thought to be a timeless One called "eternity." Luke has Yeshua say that the year of the Jubilee is the *pleroma*, the fulfillment of time, but in the Gnostic way fulfillment means eradication, that time and flesh will be wiped away. This is most pronounced in that late gospel so idiosyncratic that we often just call it the "fourth" gospel. There the kingdom of God is not a form of life but a form of afterlife, and its central narrative is a cynical story (which, interestingly and fortunately, no one else in the New Testament knows) of Jesus waiting for Lazarus to die in order to put on a show of divine power (Jn 11.4-5) by raising him from the dead.[9] Then the kingdom of God is volatilized into a kingdom of heavenly, incorruptible, docetic bodies flitting about in a timeless eternity doing God knows what. To such mythology, the best religious and theological response, as Tillich said, is atheism.

The Catholic way is to remain faithful to the carnality and materiality, to the temporality and historicality of the kingdom; to mustard seeds not metaphysics; to

---

[9] I have defended this reading of the story in *The Weakness of God: A Theology of the Event* (Bloomington: Indiana University Press, 2006), pp. 236–258. See also, Ernst Kasemann, *The Testament of Jesus* (Philadelphia, PA: Fortress Press, 1968), p. 9.

Yeshua the earthman, not the heavenman. The challenge is to be faithful to this in the face of the evidence, which is that the year of the Jubilee seems very far away, indeed sometimes farther than ever. In the Catholic way, the challenge of the God of Yeshua, of the God whose *ikon* was Yeshua, who announces good news for the poor and the coming of the year of the Jubilee, has to do not with predicting the future but with offering us a promise. The year of the Jubilee belongs neither to the timelessness of eternity nor to the chronological time of the calendar but to the time of a *promise*. Our challenge is to put our trust and confidence (*pistis*) in God's promise, a trust that is distorted when *pistis* becomes epistemology, a "faith" corrupted into a modernist creedal belief, a form of life contracted into a propositional assertion.

Then Protestants pound on their Bible, and Popes decree infallibly.
Then the kingdom of God recedes. Then Yeshua weeps over Jerusalem.

The challenge of God comes down to this—that this primal trust is for all the world the foolishness that Paul describes in I Corinthians 1. Judged by the standards of the world, the genuine wisdom of God is foolishness, and the genuine power of God is weakness. In God's kingdom, offense is met with forgiveness not retaliation, and hatred with love not a counter-attack. Such weakness and folly are a *skandalon*, a stumbling block. They are not part of a long-term *winning strategy*, or a case of deferred heavenly gratification, or a way the weak have come up with to outwit the strong and take them by surprise, which is pretty much Nietzsche's critique of Christian *ressentiment*. They are not a way to show that the children of the light are ultimately quicker on their feet than the children of darkness, which is a Gnostic mythology. The genuine wisdom and power of God is that the strength is found in the weakness, and the wisdom in the folly—of mercy, love, and forgiveness, where there is every chance, maybe even a likelihood, that the wicked will prosper and the merciful will lose.

As Margie Winters can tell you, the challenge of God is that God is not about *winning*. The kingdom of God is a form of life, not of afterlife, and not a secret way to win. The year of the Jubilee is not a world-historical event. It reaches such sporadic and fragile fulfillment as time allows. It is temporal not eternal, and its temporality is neither that of calendar time nor of an apocalyptic time which triumphantly crushes evil. It has the temporality of the *kairos*, belonging to the moment, even little quotidian kairological moments, what Richard Kearney calls "microeschatologies."[10] The kingdom of God arrives not by transcending time but letting the shoots of grace spring up in the crevices of time, by letting being be broken up and disjoined by time. Unhappily, the kingdom happens, grace emerges, when people like Margie Winters lose.

As I have argued at greater length in a little trilogy—*The Weakness of God, The Insistence of God*, and *The Folly of God*—the challenge of God is to recognize that the name of God is not the name of a supreme being (*ens supremum*), nor of being itself

---

[10] Richard Kearney, "Epiphanies of the Everyday: Toward a Micro-Eschatology," in *After God: Richard Kearney and the Religious Turn in Continental Philosophy* (ed. John Panteleimon Manoussakis; New York: Fordham University Press, 2011).

(*ipsum esse*), nor of the ground of Being, nor of a hyper-being (*hyperousios*), but of a promise.[11] The challenge of God lies not in the ontological eminence or the ontological depth of being but in the unconditionality of the challenge to make the kingdom of God come true. The operative distinctions are not ontotheological—beings and Being, time and eternity, matter and spirit, body and soul—but theopoetical: conditional and unconditional, call and response. The challenge is, otherwise than being, the name of a promise, of an unconditional call, of a solicitation issuing not from a Super-being but from the bowels of the earth, to use an earthy image, or from the spirit-in-the-world, to use a more edifying one. From time to time, in time, Spirit breaks in upon us as if from without, and from time to time breaks out among the people of God, who are filled with this spirit. This all takes place according to the Catholic Principle, the unfolding of the Spirit in space and time, in carnality and mortality, in temporality and historicality, in materiality and terrestriality.

I conclude in the same way, and with the same words, invoked by the authors of the "op ed" in the Philadelphia newspaper, a citation from Pope Francis, a man poised precariously and with great uneasiness between occupying the place of *Pontifex Maximus* and affirming the kingdom of God, "If the Christian is a restorationist, a legalist, if he wants everything clear and safe, then he will find nothing. Tradition and memory of the past must help us to have the courage to open up new areas to God."

---

[11] John D. Caputo, *The Weakness of God; The Insistence of God: A Theology of Perhaps* (Bloomington: Indiana University Press, 2013); *The Folly of God: A Theology of the Unconditional* (Salem, OR: Polebridge Press, 2016).

8

Theological Thinking and John Caputo's *Tradition and Event: Radicalizing the Catholic Principle*

John McCarthy

The immediately preceding chapter, "Tradition and Event: Radicalizing the Catholic Principle," is an instance of how a thoughtful person might think theologically in a contemporary world; it is an example of theological reflection rooted in the practicality of the everyday and the flux of a living tradition; it is a catalogue of some of the most frequent themes and ideas used by Caputo: hope, promise, event, criticism of destructive absolutes; attention to proper names and naming, to suffering, to irony and paradox, and, not least, to the name of God. It is a gift to both the mind and the heart because it does what Caputo is noted for: taking the often-jargon-filled language of philosophy and theology, and making its *sache*, its issue, not only clear, but also felt, and without loss of rigor.

In what follows I will focus on this project of "thinking theologically in a contemporary world" by exploring more closely how Caputo thinks through the central issue of all theology, namely, the challenge of God. My wager is that by first thinking along with Prof. Caputo—exploring *what* he thinks the challenge of God is and *how* he thinks through that challenge—we are then better able as fellow theologians to also face the challenge of God.

So let's begin with Caputo's *what* and *how* of theological thinking in this work. *What* is the challenge of God? Caputo begins his consideration with an institutional event: Margie Winters is dismissed from her position because she is a married lesbian and a director of religious education in a Catholic academy within the Archdiocese of Philadelphia. She was fired from that position seemingly because her marital relationship was incompatible with the doctrinal and moral position of the institutionalized religious organization which she represented, the Roman Catholic Church. So why is this anything more than an institutional event where an employee acts in a way that is inconsistent with the mission of the organization? Where is the challenge of God in this situation? It is in the alleged disjunction between the rationale and action that the Catholic Church took (and often takes) as a sacrament of God in the world, and the rationale and action that sacramentally discloses the workings of the Spirit of God in history theologically clarified. Caputo begins his theological thinking in a very specific situation understood as much more than an event in the life of Margie Winters and much more than an event that might be handled by the Human

Relations Department of an organization; it is a sacramental event in a theology of history. And it is a sacramental event in which the organization, in this case the church, has a sacramental responsibility, namely, to be disclosive of, and not blind to, the Spirit of God in history. In Caputo's judgment the church has failed its theological responsibility in the case of Margie Winters, as it has in many instances within history, by repeating a pattern of confusing its often-distorted institutionalized authority with its sacramental responsibility. In this disjunction between the institutional Church and a theology of history, the challenge of God erupts as the responsibility to discern the Spirit of God in history, to explain why this discernment is a responsible theological judgment, and then to bring that judgment to light publicly. For Caputo it is likewise important to note what the challenge of God is *not*, but where some might argue that it is located: in institutional allegiance; in doctrinal intransigence; in biblical literalism; in other-worldly spiritualities; in privatized religion. Theological thinking for Caputo has the responsibility to recognize the ambiguity which makes an event like the firing of Margie Winters a contested judgment with alternative discernments of the Spirit in history. Yet within this ambiguity theological thinking likewise has the responsibility to be able to state clearly why the Catholic Church has gone beyond a socially clumsy firing and has failed its own theological mission.

So, if this is *what* the challenge of God for theological thinking is—to identify and explain what it means to discern the Spirit of God in very real, everyday events in the world, and to recognize the responsibility and likely obstacles that such discernment entails—then *how* does Caputo carry out this theological thinking? He does this by advancing an argued theological hermeneutic of selected topics within the Catholic Christian theological self-understanding, a hermeneutic which he labels a "theopoetics of call and response." This argued theological hermeneutic consists of an analysis of what Caputo calls the "Catholic Principle," an exposition of the radicality of this "Catholic Principle," and a largely biblical analysis of the "kingdom of God" as a primary symbol of the radicality of the "Catholic Principle." Two themes are consistently invoked in advancing this theological hermeneutic, namely, (1) that the thinking involved is thoroughly hermeneutical, meaning that there is no absolute, non-historical essence of the Christian tradition or fact of the Bible which can serve as an indisputable criterion for discerning once and for all what the activity of the Spirit of God in history is, and (2) that whatever this hermeneutic understanding calls for it will always be marked by its "carnality and materiality, temporality and historicality." As he notes, from this perspective, the "worst heresy" for the Christian theological tradition is Docetism, a position that denies the historicality, carnality, and materiality of the incarnation and the Spirit of God in history.

Let us then look more closely at Caputo's theological thinking by exploring the three elements of his hermeneutic and the two themes which stitch these elements together. First, the "Catholic Principle": against the background of Paul Tillich's famous discussion of the "Protestant Principle" and the "Catholic Substance,"[1] Caputo argues for an understanding of the Catholic tradition that is thoroughly

---

[1] Paul Tillich, "The Protestant Message and the Man of Today," in *The Protestant Era* (trans. James Luther Adams; Chicago, IL: The University of Chicago Press, Abridged Edition, 1957), pp. 192–205.

historical, always unfinished, and consistently in need of self-reformation. This "Catholic Principle," this tradition, is not an essence deposited by a divine revealer, or an essential message contained within the Gospels, or a creed which brings irreformable doctrines, or an authority vested in an office or an institution. Rather this "Catholic Principle" is situated within a constant tension between that which makes an unconditional, unavoidable, and nonnegotiable claim to what is most important for us to do and be, and the recognition that we will never be able—because of both finitude and sin—to satisfy this unconditional claim. This tension is not an inner tension of the soul; it is rather an historical, practical, individual, and social tension, or, as Caputo writes:

> The Catholic Principle appropriately broadened and deepened is the principle of *historicality and temporality, materiality and carnality*. It is wider and deeper than the words of Scriptures or the datable-locatable declarations of the hierarchy; it is polyvalent, poly morphic, polyglottal. It is the very *Sache* of Christianity, which is the Spirit in the World.[2]

Radicalizing the "Catholic Principle" means that there is no room for an escape from the themes of historicity, materiality, carnality, and temporality by an appeal to the eternal, irreformable, essential, or unchangeable, or in the refuge of certainties, dogmatisms, or authoritative declaration, whether they be those of an institution or a book. A retreat to any such refuge avoids the underlying temporality of the Catholic Principle, a temporality which is the temporality of a promise and not that of an accomplishment. A promise looks to the future, and places a demand on those who are oriented toward that future. An accomplishment looks to the past, recognizes an achievement, and lives bound by the wake of that achievement. For Caputo, the radicality of the Catholic Principle requires a theological thinking whose temporal structure is that of a promise, of that which is yet to come, whose shape and texture and demand are not quite certain. Doing theology from faith in this context is simultaneously hoping and trusting in a promise, one which often seems at best improbable and at worst, impossible. And this promise, in its radicality, takes the form of a call, the call of the unconditional demand of the Spirit in history, to which the Christin must respond, often with no assurance or certainty and sometimes sinfully, more often than not, uncomfortably, but always unavoidably.

If the discussion of the radicalization of the Catholic Principle describes first and foremost the character or feel of the response to the material, carnal, historical, and temporal unconditioned, then the analysis of the kingdom of God as the biblical symbol of this unconditioned gives a shape to this call and response structure. Caputo briefly explores each of the synoptic gospels—the Gospel of John is not a favorite of Caputo because it borders on the Gnosticism and Docetism that Caputo so rejects—but sees the symbol of the Spirit in history most especially in Paul's contrast of the wisdom of the world and the foolishness of God. Here the thinking is not so much an indulgence in paradox or irony, but rather that of "corrective," the corrective to the

---

[2] John D. Caputo, "Tradition and Event: Radicalizing the Catholic Principle," in this volume, p. 104.

standard expectations of what is successful, or what is authoritative, or what is the normal. The kingdom of God is in the mustard seed, or the crucifixion, or in weakness, or in defeat, not as a consoling self-deception of the injured loser, but rather as the locale for the unsuspected unconditional—in those who are forgotten, or discarded, or hated. For Caputo, to romanticize this turn from the normal would be just one more way of lifting yourself out of the materiality, historicality, carnality, and temporality of what is genuinely discomforting and repulsive, sometimes even deadly. The Spirit of God is discernable in the real events of history.

After the argued theological hermeneutic, Caputo again returns to Margie Winters, not only siding with those who opposed the rationale and action of the Archdiocese of Philadelphia, but now also on the other side of a theological case against the very sacramental failure of the Catholic Church, as well as with a sense that such seeming defeats are exactly what theology is called to think about, to explain, to confront, and to expect. If theological thinking is ultimately to take up "the challenge of God," and if the *what* and *how* of this challenge within the Catholic tradition is correctly diagnosed by Caputo, then our project of thinking along with Caputo gives us not only an instance of Caputo's theological outlook, but also a potential model for theological thinking in a contemporary world.

So let's return to the original wager, "that by first thinking along with Prof. Caputo—exploring *what* he thinks the challenge of God is and *how* he thinks through that challenge—we are then better able as fellow theologians to also face the challenge of God." To be sure, Prof. Caputo has given us an example of a contemporary theologian squarely confronting the endless task of theology—the challenge of God. And I am sure that he would be the last to say that the model of thinking that he has demonstrated should be anything like the closure of discussion on this challenge. Everyone who calls herself or himself a theologian must somehow face this challenge of God, and so what follows is, I hope, the second part of my wager—a fellow theologian also facing the challenge of God by taking up some of the threads of Caputo's thought, redirecting some of his thinking, and offering some of my own theological thinking.

First let me identify three specific threads in Caputo's thinking that need to be taken up, and then attempt to weave them together in a way which redirects Caputo's approach to thinking through the challenge of God theologically.

One thread occurs in a passage where Caputo is reflecting on what he takes to be the Lukan contribution to the symbolics of thinking the challenge of God.

> When Luke has Yeshua announce his ministry, he uses a citation from Isaiah. Yeshua had been anointed—he is *Christos*—to bring the good news to the poor, to announce to prisoners that they will be released, to the blind that they will recover their sight, to the oppressed that they will go free, and to proclaim the year of the Jubilee, the year that follows seven times seven, in which all debts are forgiven and the people are able to make a new start, a new beginning. That is how it will look when God rules, not Caesar. You will notice the materiality and carnality of this list, the poor, the imprisoned, the blind, the oppressed, which is pretty much the same list we find in Matthew 25. So when we press Yeshua about God, he deflects

us to the kingdom of God, and when we press him about the kingdom of God, he deflects our attention again, to things like leaven, dinner parties, and treasures buried in a field. So there is a constant deflection—from God to the kingdom, from the Kingdom to the mustard seeds—not metaphysics.[3]

What strikes me about this passage is the dynamic of deflection—deflection from God, deflection from Kingdom, deflection that ends in materiality, carnality, history, and temporality. This dynamic of deflection is the central element in the critical thinking of Caputo, a dynamic opposed to any attempt that would allow theological thinking to escape the gravity of the world by flying on the wings of a nature/super-nature distinction, or by indulging in an institutionalized refuge which lifts the Spirit of God out of the world. And the constructive thinking embedded in this deflection is also apparent—a deflection to very earthly, human and non-human symbols which give rise to the kind of hermeneutic of the Catholic Principle outlined above—symbols of materiality (seed), of carnality (the poor), of historicity (treasures buried in the past), and of temporality (Jubilee years).

This leads me to take up another thread, the thread of "theopoetics." Caputo writes:

The one genuinely lethal idea in the tradition is that the body of Jesus is a phantom, that he only appeared to be a man, to suffer, and appeared to die, while in reality he is an immaterial being, which we should all hope to be someday. I am not opposing Gnostic metaphysics with materialistic metaphysics but opposing metaphysics, especially opposing metaphysics of matter and spirit. In its place I check the guns of metaphysics at the door and think instead in terms of a theopoetics of call and response, of a Spirit calling people and people responding. In those terms, the church is a concrete conditioned response, an historical response, made under contingent conditions of space and time, to an unconditioned call, to something that has seized us unconditionally.[4]

Critical deflection is again at work in this passage, deflection from an often all too unnoticed Docetism in the Catholic tradition or a comfortable ontotheology to a very human image—call and response—which immediately becomes a theological image—Spirit calling and people responding. The deflective dynamic away from a myriad of misinterpretation of theological symbols, images, and topics deflects back into the same symbols, images, and topics that have created problems for the Catholic position in the first place, and resulted in the misconstrued hermeneutic that leads to firing Margie Winters while claiming the authority to interpret the Catholic tradition authentically. This particular thread, the deflection into the same set of symbols that generates the problem symbolically and really present in the case of Margie Winters, suggests to me that there is a constructive problem with this form of theopoetics, a theopoetics that suggests that we can better respond to the challenge of God by

---

[3] Ibid., p. 107.
[4] Ibid., p. 106.

utilizing the same symbols, images, and topics that have created a problem with the challenge of God in the first place.

Let me clarify this a bit by turning to a third thread in Caputo's thinking. Early in the chapter Caputo lays out the theological as opposed to simply institutional dimensions of Margie Winter's case. In doing this he sides with the authors of an op-ed piece published in Philadelphia newspapers calling the archdiocese to task for their action against Ms. Winters. Caputo writes:

> Their (the authors of the published op-ed) argument presupposes a view of God as the Spirit working in history, and of the church as the *populus dei*, not as the hierarchy, one of the most important pronouncements of the Vatican II. The argument is theological, pneumatological and ecclesiological. For the Catholic theologian it is the promptings of the Spirit—not "Pure Reason", or the law of Dialectical Materialism, or the "masses"—that rise up in protest against the violence of history … Against the deep errancy and fallibility of Church-as-hierarchy, the unfolding of Spirit-in-history is a movement of autocorrection and reinvention. Against the calcification of dogmatic formulae, which results in simple reproduction, the immanence of the Spirit in history unfolds in productive repetition.[5]

Here is where I wonder whether the construction of a theopoetics that returns to same set of images, symbols and topics—God, Spirit, Church, Jesus/Yeshua, Kingdom—can be as self-corrective and reinventive as Caputo hopes. By excluding that which lies outside of this symbolic matrix—here identified as "Pure Reason," "Dialectical Materialism," and the "masses"—theological thinking seems to result in a rather agonistic confrontation of choices for symbolic and imaginative priorities and orderings. All sides can appeal to biblical images; all sides can appeal to selected traditions; all sides can create coherent arguments; all sides can claim that they are authentically facing the challenge of God and doing it in a theologically responsible way. To put this rather bluntly, both the theological thinking of Caputo and the theological thinking of the decision makers in the Archdiocese of Philadelphia make arguments that energize and appeal to their respective "bases." I certainly happen to be in the base that responds in a whole-hearted way to the position and argument of Caputo but not because of the theopoetic deflection that Caputo advances. The dynamic of deflection in theological thinking is critical, but I think that the deflection into the symbolic matrix that Caputo suggests is inadequate to bring about the material, carnal, historical, and temporal ends that both Caputo and I think are part of the theological task.

So having taken up some of the threads of Caputo's thinking, and having redirected them a bit, let me now offer a response to the challenge of God that might augment—not replace—the "theopoetics" by an "anthropoetics" that makes theological thinking less constrained by conventional symbols of the Catholic tradition and more welcoming of

---

[5] Ibid., p. 100.

the symbols and responsibilities that Caputo associates with the historicity, carnality, materialism, and temporality of the Catholic Principle.

I will begin with a different starting point than Caputo uses, not one opposed to beginning with the specific situation of Margie Winters, but one which approaches that situation from a different perspective. I should like to begin by understanding the challenge of God for theology as entailing an understanding of what theological thinking is. Indeed, Caputo and I agree on this—that the challenge of God demands a clarification of thinking theologically. Theology is, in short, the thinking that thinks God, and this is a facet of the challenge of God. So beginning with this notion, that theology is the thinking that thinks God, I will explore this facet of the challenge of God first.

This way of approaching theology hypothesizes that the real object of theology is thinking, human thinking, not God, God's thinking, or God's thinking as *sacra doctrina*. At one level this is a rather trivial observation, a kind of analytic statement like all triangles have three angles. If theology is thinking, it is human thinking. But it is also more than trivial for our purposes, precisely because it brings theology into proximity with other signs, symbols, and topics through the category of thinking. Signs and symbols are not the possession of religion and theology alone, nor is their interpretation and understanding. In this case, the case of Margie Winters, the theologian may certainly appreciate her location in a theology of history, but she is also located in a history which symbolizes gender, which has signs of authority, and which has images of the good life lived for and with others in just institutions. By entering theology as a form of thinking rather than a populated but constrained set of symbols, we can allow theology to learn from other conversations and not only from the conventional religious symbols. Scientists, philosophers, cultural and critical theorists, historians, and artists—as well as theologians—think and we think as, or within, the various discourses we partake in. Margie Winters is already in all of these discourse by her vary situation. The challenge of a creator God is not to limit the creation to the religious symbols that speak of creation. Rather, carnality, materiality, historicity, and temporality are part of multiple discourses.

Second, by approaching theology as the thinking that thinks God, I am quite deliberately avoiding the phrase "thinking that thinks *about* God." And why be deliberate about this? For good theological and philosophical reasons. At its best, theology has taken seriously that whatever God is, God is not one object alongside, above, or simply greater than all other objects. God is not a thing among things, and in this specific sense, God is no-thing, nothing. Christian theologies of creation emphasize this point by asserting that theologically the doctrine of creation is not a teaching about the origin of the universe; it is rather a teaching about the relationship between the Christian God and all else. Whatever is not God is created; whatever is God is uncreated. Simply put again, God is not a thing among things. It may be extraordinarily difficult to understand the interaction through which the human genome controls a particular morphological expression, or how the mind both is and is not the brain, or all the reasons that went into the decision to fire Margie Winters, but these are at least about something. Nothing is precisely that: no thing; there is not-thing to think about.[6] So part of the challenge of God is to recognize how to think simultaneously about something—the carnal, historical, material, temporal Margie Winters—and the "no-thing" that is God.

This may not be quite as odd as it first sounds, and it is why I think Caputo is on the right track with his talk of "deflection," the deflection of God and kingdom to mustard seeds and meals. So I want to linger with this category of "deflection," and expand on Caputo's mention of this with the wager that by doing this we might open a way beyond Caputo's agonistic hermeneutics of symbols and toward the incorporation of other signs, symbols, and topics that make the theological contribution to Margie Winter's case more public and less constrained by both conventional theological symbols and the ecclesiological boundaries of the institutional Church.

So how do we get a better hold on this thinking that simultaneously thinks something and nothing, thinks Margie Winters and God?

I propose to do this by briefly responding to four fundamental questions: What is theology as thinking? What is God as the thought of theology? What kinds of thinking think God? What does this thinking do? For good reason it may not be possible to separate the first two questions: What is theology as thinking? And what is God as the thought of theology? The reason for this lies in thinking itself. Phenomenology is certainly not the first form of reflection to identify the intentional structure of conscious thought as a unity prior to any analytic division between subjectivity and objectivity. Thinking is its thought, and its thought is thinking. At this purely formal level, thinking that thinks God is no different in its formal unity of intended and intending than any other form of thinking. By starting at this very fundamental, formal level of thinking as our common ground, we are asking theology to capture its own thinking as much as possible in this formal unity of intended and intending consciousness. What differentiates theology in its thinking is not its formal unity but the kind of unity that thinks God. It is here that the real struggle to articulate theology as thinking begins, not so much from thinking God, but by maintaining the unity that does not succumb to the slippage of thinking God as an object, as a thing. But beyond these formal remarks about theological thinking how do we get going on thinking God, without thinking an object, a thing?

Here I think we must attend to the character of resistance within theological thinking. No-thingness, nothing resists thought. Thinking nothing is a resistant thinking, a thinking of that which resists thinking, not so much because it is complex or arduous, but because the intended is that which is present to consciousness in and as

---

[6] The relation of the discussion of "nothing" to dialectical theology in the twentieth century is well summarized in Carl Raschke, "The End of Theology," *Journal of the American Academy of Religion* 41, no. 2 (1978), pp. 159–179. The relation of thinking God as "no-thing" to contemporary examples of fundamental theology is well summarized in Robert Scharlemann, "The No to Nothing and the Nothing to Know: Barth and Tillich and the Possibility of Theological Science," *Journal of the American Academy of Religion* 55, no. 1 (1987), pp. 57–72. The relation of thinking God as "no-thing" to contemporary postmodern theologies is well summarized in G. Collins, "Thinking the Impossible: Derrida and the Divine," *Literature and Theology* 14 (2000), pp. 313–334. The relation of thinking God as "no-thing" to the prominent postmodern theme of "alterity" is well summarized in Thomas J. Csordas, "Asymptote of the Ineffable: Embodiment, Alterity, and the Theory of Religion," in *Current Anthropology* 45, no. 2 (2004), pp. 163–185.

absence. But resistance to thinking is not the only characteristic of theological thinking as thinking nothing, since the character of this resistance does not seem to be complete withdrawal, a nothing without a trace. Rather this resistance to thought is also the lure to thinking.[7] Historically, socially, psychologically, philosophically, "god" does not seem to go away like aether, a Ptolemaic universe, or various forms of metaphysics. Despite countless ways of both asserting god and denying god, there remains a lure to thinking god. And the trace that remains from the resistance to thinking nothing seems to be the possibility to think otherwise than the thought of things. We arrive here, I would suggest, at a first dialectic in the character of theological thinking: the dialectic of resistance and the lure.[8] This is not as strange to human thinking as these phenomenological descriptions of thinking nothing might suggest: space–time is not a thing, freedom is not a thing, life is not a thing, love is not a thing, and yet we discuss these topics thoughtfully and make carnal, material, historical, and temporal decisions regarding these topics. This first dialectic of theological thinking has not sealed theology off from other forms of thinking by its involvement with no-thing, but rather opened theological thinking to other areas which likewise think "no-things." By engaging the challenge of God through some clarification of the structure of its thinking we need not demarcate theological thinking by limiting it to the conventional symbols that are associated with its practice—Spirit in history, kingdom, God, or Jesus. By identifying this lure of resistance and lure to no-thing as part of the challenge of God, we can enter theological thinking in a different way.

So what is it that the little word, "god," introduces into thinking that seems to generate a whole way of thinking, to establish theology as something other than the thought about things? Here I think we must attend to another characteristic of this thinking, that the little word, "god," is a name before it is a concept, and here Caputo would surely agree. This has been a consistent feature of Christian theology, and this feature sets theological thinking on a different, but not unrelated, track of thinking nothing in a way that is other than the nothing of space–time, freedom, life, or love. The resistance and the lure characteristic of thinking God are made present when "god" enters discourse as a name. Thinking god, this intentional unity, is first and foremost naming god, and just as thinking is its thought, and thought is its thinking, so also here naming is the name, and the name is naming. This naming calls this nothing into an interactive relationship. God becomes a locale in discourse for the resistance and lure of thinking precisely because, as a name, it is now put in play with all the other signs, symbols, and topics that make up human discourse. And there is no guarantee that this name is unlike any other φαρμακόν, simultaneously medicine and poison. This is what begs theology to think through *how* God is named. In naming God, thinking God is set in its direction; naming places the resistance and lure on a vector. This name calls nothing into presence and gives it a discourse. It may call this resistance and

---

[7] A similar approach is seen in Marina Ludwigs, "Three Gaps of Representation/Three Meanings of Transcendence," *Anthropoetics* 15, no. 2 (2010), pp. 1–22.

[8] There is a long history of this dialectic generally contained within various efforts to present a phenomenology of the holy or of religion. See here Csordas, "Asymptote of the Inevitable," and Espin Dahl, *Phenomenology and the Holy: Religious Experience after Husserl* (London: SCM Press, 2010.

lure to a discourse of power, or oppression, or authority, or imagination, or hope, or resistance, or protest, and when theology thinks the name of god, it thinks it through what nothing does within these particular discourses. Anselm was in this sense correct in his famous thought experiment to begin with what God names: that than which nothing greater can be thought, and then to call for a thinking of that name. To be sure much goes wrong with this argument that a host of thinkers from Descartes to Kant to Plantinga have struggled with. And something important with how theology struggles when thinking God as a name is clearly evident from Anselm's approach. There is in Anselm's case a slippage in naming; the name elides with the concept of necessary existence. Inevitably, it seems that when the name, "god," enters discourse, the name is renamed by the field into which it enters. God is necessary being, creator, savior, warrior, omnipotent, a person, a "he," a "she," a Yeshua, an exclusive possession of a particular tradition, an ultimate authorization to savage what is other. For the thinking that thinks God as name in the condition of resistance and lure the gravity of discourse renames a name.

This kind of slippage reveals a second dialectical characteristic of theological thinking, one that can only be recognized in the distinction between thinking god as a name and thinking god as a concept. As a name that names nothing, the resistance to thought that theological thinking encounters becomes a deflection: the name deflects the lure of thinking by resistance to some available sign system and gives this lure to thought a particular voice, a vocabulary, a grammar, a body, a history, a temporality by which discursive action becomes a possibility; nothing enters the field of meaning and truth.

This is not strange in the case of a name. Indeed, Caputo's theological thinking begins with the name of Margie Winters. If we were to ask *what* Margie Winters is, we would immediately encounter a problem: Margie Winters as a name does not respond typically to "what" questions, unless we turn Margie Winters into a concept like employee, educator, or lesbian. And when we do that, we have still not responded to the name; the name has deflected the meaning intention to a concept. More appropriate to a name like "Margie Winters" would be a deflection into a narration, a story that deflects the name into a character and supplements the name with temporality, action, memory, and the like. The deflection to the sign system that the narrative affords fills the name with what can be thought about Margie Winters. At the same time that the name deflects to a supplement, it also redirects. The deflection of the name is a redirection to choice, to the action of selection. When I am asked to think about Margie Winters as a partner in a love relation or as a participant in a religious tradition I am directed to a host of other discourses, experiences, memories, and hopes, in my case, quite remote from Margie Winters since I do not know her other than through Caputo's narration, but in other cases quite dense because some know her well. The no-thing that the name "Margie Winters" names becomes a life about which meaningful and truthful thoughts become possible, but always with the caveat that the no-thing of "Margie Winters" is never conceptually captured by these thoughts, even by Margie Winters herself.

Whatever else Margie Winters is, in the Christian theological tradition there would be strong resistance to saying that Margie Winters is God. There is much less resistance to saying that Jesus is God. And I would suggest that "thinking God" here is the kind of thinking that deflects a meaning intention to a whole host of signs and redirects by some form of recall what we choose Jesus to be. In Caputo's case, the deflection/ redirection is to Yeshua, Yeshua's announcement of the kingdom of God and Paul's interpretation of the cross as Christian foolishness/wisdom. The history of thinking about what to recall as Jesus displays a huge range of discourses: healer, warrior, sage, storyteller, etc. "Jesus" theologically is the deflection and redirection created by the name, God, within a broad historical and cultural human sign system that cannot escape the lure of God. Like the name, God, the name, Jesus, can transition easily into a concept. God becomes omnipotent, or the good; Jesus becomes savior, or liberator— or Yeshua. And in each of these kinds of moves the name is supplemented by what the name is associated with. Contemporary theology is full of struggle with the name, God: on the one hand theology seems to desperately want to preserve the resistant/deflective character of thinking that names an original unity with words like "the impossible" (Derrida); "the infinite" (Tracy); "the God who may be" (Kearney); "the totally other" (Levinas); "the event" (Caputo). On the other hand the lure and re-directive character of the name conceptually becomes evident in so many forms of critical theologies (like Caputo's), cultural theologies, and institutionally invested theologies (like that of the Archdiocese of Philadelphia).

Caputo's theopoetics preserves both aspects of this thinking of God as no-thing, the dialectic of resistance/lure and the dialectic of deflection/redirection. The Catholic Principle resists finalization while at the same time calls for a carnal, material, historical, and temporal response to the unconditional demand of existence. The radicalization of this principle deflects the talk of God and kingdom and redirects it to weakness, foolishness, mustard seeds, and meals. Indeed, it redirects it to a direct criticism of the action of the Catholic Church in the firing of Margie Winters. But why should I hold that this interpretation of the resistance and lure, deflection and redirection, is what I should be invested in. Is a theopoetics which returns to the symbols of the tradition and selects from these symbols a certain interpretation of Yeshua, kingdom and foolishness/wisdom enough to tell me why this selection should be taken up as opposed to the "theopoetics" of the Philadelphia Catholic Church that could likewise appeal to this same symbol set?

When I come to this question—and the concern that I have with Caputo's form of theopoetics—I do not think that exploring my first two questions—what is theology as thinking? What is God as the thought of theology?—are sufficient to make a response. It is in considering the other two questions that we might be in a better position to supplement Caputo's theological thinking.

Recall the other two questions I have posed: What kinds of thinking think God? And what does this thinking do? The kinds of thinking involved in responding to these two questions must be consistent with the kinds of thinking that are appropriate to the naming of God: resistance/lure and deflection/redirection. Multiple kinds of thinking must accompany the naming of God—imagination of the future, recall of dangerous memories, rigorous empirical analysis of ghettoized spiritualities, but, particularly in Caputo's construction of theopoetics, there must be attention to a kind of thinking that would better display why I should choose the symbols that construct Yeshua/foolishness rather than Church/magisterium.

Because the name of God not only deflects but redirects, there must be some kind of thinking akin to what Jean Nabert labeled "a criteriology of the divine," or what I would call an ethics of belief. The redirection that happens with the name God compels a testimony to values and choices of action. The vector or direction that the little word, "god," introduces into discourse is a φαρμακόν, a medicine and a poison. It is the introduction of a value, one that is often called on to authorize all other values. Thus one kind of thinking that thinks god is that which thinks through and calls for an account of what we value as human beings. If I were to put another name to this kind of thinking, it would be critical thought.[9] Indeed this is what Caputo does, but without acknowledging the path that he actually takes in doing this. By eliding the dynamics of deflection with a theopoetics which returns to the same symbol complex that generates the issues surrounding Margie, and by seemingly sealing this off from other equally involved sign–symbol–topics discourses, Caputo obscures this necessary project of a criteriology of the divine or an ethics of belief. The same Spirit acting in history can be appealed to by both the supporters of Margie Winters and the Archdiocese of Philadelphia. The recognition that the case of Margie Winters involves more than a carnality, materiality, historicity, and temporality that is limited to the conventional religious symbols neither diminishes the event as a theological event, nor does it endanger the power of these conventional theological signs, symbols, and images. Rather it provides a way to more publicly identify why Caputo's support of Margie Winters is not merely an idiosyncratic, liberal response to an institution too enmeshed in its own reiteration; it allows a discourse of shared reason, critically disclosive thought about gender, imaginations about new social relations, and the like to form part of the truly theological argument. Theology is thinking, thinking God; it will always risk idolatry, and it must take responsibility for that with all the discourse, signs, symbols, and topics that it can marshal. It may do this in the name of Icons—as that which show the Spirit of God in history—but it must simultaneously recognize that Icons too are carnal, material, historical, and temporal; they too are the products of human thinking, a thinking that tries to think God. They too call for critical interpretation by the best of our reasoning, by the best of our historical awareness and by the best of our sciences.

And what does this thinking do? My fourth question. This thinking accompanies other discourses—scientific, philosophical, political, economic, legal, artistic. These forms of thinking, like all "thinking God," are redirected into and with the historical and cultural sign systems of the times, and the relations that various forms of thinking create within the sign systems. Theology does not dictate; it does not command; it does not get lost in identity formation; or good wishes; or its own self-referential indulgence. It must accompany the sign systems of human thought in each era as the discourse companion whom David Tracy describes when speaking about dialogue:

> Conversation is a game with some hard rules: say only what you mean; say it as accurately as you can; listen to and respect what the other says, however different

---

[9] Paul Ricoeur, "The Hermeneutics of Testimony," *Anglican Theological Review* 41, no. 4 (1979), pp. 435–461.

or other; be willing to correct or defend your opinions if challenged by the conversation partner; be willing to argue if necessary, to confront if demanded, to endure necessary conflict, and to change your mind if the evidence suggests it.[10]

What theology does in "thinking god" is carry on this kind of conversation with hard rules, in our times about what kind of gods we create, what kind of future we imagine, what kind of memories we must recall if our thinking is to be truthful.

Finally, what might this way of approaching theological understanding contribute to the situation that Margie Winters and the Catholic Church in Philadelphia found itself in? It can accompany the institutional thought of the Church, or the professional thought of the theologian or cleric, or the social thought of those opposed to or in favor of same-sex marriage, or the local thought of those who know Margie Winters on a day-to-day basis by raising issues about the gods we create socially, ecclesiologically, and politically through our social action; it can raise questions about the futures we create and the cost of those futures; it can recall paths we have gone down in the name of absolute value and firm conviction so that we are cautious about charting paths with today's versions of these attitudes. In short, theology can remind all of our "things" about "nothing."

Four hundred years ago, in his famous letter to Christina the Grand Duchess of Tuscany, Galileo wrote that he hoped to proceed in his inquiry with a "greater piety" then those who represented the pious structures of the church and the academy at that point in time. Piety may or may not be the right word for today's cultures and issues, but what Galileo names by this phrase "a greater piety," a kind of thinking that is unafraid to think about both the greatest challenges of the day and to do that with the best available resources of the day where ever they come from—that I think is still an admirable name for what theological thinking is when it faces the challenge of God. And in the end, while we might take different paths, I think Caputo and I would agree.

---

[10] David Tracy, *Plurality and Ambiguity: Hermeneutics, Religion, Hope* (New York: Harper Press, 1987), p. 19.

9

Epic and the Crucified God

Thomas J. J. Altizer

James Joyce is perhaps unique among our contemporary visionaries in being simultaneously both deeply distant from and ultimately grounded in our deepest traditions, and yet this condition is characteristic of our great Christian epic poets, and at no other point is there a greater unity between them. Dante, Milton, and Blake are all revolutionary visionaries; all created visions of a comprehensiveness found in no other epic poetry throughout the world, and this comprehensiveness is itself a revolutionary achievement. Therein scripture itself is profoundly transformed, now disappearing as a scripture which is only "scripture," and appearing as a scripture which is world or totality itself, a scripture fully and actually speaking in these epics, epics which are scripture and actuality at once. Moreover, scripture here is a truly evolving scripture, and one evolving through deep transformations of itself, transformations wherein scripture evolves its own polar opposite, but does so only to realize a true *coincidentia oppositorum* between itself and its opposite. So it is that a deep and radical "heresy" here evolves out of a pure "orthodoxy." Nothing else is more manifest in the evolution of the Christian epic imagination than its movement from orthodoxy to heresy, yet this heresy is truly the dialectical "other" of orthodoxy, ever more fully realizing itself as a totality drawing orthodoxy into itself, so that full realizations of this scripture are totalities embodying "light" and "darkness" simultaneously.

Luther revolutionized Christianity by rediscovering the Crucified God; this is the deepest of all renewals of Paul, just as it is inseparable from an ultimate realization of the totality of guilt, an absolute guilt revealing the necessity of the Crucified God, apart from whom eternal death is our only possible destiny. It was the young Heidegger's immersion in Luther and Kierkegaard that made possible his truly new ontology, and although he disguises this in *Being and Time*, it has fully been drawn forth in recent Heidegger scholarship. So, too, Heidegger discovered an apocalyptic *Ereignis*, one making possible his deep move beyond *Dasein*, and by moving to that new apocalyptic ground, Heidegger made possible a revolutionary transformation of philosophy, one truly renewing the apocalyptic thinking of Schelling, Hegel, and Nietzsche. Heidegger is the deepest of all philosophical influences upon late modern theology, and if this resulted in a phenomenological bracketing of God, by necessity this could only be a temporary suspension or *epoché*, but one making possible an ultimate theological revolution. But it also could make possible a genuine opening to the most revolutionary faith, one truly hidden and disguised throughout our history, except insofar as it is realized in the uniquely Christian epic.

We now know that Christian orthodoxy arose as a transformation of an original Christian apocalypse, a transformation which is the most radical and total transformation in the history of religions, and this is a transformation that the Christian epic ever more decisively and more comprehensively reverses, as a truly new apocalypticism dawns in Dante, bursts forth even more deeply and comprehensively in Milton, and then seemingly becomes total in Blake's revolutionary vision. Therein we can truly see a comprehensive evolution of "heresy," but this is a heresy renewing an original Christian apocalypticism, and just as the Christ of this vision is an ever more fully apocalyptic Christ, world itself ever more fully dawns as an apocalyptic world or new aeon, even as darkness itself is ever more fully transfigured into an apocalyptic light. But Christianity has never evolved a truly or fully apocalyptic theology, so that the Christian epic has ever been alien or impenetrable to Christian theology, and this despite the fact that it is so clearly a renewal of the Bible, for here the Bible is reborn far more fully than it is in any other expression of our mind or imagination. Nevertheless, our Christian epics remain a theological cipher, and most so those of our last great epic visionary, James Joyce. Of course, Joyce is the most heretical of our epic seers, and here heresy is more total than anywhere else, and not only heresy but blasphemy as well. It seems impossible that there will ever be created a more offensive work than *Finnegans Wake*, but the truth is that there is a deep continuity between Dante and Joyce, and between Joyce and Blake as well.

One such deep continuity lies in their apocalyptic visions, and even if *Ulysses* and *Finnegans Wake* must be interpreted as reverse or inverted apocalypses, they are apocalypses nonetheless, and apocalypses fulfilling a Christian epic tradition, a tradition which had ever more fully inverted or reversed everything which the Christian tradition had known as apocalypse. Yet it is precisely thereby that an original Christian apocalypse is renewed. If nothing has been more deeply repressed in Christianity than its original ground, nothing has been more alien to our dominant Christian tradition than apocalypse, so that the renewal of apocalypticism has ever been a renewal of deep heresy, and this as early as the New Testament itself, as witnesses the Book of Revelation. All of the great Christian epic visionaries, including Joyce himself, were deeply inspired by the book of Revelation, but so likewise were they inspired by a deeply heretical apocalyptic tradition, one bursting forth not only in Dante's world but even more comprehensively in the Radical Reformation, a reformation ecstatically issuing in *Paradise Lost*, and thence realizing its purest scriptures in Blake's *Milton* and *Jerusalem*. This is an apocalyptic tradition unknown to our theologians, and inevitably so if only because theology is so alienated from biblical apocalypticism, an alienation which is also an alienation from the original apocalyptic Jesus, the very Jesus who is reborn in the Christian epic, and even reborn in *Ulysses* and *Finnegans Wake*.

Nothing is more startling in Joyce's vision than the deep and comprehensive presence of the apocalyptic Jesus; perhaps thereby he is most disguised to the Christian reader, but he is also thereby the most anonymous Jesus in our imaginative history, never bearing the name of Jesus, and ever distant from every established image of

Jesus. Except insofar as Jesus is known as the Crucified, for crucifixion is more fully and more comprehensively enacted in *Finnegans Wake* than it is in any other imaginative work, and if only at this point we must acknowledge Joyce's deep ground in the original Jesus. If Paul could only know Christ through and as the crucified Jesus, Joyce is inescapably a Pauline visionary, and one who unites as theology has never been able to do the apocalyptic and the ecclesiastical Paul. Paul could know the church as the body of Christ, a body which is an embodiment of the crucifixion, and only thereby the eschatological Adam (Rom. 12.3-8), but Joyce can know the world itself as the body of Here Comes Everybody and Anna Livia Plurabelle. This body, too, is the body of crucifixion, and only thereby is it an apocalyptic body, and just as A.L.P. and H.C.E. are polar expressions of one body, that body is an apocalyptic body, and an apocalyptic body which is totality itself. Now this is a truly new expression of that totality which Blake finally knows as Jerusalem, and just as Blake's Jerusalem is the totality of the apocalyptic Jesus, Joyce's total body, too, is the apocalyptic Jesus, but now an apocalyptic Jesus who is a wholly anonymous Jesus, yet nevertheless Jesus if only because this is a truly crucified body, and a crucified body that is not only the crucified Jesus but the Crucified God.

Nothing is more revealing about Christian theology than its deep inability to know the crucified Jesus as the Crucified God, but all too significantly this is an ever-enlarging motif in the Christian epic tradition. Just as Milton's Arianism derived most deeply from his refusal to recognize the possibility of the crucifixion of God, Blake's christocentrism ultimately centers upon the crucifixion of God (and here Joyce is deeply Blakean), but Joyce finally envisioned the crucifixion as the Eucharist of the universe, as the universe itself is realized as the apocalyptic sacrifice of God. Here Joyce is in deep continuity with Dante, as he himself realized, and there is no fuller literary presence in *Finnegans Wake* than the *Commedia*, and Joyce and Dante alone among our great visionaries finally came to know the universe itself as the body or "volume" of God.[1] Joyce envisions this body as a eucharistic body, as the *missa solemnis* is ultimately transposed into the *missa jubilaea*, and *Finnegans Wake* is our most comprehensively liturgical work, thereby being in deep continuity with *Ulysses*. Joyce and Dante are our deepest Catholic visionaries, even if Joyce's Catholicism is a totally reversed or inverted Catholicism, and thereby, if only thereby, it is in genuine continuity with Dante's Catholic vision.

The Easter celebration of Book 4 of the *Wake* opens with the Sanctus that is the great prayer of consecration in the canon of the mass—"Sandhyas! Sandhyas! Sandhyas!"— here chanted in Sanskrit because East and West are now one. An elusive motif of the *Wake* is now decoded; this is the Augustinian phrase, "securus judicat orbis terrarum," that converted John Henry Newman, and this phrase, in various transpositions, appears again and again in the *Wake*, offering yet another Catholic ground of Joyce's vision, and one that is not fully called forth theologically until the creation of this epic. This is a theological ground stating both the nature and the identity of true Catholic authority: the judgment of the world as a whole is the true authority. And now "securus

---

[1] Dante, *Paradiso*, Canto XXXIII, l. 86, in Mark Musa, trans., *The Portable Dante* (New York: Penguin, 1995).

judicat" becomes *securest jubilends*,[2] as an external and exterior authority passes into a universal *missa jubilaea*, and the No-saying of the Catholic and Christian God passes into an absolute Yes-saying, an absolute Yes-saying which is absolute joy. This is a joy that Dante alone among our visionaries had known before Joyce; it is a joy that is a recovery of the long-hidden beatitudes of Jesus, beatitudes which pass into the brute actuality of the world in this epic, and do so even in its ultimate blasphemy, a blasphemy which is here an ecstatic celebration, even an ecstatic celebration of the apocalyptic, the eucharistic, and the crucified body of Jesus.[3]

This very section culminates with the first pages of the *Wake* to be written,[4] and these center on the crucifixion of God, or the crucifixion of H.C.E., eliciting the anguished cry, *I've a terrible errible lot todue todie todue tootorribleday*. These early pages eventually became the conclusion of Book 2, chapter 3, which is both the central or axial chapter of the *Wake* and also the most difficult and complex section of this dream or night epic. And there is only one full and actual movement throughout this section: the movement of crucifixion, an eternal death which is not only the center of a historically cosmic Holy Week, but which is reenacted again and again throughout both *Ulysses* and *Finnegans Wake*. While everything is the same in this eternal recurrence or return, it is the "seim anew"[5] and the "mystery repeats itself todate,"[6] for now the primordial mystery becomes an apocalyptic mystery, a mystery even now being not only unveiled but cosmically enacted, and enacted in that universal eucharistic body which is the primordial and the apocalyptic sacrifice of God. The church knows the apocalyptic sacrifice of God only in the Eucharist, and just as the primal action of the Eucharist is the *anamnesis* or renewal of the crucifixion, an *anamnesis* which is a renewal of primordial sacrifice itself, the major action of the *Wake* is an *anamnesis* of primordial sacrifice, one here beginning with the fall of God or Satan on its first page, and culminating with that resurrection which is the resurrection of the Crucified God.

Yet this is the resurrection of Anna Livia Plurabelle, who is Dante's Beatrice reborn, and just as Dante envisions Beatrice as the incarnate body of Christ, Joyce envisions Anna as that Theotokos or Mother of God who is the mother of the universe, but now a mother who is embodied in the brute actuality of matter itself, as matter and Spirit wholly pass into each other, one prefigured in the *missa solemnis*, and finally joyously embodied in the *missa jubilaea*. Now the deep power of the Mass passes into the power of the world or of the body itself, and this is a body which is a cosmic and a historical body simultaneously, a body which is a new universal humanity, and precisely thereby a universal and cosmic body. But it is a universal body only by being a eucharistic body, a body embodying a universal sacrifice, which is the sacrifice of the Crucified God, and which is the deepest and most comprehensive action of Joyce's apocalyptic epics—an action which dawned in Homer's epics, and dawned even earlier

---

[2] James Joyce, *Finnegans Wake* (New York: Viking, 1947), p. 593.
[3] Ibid., pp. 377–380.
[4] Ibid., pp. 380–382
[5] Ibid., p. 215.
[6] Ibid., p. 294.

than this in Israel's epic sagas, epic sagas which Christians know as prefigurations of the gospels, and sagas which become universal sagas in the Christian epic. Epic above all other genres is inevitably given to a universal horizon, and just as epic is our least understood literary genre, it is theologically our most baffling genre as well, but a deep and comprehensive theology is fully present in all of our great Christian epics, and present here as it is nowhere else.

Yes, this is certainly a heretical theology, and is so already in Dante, and if that theology becomes totally heretical in Blake and Joyce, it is no less theology because of that, and in Joyce and Blake, as in no modern theologians, we are given total theologies. The truth is that all of our great Christian epic visionaries are far more deeply theological than are our theologians. Perhaps this is the source of the deepest hermeneutical barriers which their language embodies, and if here cosmos, humanity, and deity are united, this is a unity unknown to all our philosophers and theologians. And it is a unity which surely speaks in the language of *Ulysses* and *Finnegans Wake*, but so likewise does it speak in the language of the *Commedia*, and in the language of *Paradise Lost* and of *Milton* and *Jerusalem* as well. There is a power in this language which can be discovered nowhere else, a power which is clearly the power of scripture, one embodying an authority which is simply undeniable, but an authority which is a truly cryptic authority, and while such an authority may well be embodied in all genuinely epic language, this is yet another point at which epic is truly opaque for us. Could the authority of epic language derive from its very universality, if a genuinely epic language is truly universal in its own world? Did our modern epic arise from a new universal world, and a universal world which is a truly and actually comprehensive world?

Genuinely epic language is extraordinarily difficult, posing deep problems for its reader unknown in any other genre, and even as our great epic writers have been creators of language, a genuine sign of the true epic is that its revolutionary transformations are absorbed by the language which follows it, as is clearly true not only of Homer and Dante, but in our own time of Joyce, too, who is surely the greatest creator of language in the twentieth century. All of us are Joyceans now, whether we know it or not, and are Joyceans in our language, or are so when we actually speak. So likewise were the classical Greeks Homereans, and Joyce consciously intended to create a Homeric epic for his own world, yet this linguistic genius never learned Greek, just as he never learned Hebrew, and yet he created epics which were Classical and Biblical simultaneously, and that can be said of no other writer since Milton. Milton consciously knew himself to be a prophet, as he declares in the opening of *Paradise Lost*, and he created a vision of the Fall that has become more widely known than that of Genesis itself—indeed, innumerable people read the beginning of Genesis as though it had been written by Milton himself—and this is just the effect which true epic has, as it absorbs and transforms that scripture which is its source. Yet thereby scripture becomes even more fully, even more comprehensively, scripture itself, and just as something like this occurs in every religious tradition in the world, it also occurs in our imaginative traditions, but, in the epic, imaginative and religious traditions are united.

Only the Christian epic, however, is truly universal, only here are the sacred, the cosmic, the political, the psychological, and the conceptual realms truly united. Even when an absolute void or nothingness is called forth, as it is in all of our Christian epics, this void is integrally related to, if not united with, its opposite or contrary, and when it does triumph, as in Blake and Joyce, it calls forth not a simple nihilism, or a pure surd, but rather a reverse or inverted language, and one inverting not only logic and grammar and syntax, but the fullness of language itself. While this language clearly negates the language that precedes it, this negation is a transcending affirmation, incorporating into itself that language and horizon which it negates. So it is that the Christian epic is an epic of joy and affirmation; here it has no real precedent in the ancient world, yet perhaps it is most joyous when it is most negative, when it most fully negates its own world and tradition, when it is most "anti-scriptural," and this in the fullest sense. All of our great Christian epic poets are revolutionaries, and not only imaginative and religious revolutionaries, but political and social revolutionaries, too. All were not only religious but also political heretics, although at this point we have surely not yet understood Joyce.

It is simply impossible genuinely to read Joyce apart from celebration, and the deepest possible celebration; perhaps Joyce's are our only truly modern texts which can be read with such celebration today. If Joyce is our most popular modern canonical author, Joyce beyond all other modern authors has transformed our canon, as truly canonical language can only be a wholly new language today. Here, novum is truly an absolute novum, an absolute novum reflecting and embodying a new aeon, a new apocalypse which is apocalypse itself. If Joyce is our most apocalyptic twentieth-century writer, therein his language can be understood as a rebirth of biblical apocalyptic language, and therefore a rebirth of the language of Jesus itself. Our forgetting of that language is a forgetting of the revolution of Jesus, but that language has been reborn again and again in our history, and if it has truly been reborn in Joyce's epic language, that is perhaps the one real hope that is left to us today.

Apparently, the glories of the Christian epic have simply been ignored by our philosophers and theologians. But just as we can deepen our understanding of Hegel and Nietzsche by understanding them as epic philosophers, philosophy and theology themselves could be enriched if we could realize and enact them by way of an epic ground and perspective. Above all, this could make possible a profound transformation of our understanding of God. Then we could truly go beyond ontotheology by radically universalizing it, and universalizing it by truly integrating it with anthropology and cosmology. Already this is fully actualized in Dante's *Commedia*, and in Blake's *Jerusalem* as well, and even actualized in *Paradise Lost*. Thereby the Christian epic is far beyond either ancient or Asian epic, and is itself an epic both sacred and profane, even as has been our deeper philosophical theology throughout its history.

One of the ultimate failures of Christianity is the failure of its thinkers and theologians to enter the depths of Christianity itself, unless this occurs in German Idealism, even as it is occurring in our own time in the revolutionary thinking of D.G. Leahy, perhaps the most Catholic of all thinkers, and one who for the first time has created an absolute apocalypse that is a Catholic or universal apocalypse. Nothing could be more against the grain of all established Catholic thinking, but this is a Catholic thinking that is a Catholic thinking only as a revolutionary thinking, as for the first time since Augustine revolutionary and Catholic thinking are inseparable. Just as Augustine founded modern philosophical thinking in his discovery of the subject of thinking, Leahy discovered a wholly new philosophy in his discovery of the absolute apocalypse of thinking in "the thinking now occurring for the first time." This occurs most decisively in perhaps the most difficult of all philosophical works, *Foundation: Matter the Body Itself*,[7] not only our first work to fully unite Body and Spirit, but our first work wholly and fully to unite philosophy and theology. Here is an epic work, indeed, one creating an absolutely new epic, and even an absolutely new Catholic epic, but one nonetheless remaining in continuity with Dante and Joyce. Leahy began writing as an epic poet, and his work culminates in a glorious epic, and even if this epic is far too difficult now to be understood, it nevertheless succeeds in evoking that absolute apocalypse which is our ultimate destiny, and even in evoking it with an epic finality.

---

[7] D.G. Leahy, *Foundation: Matter the Body Itself* (Albany: SUNY Press, 1996).

10

Scripture, Epic, and Radical Catholicism: A Response to Thomas J. J. Altizer

Adam Kotsko

Thomas Altizer has done more than anyone to prove that even in our ostensibly secular world, Christian theology can still bring a word of scandal. He achieved this most dramatically in the "death of God" controversy of the 1960s, which resulted in the iconic *Time Magazine* cover asking "Is God Dead?" Aside from Reinhold Niebuhr, virtually no American theologians have made as big an impact in the public debate, and the ideas that drew Altizer into the public eye were much more radical and creative than Niebuhr's. Yet although Niebuhr is a familiar point of reference in the mainstream American debate—both President Barack Obama and *New York Times* columnist David Brooks are among his admirers—Altizer's work has fallen by the wayside. Although the "Is God Dead?" cover inspired the more recent *Time Magazine* cover asking "Is Truth Dead?," the very availability of this imagery as the basis for a clever joke seems to show how much the impact of the once-scandalous message has been blunted.

Within the hallowed halls of theology, however, Altizer remains a household name—indeed, arguably the most significant American theologian of the twentieth century. He has inspired the work of Theodore Jennings, Mark C. Taylor, John Caputo, and Slavoj Žižek. If only Jennings has remained squarely within the field of theology, that fact corresponds to Altizer's ambitions. He aimed emphatically at a theology *for* secular modernity, and in this regard, we could view him as a more radical, or at least emphatically less *ecclesiastical*, response to the work of Dietrich Bonhoeffer. In *The Gospel of Christian Atheism*,[1] which laid out the basic position that he would develop over the course of many books in subsequent decades, Altizer cites Bonhoeffer's idea of "religionless Christianity" with approval, but takes it a step further. Where Bonhoeffer argues that the Christian God "wins power and space in the world by his weakness,"[2] Altizer claims that God fully emptied himself into Christ, such that in the cross of Christ, God did not just display weakness, but actually *died*:

---

[1] Thomas J.J. Altizer, *The Gospel of Christian Atheism* (Philadelphia, PA: Westminster, 1966).
[2] Dietrich Bonhoeffer, *Letters and Papers from Prison* (ed. Eberhard Bethge; trans. Reginald Fuller, et al.; New York: Simon and Schuster, enlarged edn, 1997), p. 361.

The death of God in Christ is an inevitable consequence of the movement of God into the world, of Spirit into flesh, and the actualization of the death of God in the totality of experience is a decisive sign of the continuing and forward movement of the divine process, as it continues to negate its particular and given expressions, by moving ever more fully into the depths of the profane.[3]

From this perspective, the actual-existing church can only be a betrayal of the true meaning of the gospel, an attempt to enclose and enshrine the God who wants to be all in all—or, to use a phrase from Joyce's *Finnegans Wake*, the God of "Here comes everybody."

Joyce, and above all *Finnegans Wake*, is a key point of reference for Altizer's contribution to this volume, and for readers of his work, that is no surprise. If he was among our most famous and controversial theologians—though sadly also our most dismissed and ignored—what his contribution highlights is that he was above all the most *literary* of theologians. After being forced out at Emory University, he spent most of his career in the English Department of SUNY, Stony Brook, and he once told me that if he was a "critical scholar" of anything, it was the poetry of Blake. This may seem a strange trajectory for a theologian, but for Altizer it was a natural fit, because as he emphasized again and again, he believed that literature—much more than the institutional Church or traditional academic theology—is where the most radical theology is happening. In case we are tempted to view this claim as somehow figurative, he clarifies in his conclusion that the deepest goals of Christian theology are fully "actualized" in Dante, Milton, and Joyce. Dante and Milton can offer us an apocalyptic vision that challenges and even overwrites that of the Bible, so that people now read the opening chapters of Genesis as though they were written by Milton. Joyce does them one better, as Altizer attributes to him the kind of transformative power over the English language that one is accustomed to attributing to Shakespeare or the King James Bible.

This claim is difficult to understand from a common-sense viewpoint. After all, the number of people who have read *Finnegan's Wake* is very small, and it is far from having the same kind of impact on everyday speech as Shakespeare or the King James, both of whom most native speakers of English consciously or unconsciously quote virtually every day. To try to get at what he might mean, I would like to take a slight detour through the Islamic tradition. This is not as arbitrary as it may seem, because Altizer himself was deeply knowledgeable about world religions, having studied at the University of Chicago during the heydays of Mircea Eliade, a close friend as well as the topic of one of Altizer's earliest books.[4] Though Islam was not a primary area of focus, he engaged intensively with other monotheistic traditions, most notably in *The Self-Embodiment of God*, which was published as part of a series on Judaism edited by Jacob Neusner.[5]

---

[3] Altizer, *Gospel*, p. 110.
[4] Thomas J.J. Altizer, *Mircea Eliade and the Dialectic of the Sacred* (Louisville, KY: Westminster, 1963).
[5] Thomas J.J. Altizer, *The Self-Embodiment of God* (New York: University Press of America, 1987).

My initial point of contact with Islam comes in a short book on the subject by Norman O. Brown, another American thinker who made his name at around the same time that Altizer was making headlines.[6] Attempting to provide a synoptic overview of the Islamic tradition, Brown naturally devotes considerable space to a book that represents something like a combination of Shakespeare and the Bible for the Arab literary tradition: the Qur'an, which stands not only as the foundational Scripture, but as the founding work of classical Arabic literature. As Brown points out, echoing what any attentive reader of the Qur'an could not fail to notice, "Muhammad said, the only miracle is the book. He challenges doubters to produce a book like it."[7] Muhammad himself does not perform miracles in the style of Moses or Jesus, but instead recites the greatest miracle of all—the self-verifying Qur'an, which is by its own account radically self-consistent and so convincing as to render all previous poetry obsolete. Here, perhaps, we have a sense of what it means for a prophetic message to be "fully actualized" in a text—albeit a text that took a generation to be codified in writing and that still today lives on primarily as an oral recitation, memorized phonetically even by those who do not speak Arabic.

I can attest that for Western readers approaching it for the first time, this civilization-shaping authority is difficult to grasp. Indeed, the Qur'an can be very alienating. Brown acknowledges that it can be hard to get a handle on this *sui generis* text, but nonetheless suggests that "we are the first generation in the West able to perceive this book," precisely because we have access to the example of *Finnegans Wake*.[8] The comparison may seem arbitrary, but drawing on an important scholarly work on the *Wake*, Brown argues that "Joyce quotes the title of exactly 111 out of 114 surahs of the Qur'an."[9] Therefore, if "Muhammad threw down that challenge … to produce a surah like it," we are forced to conclude that Joyce "took up that challenge."[10] From this perspective, the quasi-scriptural status of *Finnegans Wake* for Altizer—who has more than once exhorted readers to take up Joyce's text and *recite*, with the promise that they will experience a deep and abiding joy, regardless of whether they fully understand what is being read—makes a certain kind of sense.

Though Brown's suggestion is an interesting and fruitful one for the study of the Qur'an (and for clarifying Altizer's intentions), it strikes me as less helpful for understanding the historical events that motivated Brown's intensive research into Islam: namely, the Iranian Revolution. Still less does it account for the subsequent evolution of political Islam. If we are to imagine an Islamic Joyce intent on "actualizing" the Islamic vision in literary form, it is difficult to picture them as anything other than exiles, as Joyce was—and as Altizer has effectively been in the theological community. In this context, any claim to have "actualized" a more authentic Islam is likely to ring hollow in the face of other, more forceful "actualizations" in the political field.

---

[6] Norman O. Brown, *The Challenge of Islam: The Prophetic Tradition* (ed. Jerome Neu and Mathew E. Simpson; Santa Cruz and Berkeley, CA: New Pacific Press and North Atlantic Books, 2009). The book reflects a transcript of lectures given at Tufts University in 1981.
[7] Brown, *Challenge of Islam*, p. 45.
[8] Ibid., p. 49.
[9] Ibid., p. 49.
[10] Ibid., p. 49.

The idea of a literary "actualization" of Islam is not my own invention. I draw it from the conclusion of a massive work by another academic of Altizer and Brown's era: Marshall G.S. Hodgson's epic three-volume *Venture of Islam*, which concludes with a reflection of the place of Islam in the modern world. Like Altizer's early work, Hodgson's study was responding to a situation of seemingly inexorable secularization, not only in the West but also in the Islamic world, which was dominated by secular Arab nationalist parties (and on its margins, by actual Soviet Republics). Hence Hodgson can ask, as we perhaps cannot, "Is the Islamicate culture to be relegated to the history books and the museums? Is the Islamic faith to merge (after whatever loyalistic but parochial resistance) insensibly into some general ecumenical religiosity, perhaps to disappear altogether in the face of technicalistic enlightenment?"[11] After a rapid but comprehensive survey of Islam's place in the modern world of his time, he concludes his life's work with the following speculation: "It is possible that eventually Islam (like Christianity already in some circles) will prove to have its most creative thrust by way of the great 'secular' literature in which its challenge has been embedded, and will move among its heirs like a secret leaven long after they have forgotten they were once Muslims."[12]

Hodgson's point is somewhat different from Altizer's—he is thinking of the tradition of "secular" Persian literature that had always formed a part of the Islamicate milieu without being strictly Islamic in the religious sense—yet the shared focus on the literary is potentially revealing. Throughout the modern period, there have been repeated attempts to make art, and specifically literature, do the work religion had once done, and so it is perhaps natural that Hodgson would reach for a literary legacy to ensure that Islam's contribution to the human project would not be entirely lost. Making all due allowances for the radical differences in their approaches—above all in their rhetorical styles—is Altizer's project really that different from Hodgson's? Is he ultimately trying to save the heritage of Christianity through his claim that it could somehow be "actualized" in literature? If so, Altizer's project could very well seem outdated or even beside the point in an era when Christianity, like Islam, has asserted itself as a political force that must be reckoned with.

Of course, Altizer is not thinking on such small timescales. Dante, after all, has far overshadowed any of the more immediately influential politicians and clerics of his time—hence the need for the burdensome footnotes in every edition of *The Divine Comedy*. Similarly, Milton's poetic vision has endured, whereas the radical theology of the Puritan Revolution—which Altizer has elsewhere highlighted—languishes in obscurity. Perhaps Joyce, too, will outlast any preacher, politician, or pope of our era through his profound impact on the English language itself. After all, if the *Wake*, like the Qur'an, carries its own authority with itself, if it "actualizes" the Christian demand as fully as Altizer claims, then its lack of immediate topical relevance is itself of no relevance. Such a long view does conflict with contemporary academic demand that every concept and argument will somehow have an immediate political "payoff,"

---

[11] Marshall G.S. Hodgson, *The Venture of Islam: Conscience and History in a World Civilization*, Vol. 3: *The Gunpowder Empires and Modern Times* (Chicago, IL: University of Chicago Press, 1974), p. 411.
[12] Ibid., Vol. 3, p. 441.

a demand that is unrealistic and increasingly tiresome (at least to me), and hence Altizer's mismatch with academic fashion may be a welcome breath of fresh air.

In any case, even if Altizer is not "political" in a reductive sense, his narrative is one of rivalry and conflict, played out over millennia as the Christian epic vies with classical epic and Hebrew saga for supremacy, an effort that is ultimately successful in Altizer's view, at least in terms of the Hebrew Bible. Much less emphasis is placed on classical epic, a choice that is puzzling to me, because that is, after all, what Christian *epic* is most directly imitating. As a professor at a Great Books school—a theologian in exile, one might say—I have spent a great deal of time with the classical epics, and I am intrigued by the resources Altizer provides for rereading the epic tradition.

The epic is a puzzling genre, one that perhaps not even Aristotle got quite right. Favoring tragedy, he claimed, effectively, that the epic wants to be a tragedy but is forced to expand its story beyond all reasonable bounds via the proliferation of episodes. Perhaps it is only the perspective of Christian epic that allows us to see what epics were really trying, and arguably failing, to do: to tell a story that can include all stories, to provide a sense of meaning in history, even to "justify the ways of the gods to man."[13] On this latter point, one thinks of Homer's very Miltonian Zeus, complaining at the opening of the *Odyssey* that humanity constantly blames its troubles on the gods:

Ah how shameless—the way these mortals blame the gods.
From us alone, they say, come all their miseries, yes,
but they themselves, with their own reckless ways,
compound their pains beyond their proper share.[14]

This complaint rings hollow, of course, in the wake of the events of the *Iliad*, where the gods micro-managed the conflict in such a way as to extend it and increase the suffering and carnage—perhaps most notably when Aphrodite extracts Paris from the one-on-one fight with Menelaus that could have ended the war with considerably less bloodshed and destruction. It is answered, equally unconvincingly, in the abrupt ending to Homer's epic cycle, when an incipient war between Odysseus and the fathers of the murdered suitors (i.e., an entire generation of young men in his kingdom) is halted by Athena's fiat.

The problem is finding a big enough frame to house the epic ambition. The Greek epics seem to give us only a cycle: of cities built and conquered, of journeys home that open out into further journeys. This gives us a worldview—the war never ends, no one ever really comes home—but not a narrative. The Roman epics have a more teleological feel, as both the *Aeneid* and the *Metamorphoses* culminate in the founding of Rome, but this frame threatens to reduce them to propaganda for a local and provisional victory. Only the Christian narrative is "big enough" to fulfill the epic longing for completion—and so one can say that Milton fulfills the tradition with *Paradise Lost*, which relates literally the entire history of the world, from the prehistory of creation to

---

[13] John Milton, *Paradise Lost: A Norton Critical Edition* (ed. Gordon Teskey; New York: Norton, 2005): l. 26.

[14] Homer, *The Odyssey* (trans. Robert Fagles; New York: Penguin, 1999), ll. 36–40.

the Last Judgment. At various points in this epic, we learn not only of the temptation in the Garden of Eden but also of the creation and rebellion of the angels, the creation of the material world, and the entire providential narrative as related in Scripture and the history of the Church. Finally, it seems, the epic task has been fulfilled.

Yet Milton is not content to outdo the classical epics. He wants to undo them, to expose them as imposters. It has long been a cliché that the devil is the hero of *Paradise Lost*, but I think it is worth taking that claim very literally. He does everything the epic hero does—rally the troops, go on dangerous voyages, make skillful use of deception, and succeed against overwhelming odds. Milton does not make the devil the hero by accident, but as part of a rhetorical strategy to expose the classical epic hero as *evil*, as no hero at all. From this perspective, Blake's claim that Milton is of the devil's party[15] is ultimately a claim that the devil remains seductive—indicating that the classical epics perhaps maintain their own autonomous force even in the wake of the Christian epic. It is, after all, the classical epic that gives form to Joyce's epic of everyday life, *Ulysses*.

If the Christian epic was able to effectively overwrite the Hebrew Bible and overcome the classical epic, it proved less mighty in the face of another potential rival: namely, the New Testament, or more precisely, the gospels. Altizer does say that Christian epic reactivates the vision of the book of Revelation, just as Heidegger can reactivate Paul—yet does anyone effectively rewrite a new Gospel? Milton tries, perhaps, but *Paradise Regained* is a historical footnote that is far from reshaping our understanding of the temptation in the wilderness.

The question of the genre of the Gospels is a vexed one, and no firm consensus has ever emerged from biblical scholarship on this question. One possibility is particularly intriguing for our purposes here, however. In what is admittedly a minority report, Marianne Palmer Bonz argues that Luke-Acts, at least, is an epic—and one that explicitly sets out to rewrite the narrative of Virgil's *Aeneid*.[16] Arguing that Luke and Acts should be read as a unit,[17] she claims that the author is not only rewriting the Hebrew Bible but putting forward the nascent Church as a counter-empire. Responding to the obvious objection that Luke–Acts is a prose narrative on a much smaller scale than the *Aeneid*, she points out the existence of prose Greek translations of the Latin epic and draws on a range of lesser-known epic poems that inform and, later, challenge Virgil's conception of the founding of Rome. She also adduces some striking parallels in the structure and rhetorical strategies of the two works.

If we grant some credence to Bonz's argument, then perhaps the reason the Christian epic does not explicitly seek to supercede the Gospels is that the Gospels *already are* the primal form of the Christian epic. In this regard, we could claim that for the tradition of Christian epic, the New Testament is the unsurpassable horizon—certainly not even Milton has so thoroughly rewritten the Hebrew Bible as the New Testament did when it cast its predecessor as the Old Testament. Or perhaps, taking into account our

---

[15] Qtd. in Milton, *Paradise Lost*, p. 389.
[16] See Marianne Palmer Bonz, *The Past as Legacy: Luke-Acts and Ancient Epic* (Minneapolis, MN: Fortress, 2000).
[17] In Bonz's reading, the repetitions and contradictions in the final chapter of Luke and the first chapter of Acts result from a later editor cutting the work in half to allow Luke to conform to the model of the other Gospels.

detour into Islam, it is a horizon that has itself already been surpassed by the work of the Qur'an, which is, if we are to believe Brown, the chief rival that *Finnegans Wake*, Altizer's ultimate point of reference, sets itself. Yet here again, the Qur'an's primary rival is not the New Testament, from which it draws at most a few vignettes, but the Hebrew Bible. The reader of the Qur'an gets only a vague impression of Jesus and Mary, most of which serves to undo the key claims of the New Testament: about Jesus's divinity (ambiguously affirmed in much of the New Testament but unambiguously rejected by the Qur'an), about his crucifixion (which for the Qur'an, here embracing Docetism, never actually occurred), about the Christian claim to supersede Judaism (which is undercut by the implication that Jesus was actually a prophet to the Romans, not the culmination of the Hebrew prophetic tradition). This is not a rewriting so much as a repudiation of a potential rival.

Dante, of course, puts both Muhammad and Ali not among the heathens or even the heretics, but among the schismatics. As Dante's interlocutor describes the pair:

> See how Mahomet is deformed and torn!
> In front of me, and weeping, Ali walks,
> His face cleft from his chin to the crown.
>
> The souls that you see passing in this ditch
> were all sowers of scandal and schism in life,
> and so in death you see them torn asunder.[18]

When this interlocutor demands an explanation of who the unexpected visitors are, Virgil responds that Dante has not yet died but is in hell "that he may have full experience" (XXVIII.48). This phrasing echoes that of an inmate of a nearby circle—namely, Ulysses (Odysseus), who claims to have undertaken his last fatal voyage (an invention of Dante's) because nothing

> could quench deep in myself the burning wish
> to know the world and have experience
> of all men's vices, of all human worth. (XXVI.97-99)

This is a "radical Catholicism" of a sort, an attempt to grasp human experience *kath' holikos*—according to everybody, according to the whole. But it is a strange kind of Catholicism in that it is expressed by a figure who comes before and outside of the Christian revelation and echoed immediately after an encounter with two figures who claimed—and yet, in Dante's view, in some unspecified sense failed—to supersede that revelation and wind up tearing it, and themselves, to shreds.

And this brings us, belatedly, to the question of what exactly this "radical Catholicism" of Altizer is supposed to consist of. Catholicism, radical or not, is an unexpected topic for Altizer, who for all his philosophical and religious promiscuity

---

[18] Dante, *Inferno*, Canto XXVIII, ll. 31-36, in Mark Musa, trans., *The Portable Dante* (New York: Penguin, 1995). Subsequent references in text, by Canto and line.

remained very much in the Protestant tradition. Indeed, his enthusiastic embrace of secularism as the very outpouring of God—and his rejection of anything like the traditional Church—could be taken to be the most radically Protestant move of all, a Protestantism that undoes Protestantism itself.

What remains for Catholicism in this context? Altizer himself does not give us much to go on in a contribution that does little to explicitly situate itself in connection with any institutional form of Catholicism, leaving us to assume that Dante and Joyce are the representatives of the radical Catholicism he has in mind—though the reference to Milton, a devout anti-papist, is difficult to reconcile with this intuition. Picking up on the few hints he gives us, we might speculate that the "Catholicism" he wants to show us is the small-c catholicism of the "Here comes everybody," the *kath' holikos* that Christianity allows the epic tradition to grasp. And drawing on another thinker of the whole who has deeply influenced Altizer down to the very texture of his prose, namely Hegel, perhaps we could view the literary "actualization" of Christianity as a supersession in its own way—a preservation and abolition of Christianity by means of a synthesis with its rival, the classical tradition.

Yet if we grant Bonz's theory about the relationship between Luke–Acts and the *Aeneid*, then we are forced to concede that this movement is what Christian literature was always doing from the very beginning and hence to admit that the establishment of the institutional Church and its alliance with Empire may not be a straightforward betrayal, as Altizer and so many others have asserted. From this perspective, Altizer's narrative of the birth of secular modernity out of the death of God would not be qualitatively different from the narrative within which the death of the messiah turns out to redeem the Empire—a more radical catholicism in the sense of being more all-embracing, but still a radical *Catholicism*, with all the compromises and betrayals that implies.

11

Anatheism: A Theopoetic Challenge

Richard Kearney

Why is "making" considered a sacred activity for gods and mortals alike? Making something out of nothing. Making something in the image of something else. Creators making creatures while creatures in turn make their creators. Making out, making up, making and remaking worlds in one's image and likeness. In shapes and songs, paintings and poems, dreams, and crafts. From the beginning to the end of time. One great game of holy imagination played with hands, mouths, ears, and eyes. With bodies and souls. Art as divine–human interplay, again and again.

Theopoetics names how the divine (*theos*) manifests itself as making (*poiesis*). The term dates back to the early centuries, meaning both the making human of the divine and the making divine of humanity. As the poet scholar, Ephrem of Syria, wrote: "He gave us divinity, we gave Him humanity." Or as Athanasius said in the fourth century: "God became human so that the human could become divine." Catherine Keller puts it succinctly: "The term theopoetics finds its ancestor in the ancient Greek *theopoiesis*. As poeisis means making or creation, so theopoiesis gets rendered as God-making or becoming divine."[1]

---

[1] These quotes are from Catherine Keller, "Theopoetic Becomings: A Brief, Incongruent History," in *Intercarnations: Exercises in Theological Possibility* (New York: Fordham University Press, 2017). Keller traces the origins of theopoetics from the participatory mysticism of Patristic authors and the cosmo-theology of Cusanus to a third millennium process cosmology inspired by Whitehead's notion of God as "Eros of the universe"—"Poet of the world, with tender patience leading it by his vision of truth, beauty and goodness" (*Adventures of Ideas* [New York: The Free Press, 1961]), p. 253. Developing a radical notion of "cosmic theopoiesis," Keller comments on Whitehead's statement that "as God creates the world, the world creates God" thus: "Theopoiesis takes on a new and risky double meaning: we are at once making ourselves God—and making God." For Keller, theopoetics is also cosmopoetics: world-creating as well as person-creating and thing-creating, in such a way that it is less a matter of theist believing or atheist disbelieving than an ana-theist "making and materializing of God ... a doing God ... doing the prophetic justice, the love thing." In her groundbreaking work, *Cloud of the Impossible* (New York: Columbia University Press, 2015), Keller amplifies further theopoetic insights by Cusanus and Whitehead concerning the "creatable-creating" character of God in dialogue with ideas of infolding–exfolding from Leibniz, Deleuze, and the contemporary physics of "planetary entanglement" (see especially pp. 209–210 and 306–316). See also our notion of a poetic-dynamic divinity in R. Kearney, *The God Who May Be* (Bloomington: Indiana University Press, 2002) and *Anatheism: Returning to God after God* (New York: Columbia University Press, 2014).

Theopoetics carries an attendant claim that first creation calls for second creation—re-creation or creation again (*ana*): a double act where humanity and divinity collaborate in the coming of the Kingdom. This play of recreation goes by the name of "ana-theism."

Most wisdom traditions involve an original story of creation—or cosmogony—which serves as paradigm for their subsequent spiritual narratives. In what follows I will draw mainly on Abrahamic and Hellenic narratives to trace a short history of theopoetics before illustrating the notion of sacred play with reference to the work of Andrei Rublev. My overall suggestion is that certain expressions of artistic imagination offer ways of responding to the call of creation which precedes and exceeds the abstract systems of philosophy and theology. Theopoetic imagination gives flesh to word and word to flesh. It works both ways.

I Theopoiesis

i

The use of the term *poiein*—to make, shape, or form—occurs often in the Bible in relation to divine creation. This theopoetic motif features from the start in Genesis (1.1, 1.7, 1.27) where we read, famously, that "In the beginning God created (*epoiesen*) heaven and earth" (1.1); or, again, "Let us make (*poiesomen*) man" (1.26). In Proverbs 8 (22-26), we witness the great primal scene of God's creation (*poiesis*) of Wisdom:

> The Lord brought me forth as the first of his works, before his deeds of old;
> I was formed long ages ago, at the very beginning, when the world came to be [*poiesis*], when there were no watery depths, I was given birth, when there were no springs overflowing with water; before the mountains were settled in place, before the hills, I was given birth, before he made (*epoiesai*) the world or its fields or any of the dust of the earth ... Then I was constantly at his side. I was filled with delight day after day rejoicing always in his presence. (Prov. 8.22-29)

In the Wisdom of Solomon, the formative power of *Sophia* is even more explicit:

> God of my fathers and Lord of mercy,
> who by your Word (*logos*) made (*poiesas*) all things,
> and through your Wisdom (*sophia*) framed man. (9.1-2)

These early panegyrics of the divine play of *Sophia* echo the first chapter of Genesis where God creates humans in his own image and likeness. The original Hebrew term—*yzr*—plays on the mirroring between (1) the divine Creator (*yotzer*) who creates (*yazar*), and (2) the human power to form and shape (*yetzer*) according to the secret alphabet of creation (*yetsirah*).[2] It is telling that the Lord did not make anything on the seventh day of genesis, leaving it free for humans to complete. The unfinished Sabbath is a gap calling for perpetual recreation—in imagination and action. And Adam and Eve, as the first creatures shaped from earth (*adamah*), deployed their power of "good imagination" (*yezer hatov*) to engender a human race capable of fashioning a Kingdom in the image of their God.

This play of mutual recreation between human and divine is what we call theopoetics. It involves creatures co-creating with their Creator. In this view, God co-depends on us so that the promissory word of Genesis may be realized in embodied figures of time and space, image and flesh, art and action. Or as Thomas Mann aptly observes in *Joseph and His Brothers:* "God created for himself a mirror in his own image ... as a means of learning about himself. Man is a result of God's curiosity about himself."[3] But greater than curiosity was desire. For in forming the human, God bore witness to a gap within divinity, a sabbatical crack or fracture from which the life-force of eros could emerge as desire for its other. God created because he desired a play mate, someone to consort with, as we know from Hosea and the Song of Songs. Or as the contemporary Jewish philosopher, Emmanuel Levinas, put it: "*Dieu a*

---

[2] See our chapter on the "Hebraic Imagination," in *The Wake of Imagination* (ed. Richard Kearney; London: Hutcheson, 1987). For recent pioneering work on theopoetics, in addition to Catherine Keller's work cited above, see Callid Keefe-Perry, *Way to Water: A Theopoetics Primer* (Eugene, OR: Cascade Books, 2014); Roland Faber and Jeremy Frankenthal, *Theopoetic Folds* (New York: Fordham University Press, 2013); John Caputo, "Theopoetics of the Kingdom of God," in *The Folly of God* (Salem, OR: Polebridge, 2016); Amos Wilder, *Theopoetic: Theology and the Religious Imagination* (Lima, OH: Academic Revival Press, 2001); Colby Dickinson, *Words Fail: Theology, Poetry and the Challenge of Representation* (New York: Fordham University Press, 2016); Noirin Ni Rian, *Theosony: Towards a Theology of Listening* (Dublin: Veritas, 2011), Patrick Hederman *The Haunted Inkwell: Art and the Future* (Dublin: Columba Press, 2001) and John Manoussakis, *God after Metaphysics* (Bloomington: Indiana University Press, 2009). It is worth noting here that there are three main terms used to designate "creation" in the Hebrew Bible—*poiesis, ktizis,* and *bara*. It would require another work to fully explore the different nuances of these usages.

[3] Kearney, *The Wake of Imagination*, p. 37. On the theme of divine–human mirroring see Hildegard of Bingen, who has God say that he "created mirrors in which he considers all the wonders of his originality which will never cease" (*Hildegard of Bingen's Book of Divine Works* [ed. Matthew Fox; Santa Fe, NM: Bern and co, 1987], p. 128) and Bonaventure who claimed that on the soul's journey to God "we must present to ourselves the whole material world as the first mirror through which we may pass over the supreme [Artisan]" (*The Soul's Journey to God* [vols 1, 9; New York: Paulist Press, 1978], p. 63). I am grateful to Richard Rohr for these two quotations and to Emmanuel Falque for his deep insights into the idea of divine–human mirroring in both Bonaventure and John Scotus Eriugena in *God, Flesh and the Other* (Evanston, IL: Northwestern University Press, 2015). Eriugena's notion of "theophany"—God's theopoetic self-creating in and through his creatures—is expressed in the following formulae in Eriugena's ninth-century *De Divisione Naturae*: "God and the creature do not constitute two distinct realities but constitute a single and same reality because it is by a mutual concurrence that the creature subsists in God and that God is created ... in the creature, manifesting Himself there" (p. 63); or again: "Because the divine Nature ... becomes visible in everything that exists, it is not incongruous to say that it is created in everything that exists" (p. 64). In short, theophany is theopoetics to the degree that for God to create is to be created in and by His creatures. God thus sees himself "as in a mirror, carrying in Himself all existing beings." God-mirroring is God-making in and through creation (p. 65 f).

crée l'homme car on s'amuse mieux à deux." Creation is a love affair.[4] Theopoetics is theoerotics.

It is important to repeat that both Genesis and Proverbs declare that God is relation. Not a self-subsisting remote substance but a relationship between two—Yahweh and Sophia, Elohim and Adam—through the medium of a third (the breath of language). Indeed the fact that the Creator is also called by a plural name, Elohim, itself reveals that God is originally a community rather than some autonomous Supreme Being— "Let *us* make man." Divine creating is divine speaking from the start, as evidenced in the Hebraic word play on the first and last letters of the alphabet in Genesis 1.1.[5] The first word of Genesis is dialogue not monologue, and this is echoed in the opening of St

---

[4] Emmanuel Levinas in Kearney, *Dialogues with Contemporary Continental Thinkers* (Manchester Manchester University Press, 1984). See also Aviva Zornberg, *The Beginning of Desire: Reflections on Genesis* (New York: Image Books/Doubleday, 1995). Just as a certain Jewish teaching claimed that the Torah (Law) existed before the Creation of the world, so too the spirit of loving Wisdom (Sophia) may be said to serve as an originary act of divine pro-creation (Prov. 8). This finds a Christian variation in Paul's claim in Ephesians (1:4) that Christians exist in a loving relation with Christ before the foundation of the world—and ever since in the work of ongoing creation, incarnation, and salvation (Rom. 8). The notion of a primal Cosmic Creative Christ is revisited in Colossians 1.15: "He is the image of the invisible God, the firstborn of all creation. For in him were created all things in heaven and on earth." The Trinitarian relationship of Father–Son–Spirit as a primordial dance of mutual co-creation finds expression in the Patristic notion of perichoresis which first arose in third- and fourth-century Cappadocia, a theme we explore in the final part of this chapter. See Richard Rohr with Mike Morrell, *The Divine Dance: The Trinity and Your Transformation* (Kensington, PA: Whitaker House, 2016): "This flow of love goes full circle. The 'Son' also creates the 'Father' precisely as Father." And Rohr does not hesitate to explore the gender fluidity of the persons of the dance, to include "mother" and "daughter," reminding us that the Pauline view of creation in Romans 8.22 ("From the beginning until now, the entire creation has been groaning in one great act of giving birth") is "very feminine"—in keeping with the feminine Sophia of the books of Wisdom. Which is why, Rohr notes, "men were historically so opposed to it" ("One Great Act of Giving Birth: The Cosmic Christ," November 2, 2016, Meditations@cac.org). In this connection he cites a number of great Christian mystics, including (1) Hildegard of Bingen—"Humanity is called to assist God … to co-create"; (2) Thomas Merton's notion of creation as a "general dance" (*New Seeds of Contemplation*); and Teilhard de Chardin: "'The world is still being created, and it is Christ who is reaching his fulfillment in it.'" When I heard that saying, I saw as though in ecstasy that through all nature I was immersed in God" ("Cosmic Life" in *Writings in Time of War*).

[5] I am grateful to the biblical scholar Stephen Rugg for the following analysis: "The first line of the Hebrew text of Genesis (1.1) is *bᵉrēšîṯ bārā' 'ĕlōhîm 'ēṯ haššāmayim wᵉ 'ēṯ ha 'āreṣ*
In the beginning he created God/gods the heavens and the earth."
There is a Hebrew "word" that doesn't translate. The "word" is constructed of two consonants the *aleph* (first letter of the Hebrew alphabet) and the *tav* (the last letter of the Hebrew alphabet); it is like seeing AZ or AΩ. That "word" has a grammatical purpose in this sentence as the "direct object marker." Hebrew doesn't have noun cases and word order is not absolute, so when a direct object needs to be specified this "word" is placed before the direct object(s). Rhetorically (and theologically) every "jot and tittle" would also be significant. Here we could suggest that the grammatical marker is a sign. "In the beginning God created aleph-tav," where aleph-tav is a merism for the alphabet and a synecdoche for language. The aleph-tav appears twice (because there are two noun objects) In the second instance it mediates (with the conjunction) "'the heavens' and 'the earth'. Language graphically 'holds/pulls together' the merism of heaven and earth. Interpreted thus we could suggest that *Eros*/language operates primordially as a bridge between two oppositions stuck in *thanatos*. So to hazard a more contemporary interpretive translation we might read: 'At the origins (of time) God created *langue*, and the heavens and the earth with *langue*'. [To expand the play of the aleph-tav in Hebrew—the word is sometimes a preposition, translated as 'with.'] *Langue* is then creatively employed as God's *parole* (because time and *langue* are in a sense simultaneous first-creations. *langue* participates with chronic force and can now be expressed as *parole*), where God speaks and 'there is'. What follows in the story is then a series of distinctions that cannot be maintained

John's Gospel which declares that "In the beginning was the word (*logos*) and the word was *with* God." The preposition "with" (*pros*) here actually means "toward" or "before," revealing a relation of face-to-face or person-to-person (*prosopon*): a dynamic liaison which mirrors the inaugural scene of Sophia (a feminine noun) playing before the face of the Lord (Prov. 8). These Jewish and Christian claims to the primacy of relation between persons are reinforced in the later Patristic figure of creation as a trinitarian dance (*perichoresis*).[6] We shall return to this point in our commentary of Rublev's icon of the perichoresis below.

separately; each separation is imbued with inherent boundary crossing—evidence of eros at work." I am very grateful to Stephen Rugg's presentation at my "Eros/Thanatos" seminar at the Philosophy dept, Boston College, Fall, 2016. See also Jonathan Yovel, "The Creation of Language and Language without Time: Metaphysics and Metapragmatics in Genesis 1," *Biblical Interpretation* 20 (2012), pp. 205–225; Naomi Janowitz, "Recreating Genesis: The Metapragmatics of Divine Speech," in *Reflexive Language: Reported Speech and Metapragmatics* (ed. J.A. Lucy; Cambridge: Cambridge University Press, 1993), pp. 393–405. See also Gerhard F. Hasel, "The Significance of the Cosmology in Genesis I in Relation to Ancient Near Eastern Parallels," *Andrews University Seminary Studies* 10, no. 1 (1972), pp. 1–20, and Tzahi Weiss, "On the Matter of Language: The Creation of the World through Letters," *The Journal of Jewish Thought and Philosophy* (Fall, 2009). One might also cite here a number of contemporary hermeneutic readings of Genesis in terms of language and eros. Jacques Derrida declares: "In the beginning was hermeneutics" and associates Genesis with the ongoing play of "dechemination/ dissemination/ diaspora/ differance"; while Paul Ricoeur explores the primary role of nuptial metaphoricity and creation in another inaugural Wisdom book of Solomon, namely, the Song of Songs (see Ricoeur, "The Nuptial Metaphor," in *Thinking Biblically* [with André La Cocque; Chicago, IL: University of Chicago Press, 2004]). See also the opening chapters of Aviva Zorberg's extraordinary hermeneutical–Rabbinical reading of Genesis as a language of eros in *The Beginning of Desire: Reflections on Genesis*; and Emmanuel Falque's claim, in his hermeneutic reading of Genesis 1, that "In the beginning was sexual difference" (*The Wedding Feast of the Lamb: Eros, the Body and the Eucharist*, [New York: Fordham University Press, 2016], p. 140).

[6] *Perichoresis*, or the divine dance of Trinitarian relation, was there from the beginning (see Rohr, *The Divine Dance*). In Christianity, Sophia—which Proverbs said was created in the beginning—was sometimes identified with Christ as the second person of the Trinity (viz, the famous Hagia Sophia basilica in Constantinople). Sophia was associated at times with the "Word" (*Logos*)—for example, in the Wisdom of Solomon (9.1-2) as we noted above, where *logos* and *Sophia* are used synonymously as equiprimordial powers of creation (of the world and humans): a theme echoed in certain late commentaries on the Prologue of John's Gospel. It should be noted, however, that in the Nicene Creed (381 AD), the Church Fathers spoke of the Father "engendering," rather than "making" the Son—"*genitus non factum (poiethenta)*." And the later controversy over the "*Filioque*" (seventh–ninth centuries), which hierarchically subordinates the third person of the Trinity (*pneuma*) to the Father "and" (*que*) the Son, further diluted the radical equity of face-to-face (*prosopon*) relations between the three divine persons. It is very revealing, nonetheless, that the term "*pros*" features in the opening sequence of John's Prologue—"The Word was with (*pros*) God—indicating that the Word-Logos-Christ-Son plays 'before/in front of/face to face with' the Father (*prosopon* means face). I am grateful to John Manoussakis for his readings of Sophia and *prosopon* in 'Toward a Fourth Reduction' in his *After God*" (New York: Fordham University Press, 2009). I am also indebted to Richard Rohr in *The Divine Dance* for his insistence that the human person see itself in continuity with divine creation, in perpetual personal face-to-face relation, and not as some isolated autonomous self. We are "chosen in Christ before the foundation of the world" (see Eph. 1.4). For more on our understanding of *prosopon/persona/person* see also the opening Chapter of Kearney, *The God Who May Be*. While perichoresis is primarily a Christian image of the Trinity it is important to note, as we shall below, that Rublev's famous image portrays the Trinity in terms of the Jewish Bible scene of three strangers visiting Abraham and that many other passages in the Torah and Psalms depict God in terms of imaginative figures and metaphors—nursemaid, shepherd, eagle, lion, father, burning bush, still small voice, etc. See also Numbers 12.8 where Moses is reported as seeing the "image" (*doxa*) of the Lord. It is telling, I think, that one of the most powerful contemporary paintings of the three strangers visiting Abraham at Mamre—after Rublev—is that by the Jewish painter, Marc Chagall.

In Jewish Scripture the leitmotif of *theopoiesis* extends well beyond Genesis and the books of Wisdom to the Psalms and Prophets. Think, for example, of Isaiah 29.16 where the human creature is described as the clay of the potter, the handicraft of the craftsman, the art of the artist. Or, again, recall the Rabbinical and Kabbalistic commentaries on the making of Golems—human-like figures shaped from clay according to the Book of Creation (*Sefir Yetsirah*). One such version tells of how Abraham and his teacher, Seth, were invited by God to study the *Sefir Yetsirah* for three years "until they knew how to create a world."[7] But lest they succumb to the temptation of idolatry—like Enosh who worshipped his own clay image—humans were admonished not to replace God's creation but only to repeat it so as better to appreciate the power of divine making. It was good to experiment with the divine letters of creation as art, exploration, invention, but not to actually substitute God with an idol. If one yielded to the temptation of literal imitation, the Golem risked becoming a monster who turns on its creator. And so to prevent such idolatrous destruction, the makers of Golems were exhorted to remove the "shem" (a parchment spelling *emeth*, meaning "alive") from their creature's lips so as to respect the difference between human and divine creation. The point was for humans to participate in divine *yetsirah/poiesis* in the right manner—namely, abiding by the Way (*Torah*) of the Creator (*Yotzer*)—rather than set themselves up as mini-Gods in their own right.[8] According to Jewish wisdom, then, we are not divine makers but human makers—finite creatures called to collaborate with God in the completion of Creation.

In the later Christian tradition we find similar calls to cooperate in the coming of the Kingdom by joining the Trinitarian dance of perichoresis, thereby repeating the original act of genesis. Such a collaborative theopoetics between the divine Logos and human action seeks to follow Christ the God-Man in completing the "New Creation" (Gal. 6.15). We read in Ephesians 2.10 that "we are the handiwork (*poiema*) created by Jesus Christ for good works ... that we should live in them." As such, Christianity may be understood as the historical–cultural task of carrying on and carrying out this "poem." Whence the notion of Christ as Lord of the Dance and Supreme Artist—echoed in the vibrant Christian culture of image-making both in the iconography

---

[7] Cited in Kearney, *The Wake of Imagination*, p. 55.
[8] On the Talmudic and Kabbalistic readings of the Golem, see R. Kearney, chapter 1, section 3, *The Wake of Imagination*. See also Gershom Scholem's illuminating account of the Jewish literature of Golem-making in the *Mystical Symbols of Judaism*: "Just as the human mind remains infinitely inferior to the all-encompassing divine intelligence of God, so does the Golem's intelligence lag behind the human ... Still, the Golem remains a representation of man's creative power. The universe, so the Kabbalists tell us, is built essentially on the prime elements of numbers and letters, because the letters of God's language reflected in human language are nothing but a concentration of His creative energy. Thus by assembling these elements in all their possible combinations ... the Kabbalist who contemplates the mysteries of Creation radiates some of this elementary power into the Golem. The creation of the Golem is then in some way an affirmation of the productive and creative power of man. It repeats, on however small a scale, the work of creation" (cited in Kearney, *The Wake of Imagination*, p. 59). Scholem does not hesitate to note the implications of this for contemporary cybernetics and the new technology of virtual simulation and cloning. His critical conclusion is that we should explore the power of making (*poiesis*) to experiment with "creations of imagination and mind" (*tetsirah mahshartith*) but not to substitute ourselves for God (cited in *The Wake of Imagination*, p. 61).

of Eastern Orthodoxy and the religious art of the Italian humanist Renaissance and after.[9] We will return to a discussion of this iconographic culture in Part III and ask the related question of how divine *poiesis* relates to human *praxis*.

ii

It is worth noting briefly here that when, in the Greek philosophical tradition, Aristotle seeks a term for the divine mind, he chooses *nous poietikos*—the mind that "makes." And in his *Poetics (Peri Poietikes)*—though now talking of human not divine making—Aristotle describes poetic creation as a mirroring–emplotting (*mimesis-mythos*) of life: an art of recreation involving, in Paul Ricoeur's words, a radical "configuring" of our world. The term *poiesis* occurs in the very first line of Aristotle's classic text and regularly thereafter, referring to the transformation of everyday haphazard events (one thing after—*meta*—another) into a meaningful configured plot (one thing because of—*dia*—another). And it is by means of such creative re-making of our experience that we achieve healing catharsis: namely, a poetic distillation of our basic drives of "pity" (*eleos*) and "fear" (*phobos*) into compassion and serenity. Poetics, in short, involves a "creative redescription" of experience which replays our actions and sufferings in a storied way that issues in the pleasure and wisdom of art. Configured

---

[9] Kearney, *The Wake of Imagination*, chapter 3, pp. 133–138. Since, for Christians, God is made man in the person of Christ, images are permitted and even encouraged, for there is now said to be a legitimate analogy or *similitudo* between the finite and the infinite, overriding Deuteronomy's prohibition ("Thou shall have no graven images"). Image becomes the mediator or chiasm between word (*logos*) and flesh (*sarx*). On the notion of Christ as artist-dancer-player see our hermeneutic analysis of the mystical tradition of *deus ludens* in Kearney, *La Poétique du Possible* (Paris: Beauchesne, 1984), pp. 269–272. The notion of divine play has played an important role in popular religious culture in Christian culture also, involving different forms of public liturgies, pageants, processions, and Passion plays on Holy Feasts and rituals—Mardi Gras, Corpus Christi, Good Friday, All Saints (Halloween), All Souls, Christmas, the Epiphany, etc. A common feature of many Latin Catholic cultures in particular to this day. We also find it in the notion of Christ as "Holy Fool" and "Lord of the Dance," where in certain sacred moments in the liturgical calendar—for example, Shrove Tuesday and the Feast of Saint John (June 21, the summer equinox), the faithful are invited to don masks and costumes in a time of Carnival where the normal rules of time, space, gender, class, and behavior are traversed and reversed, in a divine comedy of fantasy experimentation and play where the conventional logic of non-contradiction no longer applies. This gives popular currency to Samuel Coleridge's definition of poetic imagination as "the yolking together of opposite and discordant qualities." On this notion of Carnival as sacred time and space, see Charles Taylor, *A Secular Age* (Cambridge, MA: Harvard University Press, 2013). See here also Simon Critchley's fascinating reflections on Oscar Wilde's account of Christ as supreme artist in *Faith of the Faithless* (New York: Verso, 2013). One finds similar accounts in the work of William Blake, for example: "Jesus and His Apostles and Disciples were all Artists .... A Poet, a Painter, a Musician, an Architect; the man or woman who is not one of these is not a Christian. The Old and New Testaments are the Great Code of Art. Art is the Tree of Life ... The Eternal Body of Man is the Imagination; that is God Himself, the Divine body (Hebrew) Jesus; we are His Members. It manifests itself in His Works of Art ... Prayer is the study of Art. Praise is the practice of art" ("Engraving on the Laocoon"). It is important to recall in this context, that theopoeisis is not confined to works of high art but is also to be found in the most basic forms of everyday sacred making—of food into feast, of sound into chant, of wool into sacred weaving and couture, of wood and stone into sacred architecture and furniture (from simple Shaker cabinets to holy chapels and cathedrals). In these forms of common sacred practice, making God is a making good and making beautiful of everyday existence. Religious culture as popular culture. The Sacred in the profane.

by the poetic work we, the audience, refigure our own lived existence.[10] We refine our passions (*pathemata*) and are invited to become, in Aristotle's terms, more serene and compassionate citizens of the polis.

iii

Before concluding our preliminary note on theopoetics, let me recite what I consider to be a telling example from modern religious literature. Gerard Manley Hopkins was a Jesuit poet who combined a Scotist–Aristotelian aesthetics of singularity (*haeceitas*) with a Biblical–Ignatian belief in the inherent divinity of "all things." He describes the moment of literary epiphany as a recreation of creation; or as he puts it—an art of "aftering and seconding," a motion of "over and overing" which replays secular experience as sacred.[11] Hopkins speaks of a retrieval of past time that, like Proust, repeats forward, proffering new life to memory, giving a future to the past. This poetic revisiting involves a detour of distance and disenchantment after which we may return to our first experience in a new light, in a second naïveté, over and over. Freud calls this temporal retrieval *nachträglichkeit*; and although he is speaking of "trauma," the same après-coup structure is operative in poetic "wonder": both terms come from a "wound" of shock or surprise which explodes our normal sense of time and space. In Hopkins's work, this wounding expressed itself in a series of dark sonnets which prefaced his poetic epiphanies:

"I wake and feel the fell of dark not day … "
"Oh the mind, mind has mountains,
sheer, frightful, no-man fathomed.
Hold them cheap may those who ne'er hung there … "

---

[10] See Paul Ricoeur on Aristotle's account of poetics as catharsis and narrative emplotment in *Time and Narrative* (vol. 1; Chicago, IL: University of Chicago Press, 2005), chapter 2. Aristotle's philosophy was to exert a considerable influence on Western Christian intellectual culture, especially during the great medieval Scholastic period following Thomas Aquinas in the thirteen and fourteen centuries; but his potential impact on a Christian aesthetics of *poiesis* was often overshadowed by the Platonic critique of imagination as a mimetic and mendacious act subordinate to reason. For Plato the power of making (*techne demiourgike* in his dialogue, *Protagoras*) belongs properly to a quasi-divine maker or demiurge half way between the eternal Forms (which are not made but exist outside time and spaces) and human mortals who are condemned to replicate mere copies and imitations, removing themselves further from the original truth of the Transcendental Ideas, which remain timeless, immaterial, and immutable. See our account of the Platonic and Aristotelian theories of imagination in "The Hellenic Imagination," *Wake of Imagination*, and our analysis of narrative catharsis in "Narrating Pain: The Power of Catharsis," *Paragraph* 30, no. 1 (2007), pp. 51–66; "Writing Trauma," *Giornale de Metafisica* 2 (2013), pp. 7–28 and "Narrative Matters," in our *On Stories* (New York: Routledge, 2003).

[11] See our discussion of Hopkins's anatheist poetics in Kearney, *Anatheism: Returning to God after God* (New York: Columbia University Press, 2010), pp. 11–12; in "God after God: An Anatheist Attempt to Reimagine God," in *Reimagining the Sacred* (ed. Kearney and Jens Zimmerman; New York: Columbia University Press, 2015), pp. 6–18. See also our recent essays, "Secular Epiphanies: The Anatheistic Hermeneutics of Gerard Manley Hopkins" in "Secular Theologies and Theologies of the Secular," *Dialog: A Journal of Theology*, 54: 4 (Winter 2015), guest editor, Whitney Bauman, Blackwell, Oxford, 2015; and "Épiphanies: Hopkins, Scotus, Joyce," in *Métaphysique et christianisme* (ed. Philippe Capelle-Dumont; Paris: Presses Universitaires de France, 2015).

Traversing such dark nights of the soul, the poet returns to a celebration of ordinary things as micro-theophanies:

"Flesh fade, and mortal trash
Fall to the residuary worm; world's wildfire, leave but ash:
In a flash, at a trumpet crash,
I am all at once what Christ is, since he was what I am, and
This Jack, joke, poor potsherd, patch, matchwood, immortal diamond,
Is immortal diamond" (*That Nature Is a Heraclitean Fire*).

A Catholic author, Hopkins performs a sacramental reimagining of everyday experience. But this notion of holy repetition is not confined to any particular religion. It extends to any poetic movement of returning to "God *after* God." God *again* after the loss of God. As in the replay of a child's game, "gone, back again." "*Fort/Da.*" We learn young that what disappears as literal comes back again as figural—that is, as sign and symbol, as a second presence in and through absence. And by symbol here we do not mean *untrue* or *unreal*. The return of the lost one—in the case of religion, the lost God— may well be the most "real presence," theopoetically speaking. It may in fact be a more powerful and moving presence precisely because of the detour through separation and letting go. This involves a new notion of time—kairological rather than chronological—a time which traverses and reverses time, as in the Eucharistic formula: "We do this in memory of Him until he comes again." *Theopoiesis* is about coming back again (*ana*)— creating again time after time. In a word: *ana-poiesis*. Theopoetics is anapoetics.

II Anatheism

"Ana" is a prefix defined in the Shorter Oxford English dictionary as: "Up in space or time; back again, anew." So understood, the term supports the deeper and broader sense of "after" contained in the expression "God after God." *Ana* opens a semantic field involving notions of retrieving, revisiting, reiterating, and repeating. But, as already mentioned, repeating *forwards* not *backwards*. It is not about regressing nostalgically to some prelapsarian past. It is a question, rather, of coming back "afterwards" in order to move forward again. *Reculer pour mieux sauter!*

So it is in this sense that we use the term ana-theism as a "returning to God after God": a critical hermeneutic retrieval of sacred things that have passed but still bear a radical remainder, an unrealized potentiality or promise to be more fully realized in the future. In this way, ana-theism may be understood as "after-faith," which is more than an "after-thought" or "after-effect." After-faith is eschatological—something ultimate in the end that was already there from the beginning. And that is why the "after" of *ana* is also a "before." A before that has been transposed, so to speak, into a second after. As Sophia says when she plays before the face of the Lord: "Before he made the world I was there … constantly at his side … filled with delight, rejoicing always in his presence" (Prov. 8.26-29). And this Hebraic sense of ana-chrony is echoed in Jesus's claim: "Before Abraham was I am."

But let us be clear from the outset: anatheism is not a dialectical third term which supersedes theism and atheism in a sort of Hegelian synthesis or final resolution. True, anatheism contains a moment of atheism within itself as it does a moment of theism. Or to be more precise: anatheism pre-contains both—for it operates from a space and time *before* the dichotomy of atheism and theism as well as *after*. The double "a" of anatheism holds out the promise, but not the necessity, of a second affirmation once the "death of God" has done its work. But it differs radically from Hegel's "negation of the negation" which sees the return as an ineluctable synthesis or sublation (*Aufhebung*). In contrast to such a theodicy, the "ana" of theopoetics is always a wager—a risk that can go either way. It is a matter of discernment and decision on our part. A replay of wisdom, again and again. The event does not take place behind our backs, irrespective of our agency, like Hegel's dialectic of Absolute Spirit. There is no "Ruse of Reason." Anatheism is not some predetermined dialectic leading to a Final Totality. It is not about Upper Case Divinity. *Au contraire!* Anatheism has nothing to do with Alpha-Gods or Omni-Gods. It is about re-imaging—and re-living—the sacred in the "least of these." It is lower case from beginning to end.

Anatheism concentrates, therefore, on unrealized or suspended possibilities which are most powerfully reanimated if one also experiences a moment of a-theism; the "a-" here being a gesture of abstention, privation, withdrawal, emptying.[12] A moment which is less a matter of epistemological theory than a pre-reflective lived experience of ordinary lostness and solitude—a mood of *Angst* or abandon, an existential "dark night of the soul" which everyone experiences at some moment in their lives. Even Christ on the Cross or weeping for Lazarus. This privative "a" of atheism is indispensable to anatheism. But in "a-n-a" we have two A's. And the second "a" is the "not" of the "not." The yes after the no which repeats the first yes of creation. The double A-A of anatheism. A reopening to something new. A dance of twelve steps and more. After all.

So, I repeat, the *ana-* is not a guarantee of ineluctable rational progress. The end of religion brings us back to the beginning of religion—to a fore-time preceding the division between theism and atheism. And in this respect, we might think of John Keats's famous definition of poetic faith a "willing suspension of disbelief," a returning again to Adam's experience on the first day of creation when everything was fresh and up for grabs, when anything could happen, for better or for worse. Keats calls this originary moment of not-knowing "negative capability"—"the ability to experience mystery, uncertainty and doubt, without the irritable reaching after fact and reason." And it has echoes, I think, of Kierkegaard's famous "leap of faith" in *Fear and Trembling*. A sacred repetition—not to be understood as a regression to some original position but as an originary *disposition* of openness to the radical incoming Other.[13] Abraham has to lose his son as given in order to receive him back as gift; he has to abandon Isaac as possession in order to welcome him back as promise. Isaac is not Abraham's (as extension, acquisition, property, projection); he is another's, another, a gift of the Other (the return gift of what Kierkegaard calls the "Absolute").

---

[12] See our analysis of Paul Ricoeur's "Religion, Atheism, Faith" (*The Conflict of Interpretations*) in Kearney, *Anatheism*, pp. 71–81.

[13] Kierkegaard, *Fear and Trembling* (New York: Penguin, 1985).

In short, anatheistic faith is a retrieval of something after you have lost it. It involves the repeating of the former as latter, of the earlier as later—a replay which surpasses the model of linear time as one moment succeeding another in favor of a time out of time: an epiphanic moment (*Augenblick* or *Jetzzeit*) where eternity crosses the instant.[14] "Ana" is a prefix that seeks to capture this enigma of past-as-future, before-as-after.[15]

To say this is not, however, to deny that *ana* also involves historical time. Far from it. Infinite time is in-finite, as Levinas reminds us; it traverses finite temporality and cannot exist without it. As such, ana-theism in its current manifestation does indeed coincide with a concrete historical situation that comes after the death of God, culturally, socially, and intellectually. It is marked by the announcements of Nietzsche, Marx, and Freud, by the atheist exposés of the Enlightenment, the French Revolution, the modern critique of Ideology, and so on. It is something that very much expresses a typical modern anxiety in the face of what Max Weber terms the "disenchantment" of the world, the desacralizing of society, the general malaise of the abandonment of God and loss of faith. In this sense anatheism is indeed a historical–cultural phenomenon which engages with our contemporary secular humanist culture. But not in any teleological manner, i.e., in the sense that we were ignorant and have now seen the light—that all faith was delusion and we are finally free at last! For anatheism, losing the illusion of God (as sovereign superintendent of the universe) offers the possibility of re-opening oneself to the original promise of the sacred Stranger, the absolute Other who comes as gift, call, summons, as invitation to hospitality and justice in every moment. In sum, as someone or something that was lost and forgotten by Western metaphysics—and needs to be recalled again.[16] And here, I think, we can move from the *historical* formulation of the anatheist question—what comes after the disappearance of God?—to the more *existential* one: How do we experience this today in our concrete lived existence?

This is why anatheism calls not for new theories as such but for new "examples" and "testimonies" of the anatheist moment in art and action. It is why anatheism needs theopoetics: scriptural, literary, visual portraits of lived abandonment and disillusionment followed by a turning (what Socrates called *periagoge*, what Augustine called *conversio*). The negative moment of letting go is, let me repeat, indispensable to a proper appreciation of anatheism. Without it we have cheap grace—God as comforting illusion, quick fix, opium of the people. I often think here of Dostoyevsky's sense of faith through radical alienation ("true faith comes forth from the crucible of doubt") or the "dark night of the soul" powerfully depicted in the mystical poetry of John of the Cross or Gerard Manley Hopkins, mentioned above; or of Christ's radical sense

---

[14] For philosophical interpretations of this epiphanic moment see Kierkegaard's treatment of the "Instant" (*Augenblick*) and "Repetition" (*Wiederholung*) and Heidegger's ontological readings of these terms in *Being and Time* as well as the later deconstructive readings by Derrida and Caputo. See also Walter Benjamin's related reading of the Messianic time of *Jetzzeit*, and Giorgio Agamben's reading of the eschatological "time that remains."

[15] For kairological and eschatological notions of ana-time, see our "Epiphanies of the Everyday: Toward a Micro-Eschatology," in *The Ethics of Time* (ed. John Manoussakis; Continuum: New York, 2016).

[16] On the critique of onto-theology as a double forgetfulness of Being and God see the deconstructive readings of Heidegger, Derrida, and Caputo and our own hermeneutic treatment of this theme in Kearney, *La Poétique du Possible* and *The God Who May Be*.

of abandonment on the Cross. These are all concrete moments of emptying (*kenosis*) which open the possibility of a return to the inaugural moment of *anatheism*: the wager of yes to the Stranger. This primal wager is first and foremost an existential one—not a purely logical one *à la* Pascal (which is more a wager of knowledge than of flesh, epistemological rather than ontological). The anatheist wager—to turn hostility into hospitality—signals the inaugural moment of all great wisdom traditions. And with respect to Abrahamic theopoetics specifically, it invites us to recall certain "primal scenes" of hospitality in the Scriptures illustrated in many great works of religious art: for example, Abraham and Sarah as they encounter the strangers in Mamre; Mary faced with the stranger called Gabriel; the disciples meeting the risen stranger at Emmaus.[17] Which brings us to the final part of our reflection—anatheism as theopoetic art.

III Theopoetic art: Anatheist imagining

Let me conclude with an example of theopoetic art—Andrei Rublev's Trinity.

My suggestion is that works of art and imagination are more likely to express the superabundance of meaning, seeded by the ongoing process of theopoiesis, than the purely conceptual systems of speculative metaphysics or dogmatic theology. The polysemantic excess of theopoetics expresses the continuous creation of God which, in Teilhard de Chardin's words, "prolongs itself in history and culture." Paintings are more embodied than doctrines. Art is more incarnate than dogma. Orthopoiesis—like its twin orthopraxis—precedes orthodoxy. Indeed it is important to recall that theory is itself a faded form of *poiesis*, and only retains its pedagogical force by acknowledging its creative origin in the latter.[18] More simply put: images are more powerful than ideas because they are more sensible, more tangible, and more down to earth. They invite us to a "carnal hermeneutics" of sight, sound, taste, and touch. They move and mobilize our being. And here we should not forget that the Latin word for Sophia is *sapientia*, reminding us that primal wisdom originally comes from *sapere*, to savor and taste. The

---

[17] On other theopoetic paintings of hospitality and strangers—in addition to Rublev's Trinity—see also our mention in *Anatheism* of Botticelli's Cestello Annunciation (1490), Rembrandt's famous etching series of Emmaus and Chagall's Abraham and Strangers. One might also mention our treatment elsewhere of Antonio da Massina's Annunciata and Sheila Gallagher's recent Pneuma Hostis, as well as such contemporary films as *Babette's Feast* (based on a story by Karen Blixen) and Andrei Tarkovsky's *Andrei Rublev*. On the notion of art making (icon making and bell making) as a divine call to human co-creation—which excludes no-one—see Anthony Steinbock, "Transcendence as Creativity: Vocation in Andrei Tarkovsky," in *The Yearbook on History and Interpretation of Phenomenology* (ed. Jana Trajtelova; Frankfurt am Main: Peter Lang, 2016). Theopoetic art is exemplary of human–divine co-creation but it is not exclusionary (or elitist). Everyone is called to participate in the art of ongoing *poiesis* in many different mansions, great and small, sacred and secular, miraculous and banal. Every time anyone acts, speaks, or makes one is participating, for better or worse, in the creation or de-creation or re-creation of the Kingdom.

[18] On the derivation of intellectual concepts from imagination, see Kant's argument for the primacy of transcendental productive imagination in *The Critique of Pure Reason*, Schelling's claim that philosophy and theology are derived forms of an "unconscious poetics of nature" or Nietzsche's argument that metaphysics is a form of masked mythology—"an army of mobile metaphors"—that has forgotten its own mytho-poetic origin (a point later developed by philosophers such as Heidegger, Derrida, and Ricoeur).

savvy of imagination precedes all speculative *savoir*. And it is important to recall that theopoetic imagination is not confined to high art but more commonly manifests itself in ordinary ritual cultural practices around icons, statues, paintings, and moving images.

When Rublev painted the Trinity in 1425 he did not try to represent Father, Son, and Spirit as abstract deities but rather as three human-like persons sharing a meal at a table. To be moved by the Trinity, Rublev realized, we need to be able to sense it, see it, and touch it. (Oriental Christians touch icons with their foreheads, lips, and hands). And to this end, he resolved to embody the mystery of divine relation in a created work

Figure 1 Andrei Rublev's Trinity.

of art, where paint, volume, form, and style configure something invisible as visible. He made an image which told a story, bearing out the teaching of the Church Father, John of Damascus, that we "need the Gospel in one hand and the painted expression of the same in the other, because the two have equal value and should receive equal veneration" (*Ep. II, 171*).

Rublev was a Russian Orthodox monk who, faithful to both the apophatic tradition of discretion and the kataphatic tradition of embodiment, did not try to paint God as some transcendent Form. Instead he painted the three strangers who visited Abraham and Sarah in Mamre (Gen. 3). The primal biblical scene exemplifies the Trinity as a drama of lived hospitality: the original title of the icon was "The Hospitality of Abraham" referring to how Abraham responded to the three strangers who appeared out of the desert not with hostile fear but by hosting a lavish meal. In the sharing of food from an open bowl—depicted at the center of Rublev's painting—the event marks a space, a chalice, a chora, a womb, where a future child is conceived: Isaac.

Rublev revisits the inaugural drama of Abrahamic hospitality to manifest the mystery of a Triune God. In the making and sharing of food, the divine becomes human and the human divine. Once they participate as guests in the feast, the "three" strangers, Genesis tells us, become "one." Three in one and one in three. Human as divine and divine as human. The impossible made possible.

Rublev's icon features three persons circling around a table, each offering its place to the other in a gesture of endless hospitality. Their roles as father, son, and spirit are not depicted in terms of hierarchy or seniority but as equal partners in an open-ended dance. The dance is not self-regarding but opens onto a fourth person—an empty place at the base of the table where a stranger is invited, an outsider welcomed, a guest hosted: humanity in the person of each viewer of the painting itself. That is why a small rectangle still marks the lower part of the circle where a mirror once looked out—at us looking in. A mirror revealing to us that we are the reflection of divinity, made in its image and likeness—the fourth dancer invited to the dance.[19]

---

[19] On the "fourth person of the Trinity"—invited to the perichoretic dance through the mirror-image—see Rohr, *The Divine Dance*: "Don't try to start with some notion of abstract Being and then conclude, we also found out [through Jesus] that such a being is loving. No, Trinitarian revelation *begins* with the loving—and this is the new definition of being. Most start with the One and then have trouble making it into the Flow between the Three. How about starting with the Three, and know that this is the shape of true Oneness? There is now a hidden communion, an Absolute Friendship at the heart of everything. The final direction of history is inevitably directed toward resurrection as Alpha becomes Omega (see Rev. 1.8; 21.6; 22.13), as both Bonaventure and Teilhard de Chardin would put it. Resurrection is no longer a one-time anomaly in the body of Jesus, but the pattern of the universe ....The Trinitarian flow is like the rise and fall of tides on a shore. All reality can be pictured as an Infinite Outflowing that generates an Eternal Infolding. This eternal flow is echoed in history by the self-emptying of the Incarnation and the Holy Spirit's seducing us back to God. As Meister Eckhart and other mystics say in other ways, the infolding always corresponds to the outflowing. I love the German word for Trinity, *Dreifaltigheit*, which literally means 'the three infoldings'. The foundational good news is that creation and humanity have structurally been in this flow from the very beginning (Eph. 1.4, 9-10; Rom. 8.21-25, 29). We are not outsiders or mere spectators but inherently part of the divine dance, while ever being drawn deeper into the Divine Two-Step. Jesus said, 'I will come back again and take you to myself, so that where I am you also may be' (John 14.3). Some mystics who were on deep journeys of prayer took

This dance motif is captured in the original Greek term for the Trinity—*perichoresis*—meaning to dance around. The three persons circle around (*peri*) a receptacle (*chora*) which may be read as a bowl of hospitality, a eucharistic chalice, a womb of natality (Sarah prefiguring Mary for the Christian monk, Rublev). This latter reading is significant for in early Christian churches, such as the Monastery of Khora in Constantinople, we find icons and frescoes depicting Mary bearing Jesus in her womb with the inscription *Chora tou Achoratou*: the Container of the Uncontainable.[20] The *chora* at the center of the dance may thus be seen as the core of finitude at the heart of infinity—the chalice-womb of bread and wine which hosts the human to come, the child to be born again and again. *Chora* thus marks a space of endless possibility for endless life, a site of eros and creation, of play and feasting. A feminine space where the three persons of the Trinity give birth to each other and to a fourth: each human who participates in the visual dance. As the medieval mystic, Meister Eckhart, puts it: "Do you want to know what goes on in the core of the Trinity? I will tell you. In the core of the Trinity the Father laughs and gives birth to the Son. The Son laughs back at the Father and gives birth to the Spirit. The whole Trinity laughs and gives birth to us."[21]

---

this message to its consistent conclusion: creation must then be seen as 'the fourth person of the Blessed Trinity'. Once more, the divine dance isn't a closed circle; we're all invited in ... This fits the 'dynamic' metaphysical principle that 'the inter-weaving of the three [always] produces a fourth' (Cynthia Bourgeault, *The Holy Trinity and the Law of Three* [Boulder, CO: Shambhala, 2013], 89). This may sound like heresy—especially to a contracted heart that wants to go it alone. But this is the *fourth place* pictured and reserved as a mirror in Andrei Rublev's fifteenth-century icon of the Trinity." For further philosophical analysis of the "fourth dimension" of the divine–human relation, see John Manoussakis, "Toward a Fourth Reduction" and Kearney, "Epiphanies of the Everyday" in *After God: Richard Kearney and the Religious Turn in Continental Philosophy* (New York: Fordham University Press, 2006), pp. 21–38.

[20] On the depictions of the divine mother and son as *"chora achoraton,"* see Kearney, "God or Khora?" in *Strangers, Gods and Monsters* (London: Routledge, 2003), p. 191. I am grateful to John Manaoussakis for this reference. See also the more common ritual formulations of Mary as Bearer and Mother of her Creator, for example, "Blessed are you, O Virgin Mary, who bore the Creator of all things: You became the Mother of your Maker" (Entrance Antiphon of the Catholic Feast of the Virgin Mary, October 8).

[21] Meister Eckhart, *Meditations with Meister Eckhart* (trans. and ed. Matthew Fox; Santa Fe, NM: Bear and Company, 1983), p. 129. In *The Divine Dance*, Richard Rohr explores the liberating gender implications of this perichoretic dance between the three persons: "God has done only one constant thing since the beginning of time: God has always, forever, and without hesitation loved 'the Son'—and yes, you can equally and fittingly use 'the Daughter'—understood in this sense as creation, the material universe, you, and me. The quality of the relationship toward the other is the point, not gender or even species. God cannot not love God's self in you (see 2 Timothy 2.13)! The 'you' that holds the indwelling Spirit, which many of us call the soul, is always considered eternal and intrinsically good because of its inherent connection to God." The fact—as we said in Note 3 above—that the word for originary divine Wisdom (*Sophia*) is feminine in Greek and that the word for the originary divine Spirit (*Ruach*) is feminine in Hebrew is also highly relevant here. (See Wis 8.1, Jerusalem Bible: "She deploys her strength from one end of the earth to the other, ordering all things for good"). Not to mention the fact that the "chora"/chalice/womb at the heart of the perichoresis—around which the three persons circulate—is inherently feminine. Rohr makes the additional point that the paradigm of the perichoresis marks a pluralist opening not only to the feminine but also to the interreligious: the impossibility of inclusive patriarchal closure and dogmatism. On the role of interreligious hospitality and narrative imagination see also Kearney and Kascha Semonovitch, eds., *Phenomenologies of the Stranger* (New York: Fordham University Press, 2011) and Kearney and James Taylor, eds., *Hosting the Stranger: Between Religions* (New York: Continuum Press, 2012).

The term *perichoresis* is translated into Latin as *circumincessio*. This word can be spelled with a "c," meaning *cessio-cedo* (ceding, releasing, letting go, offering one's place to the other); or it can be spelled with an "s" meaning *sessio-sedo* (sitting, assuming one's place, immanence). This movement of persons around the *chora* thus performs an act of inflowing–outflowing, ebbing–flowing, approaching–departing, *kenosis–hypostasis*: a two-step dance in which divinity invites humanity to join.[22] And this ingenious word play between *cedo* and *sedo*, of one step forward and one step back, finds a telling linguistic equivalent in the double entendre of the age-old greeting *adieu*. The double a-dieu with which the persons greet each other may be said to dramatize what we call the two A's of ana-theism. First, *A-dieu* as welcome (as in original Latinate usage, *addeum*), meaning an opening toward (*ad*) the other. And second, *A-dieu* as goodbye (as in later usage, *ab-deo*, meaning a releasing or letting go). Emmanuel Levinas explains this by saying that the original act of Creation is an act of love which leaves open a gap for the coming and going of the other—a gesture captured in the simple phrase "after you"/ *après-toi*. This is the "aftering" of Ana which is the first word of hospitality. As at a meal where one offers food to the guest who becomes a host to another guest in turn. Or as in dance where one retreats to let the other move in—ceding one's space so that the partner can succeed one in a circular movement, a mutual participation where, in Yeats's words, we can "no longer tell the dancer from the dance" (*Among School Children*). It is this perichoretic dance around (*chorein*) the still point of the turning world which opens onto the fourth person still be come, again and again, dying to itself and rising again, passing away and rebirthing in an ceaseless motion of rebeginning. Forever arriving and departing in the persona of strangers (*hospes*) who ask for bread and water, and receive it in turn. (Christ identifies himself as this *hospes* five times in Mt. 25, just as later he will reveal himself as a Lord of the Dance. Emmaus meets eschaton in the banquet of the Kingdom.)[23]

But let us return to the icon itself. If the devil is in the detail so is the divine. We have already noted that in Rublev's painting the three persons are not presented doctrinally as Pater, Filius, and Spiritus but as the three strangers who share food at the table of Abraham. They are seated in a circle and wear three different colored robes, gold, blue, and green. This visual differentiation into three colors represents the three aspects of the Holy One. As Richard Rohr explains in *The Divine Dance:* "Gold: 'the Father'— perfection, fullness, wholeness, the ultimate Source. Blue: 'the Incarnate Christ'—both sea and sky mirroring one another ... Christ wears blue and holds up two fingers,

---

[22] See my previous treatments of perichoresis in "God or Khora?" in Kearney, *Strangers Gods and Monsters* (in critical debate with Derrida and Caputo) and later in *Anatheism* and *Reimagining the Sacred*. See also the recent work on the Trinity and perichoresis in Emmanuel Falque, *St. Bonaventure and the Entrance of God into Theology* (Notre Dame, IN: Notre Dame University Press, 2017) and Tina Beattie "On the Matter of God: Conversations in the *Khora*," in *Mysticism in the French Tradition: Eruptions from France* (ed. Louise Nelstrop and Bradley Onishi; Farnham, UK: Ashgate, 2015), pp. 59–80. While Tina Beattie offers a powerful feminist reading of the Trinity and Chora, she misreads my own hermeneutic interpretation of Chora in "God or Khora?" I hope that I have clarified my position in this present essay.

[23] See our treatment of the *deus ludens* and *homo ludens* in Kearney, *Poétique du Possible* and "Anatheism." For our previous work on hospitality and the stranger, see *Strangers, Gods and Monsters, Hosting the Stranger*, and *Phenomenologies of the Stranger*.

telling us he has put spirit and matter, divinity and humanity, together within himself. The blue of creation is brilliantly undergirded with the necessary red of suffering. Green: 'the Spirit'—the divine photosynthesis that grows everything from within by transforming light into itself (Hildegard of Bingen called this *viriditas*, or the greening of all things.) The icon shows the Holy One in the form of Three, eating and drinking, in infinite hospitality and utter enjoyment between themselves."[24]

Many spectators of Rublev's three Abrahamic strangers at Mamre may have thought not only of the three persons of the Trinity but also of the three visiting kings at Bethlehem, or the three guests at Emmaus where the divine, as risen stranger (*hospes*), returns to share bread with his two disciples. These great scenes of visitation and hospitality were often conflated in Orthodox icons, suggesting how Rublev's perichoresis may operate as a form of visual palimpsest pregnant with serial beforeings and afterings. Or to use more technical language, an "overdetermined signifier" inviting multiple semantic successions and repetitions. Each viewing of the Trinitarian image signals a new visitation, a new rereading of the original scene. Hence the importance, as noted, of the rectangular mirror-frame at the base of Rublev's circle, serving as portal welcoming each spectator to the table—asking not just for vision but participation, not just for seeing but for moving and being moved, touching and being touched, loving and being loved, hosting and guesting. "Eternal beatitude," as Anne Carson put it, "will be where to look and to eat are the same state."

If we take the portrait of God in Rublev's icon to heart, we have to admit that "In the beginning was the Relationship." Far from being a picture of internal self-regard—a self-loving-love, a self-thinking-thought, a self-causing-cause, *ens causi sui*—the perichoresis of three persons expresses the desire for a fourth. Returning to the theme of the mirror at the base of the icon, Rohr writes:

> The gaze between the Three shows the deep respect between them as they all share from a common bowl. Notice the Spirit's hand points toward the open and fourth place at the table. Is the Holy Spirit inviting, offering, and clearing space? ... If so, for what, and for whom? At the front of the table there appears to be a little rectangular hole. Most people pass right over it, but some art historians believe the remaining glue on the original icon indicates that there was perhaps once a mirror glued to the front of the table. It's stunning when you think about it—there was room at this table for a fourth. The observer ... and all creation.[25]

This radical openness to the other, the stranger, the guest, signals the deeply ecumenical nature of Rublev's icon, now displayed in Christian churches of almost every denomination; but this icon also extends, as suggested, the interreligious radius in its visual superimposition of the primal images of Judaism and Christianity—the three strangers of Abraham and the persons of the Trinity. This Jewish–Christian interplay in turn invites hermeneutic readings of the chora-chalice at the heart of perichoresis as both Sarah's womb and Mary's womb open, in each case, to an "impossible" child:

---

[24] Rohr, *The Divine Dance*, p. 28.
[25] Ibid., pp. 28–31.

Sarah is barren, Mary is a virgin. Or more exactly, the chora incubates a divine possible (*dunamis*) beyond the impossible (*adunaton*) of the humanly possible. And it is interesting to recall here that the same terms used in the Septuagint to describe Sarah's exchange with the Strangers who visit Mamre (Gen. 18.14) are used to describe Mary's exchange with Gabriel in the Gospel of Luke (1.30). "Nothing is impossible to God." Hearing the respective annunciations of a future child, Sarah laughs and Mary says Amen. In both inaugural scenes, an impossible child is conceived. Isaac to Sarah, Jesus to Mary. Both miraculous natalities reside at the heart of the Trinitarian dance.

Rublev's icon of the perichoresis, I am suggesting, offers a theopoetic artwork which reveals the trinitarian mystery of creation in a manner which goes deeper and wider than any treatise of theoretical theology—and is thereby more affective and effective in its testimony of divine *poiesis*. Indeed one might add that Rublev's picture of reciprocal inclusivity between persons is not just a hermeneutic bridge between Jewish and Christian hospitalities but also between these and other non-Abrahamic wisdom traditions celebrating triple divinities and trimurtis who are equally welcome at the table.[26] Rublev's icon is an open gateway to interreligious hospitality.

---

[26] On the interreligious power of this work and other non-textual icons and rituals, see not only Richard Rohr but also Patrick Hederman, "Cinema and the Icon," in *Anchoring the Altar* (Dublin: Veritas, 2002); and the recent work of Marianne Moyaert, "Toward a Ritual Turn in Interreligious Theology," *Harvard Theological Review* 111, no. 1 (2018), pp. 1–23.

12

The God Machine: Techno-Theology and Theo-Poetics

John Panteleimon Manoussakis

Philosophical Propaedeutics

Philosophy's very first utterances, according to Aristotle,[1] present us with two seemingly incompatible positions: the unity of all, as posited by one causative principle (*archē*) to which Thales, lacking a better term, calls water, and the multiplicity of all, infested with an equal number of gods (πάντα πλήρη θεῶν εἶναι). Throughout its course, Greek philosophy remains incapable of reconciling these two positions.[2] Even Plato, who, following Thales's first insight, grounds the multiplicity of particular things to a universal idea, refrains from calling the Ideas gods or from assigning to gods the unifying function of the ideas, thus leaving his theology somewhere in-between Greek mythology and his conception of a demiurge who, contrary to the Christian connotations of the term, is not the creator of the world but merely the decorator that bestows upon the cosmos its cosmetic element by conforming to the formal patterns of the forms.[3]

The difficulty of uniting Thales's philosophical monism with mythological polytheism—or, as the authors of the *System in German Idealism* demanded, in their nostalgia to return to the Greek beginnings, a "monotheism of reason" and a "polytheism of the imagination and art"[4]—was for the Greeks their conception of nature (*physis*). Nature, as that which keeps flowing out of a primordial source which

---

[1] Aristotle, *Metaphysics*: Volume I: Books 1–9. trans. Hugh Tredennick. Loeb Classical Library. Cambridge, MA: Harvard University Press, 1933, A 3 (983b) and *De Anima*, A 5 (411a), respectively. See also, H. Diels and W. Kranz, *Die Fragmente Der Vorsokratiker* (vol. I; Zürich: Weidmann, 1996), pp. 76 and 79; and Aristotle, *On the Soul. Parva Naturalia. On Breath*. Trans. W.S. Hett. Loeb Classical Library. Cambridge, MA: Harvard University Press, 1957.
[2] For a discussion on the tension between these two principles with respect to Greek theology, see Etienne Gilson, *God and Philosophy* (New Haven, CT: Yale University Press, 1969), pp. 1–37.
[3] Plato, *Timaeus. Critias. Cleitophon. Menexenus. Epistles*. Trans. R.G. Bury. Loeb Classical Library. Cambridge, MA: Harvard University Press, 1929, 28–29.
[4] For the text and the problem of its authorship, see David Farrell Krell, *The Tragic Absolute: German Idealism and the Languishing of God* (Bloomington: Indiana University Press, 2005), pp. 16–26.

itself remains "hidden,"[5] is itself its own origin or, rather, lack of origin (*Abgrund*). Several ideas find their birthplace in this image of the aboriginal flowing of nature. For example, nature's anarchy and thus eternity, nature's perennial emanation, and nature's divinity—for a world "full of gods," as Thales intimated, is itself divine. What held these ancient ideas together was an understanding of nature as *necessary*. For classical thought, *physis* exists necessarily and its necessary character renders any robust theology unnecessary. Thus ancient polytheism, structured as it was around this cluster of concepts associated with nature, remains unable to resolve the opposition between the world's *one* cause or principle and its *many* gods. The need of a reduction back to one principle was deeply felt in the Greek mind, yet no Greek god could be raised to the dignity of a first principle. Hence, Simplicius, the last of the pagan philosophers, can call Thales an atheist[6] without fear of contradicting the thinker who conceived of a world asphyxiating with gods. As Origen was quick to realize, all polytheism is essentially atheism in disguise.[7]

Aristotle's philosophy operates precisely on the distinction between what is man-made (*technē*) and what is independent of human craftsmanship (*physei*, i.e., the natural).[8] The very concept of *physis* makes sense only within such a schema that distinguishes the natural from the artificial. Heidegger's reading of Aristotle discovers in the distinction between *physis* and *technē* "two kinds of generation" that "are contrasted with each other."[9] He then continues: "When Aristotle time and again characterizes growing things by way of analogy with artifacts, does this mean he already understands the φύσει ὄντα as self-making artifacts? No, quite the contrary, he conceives of φύσις as self-production."[10] The difference between *physis* and *technē* inscribes them in an identity as the one can only be conceived by means of the other: indeed, either concept describes the same phenomenon, that of origination; it is only the manner of origination that differs. And their difference is man. *Technē* is man-made. Nature is not man-made (thus, it must make itself); rather, nature is what makes man. Although nature "makes" man, no man is technically a man by nature, for it is *technē* that makes man him who makes (*homo habilis*). By the first tool man makes for himself a hand—for the hand becomes a hand when it ceases to be a tool and becomes that which handles tools. By the hand, man acquires the word (man speaks with his hands). The man of words stands up. By standing up (*homo erectus*) man also stands over against nature.

To these two kinds of generation correspond two God-conceptions: to nature what has been called a "natural theology"—a god restricted within nature (or, in

---

[5] On Heraclitus famous fragment φύσις κρύπτεσθαι φιλεῖ (Diels-Kranz, fr. 123) see Pierre Hadot's *The Veil of Isis: An Essay on the History of the Idea of Nature* (trans. Michael Chase; Cambridge, MA: Harvard University Press, 2006).

[6] Simplicius, *On Aristotle's Physics*, 23, 21 (DK, 13: "ὃς δοκεῖ καὶ ἄθεος γεγονέναι").

[7] Origen speaks in his *Exhortation to Martyrdom* of a "polytheist atheism" (paragraph 32) and in *Contra Celsum* of an "atheist polytheism" (Book III, section 72).

[8] See, for instance, Aristotle, *Physics* B, 192b.

[9] Heidegger, "On the Essence and Concept of Φύσις in Aristotle's Physics B, I," in *Pathmarks* (ed. William McNeill; trans. Thomas Sheehan; Cambridge: Cambridge University Press, 1998), p. 220.

[10] Ibid., p. 221.

Kant's version, reason) alone. The other, following the paradigm of *technē*, is what we recognize as properly theological, especially in the wake of the Judeo-Christian conception of God.

Deus ex Machina

The origin of humanity, as both historians and anthropologists agree, is to be traced back to the invention of tools. But even before the first tool came to be, I was equipped with the hand. It was after the hand that the tool was made, as we often say, a "second" hand, only better and more effective. Thus, the hand became emancipated from being used only as a tool—it now manipulates the tools it had itself produced. With much of its duties transferred to the tools, the hand became free—it became creative. In fact, the two moments must have coincided: the creation of the first tool by the hand marks the moment when the hand ceases to be a tool. It is now recognized as that which has always been but which I can only now become aware of: *my body*.[11] The awareness of my body and consequently, as we shall soon see, my self-awareness as a subject have always been dependent upon this dialectical relation between the grasping hand and its tool.[12] The tool always refers back to the hand, for the one is meaningful only in relation to the other. The tool is precisely what is *graspable*: our first concept (*Begriff*). It is not an accident that even for such a sophisticated analysis of our being-in-the-world as Heidegger's in *Being and Time* the world *is* this referential totality of "tools" that, in turn, reveal themselves according to two modes of "handiness" (*Handlichkeit*): as ready-at-hand (*Zuhanden*) and as present-at-hand (*Vorhanden*).

In more than one way, man was able to develop the ability to speak thanks to his hands. As he didn't have to use his mouth as a hand—in order to fetch or hold things, as most animals do—his mouth became available for speech. Moreover, "as a man watched his hands at work, the changing shapes they fashioned must gradually have impressed themselves on his mind. Without this we should probably never have learnt to form symbols for things, nor, therefore, to *speak*."[13]

Indeed, in one of his characteristically dense passages, Heidegger attempts to establish such a connection between the hand and the word:

---

[11] According to Sartre's analysis, first I learned to use my body as an instrument and then to recognize it as my body: "The child has known for a long time how to grasp, to draw toward himself, to push away, and to hold on to something before he first learns to pick up his hand and to look at it. Frequent observation has shown that the child of two months does not see his hand as *his* hand. He looks at it, and if it is outside his visual field, he turns his head and seeks his hand with his eyes as if it did not depend on him to bring the hand back within his sight." *Being and Nothingness* (trans. Hazel E. Barnes; New York: Washington Square Press, 1956), p. 469.

[12] "Far from the body being first *for us* and revealing things to us, it is the instrumental-things which in their original appearance indicate our body to us. The body is not a screen between things and ourselves; it manifests only the individuality and the contingency of our original relation to instrumental-things." Jean-Paul Sartre, *Being and Nothingness*, p. 428.

[13] Ibid., p. 217.

> Man himself acts [*handelt*] though the hand [*Hand*]; for the hand is, together with the word, the essential distinction of man. Only a being which, like man, "has" the word (μῦθος, λόγος), can and must "have" "the hand". Through the hand occur both prayer and murder, greeting and thanks, oath and signal, and also the "work" of the hand, the "hand-work", and the tool. The handshake seals the covenant. The hand brings about the "work" of destruction. The hand exists as hand only where there is disclosure and concealment. No animal has a hand, and a hand never originates from a paw or a claw or talon. Even the hand of one in desperation (it least of all) is never a talon, with which a person clutches wildly. The hand sprang forth only out of the word and together with the word. Man does not "have" hands, but the hand holds the essence of man, because the word as the essential realm of the hand is the ground of the essence of man.[14]

Dare we say that without his hands man would have been also unable to think? That man began thinking, and still thinks, *with* his hands, that is, according to a fundamental structure implied by paradigms of touch? That "every motion of the hand in every one of its works carries itself through the element of thinking" so that "all the work of the hand is rooted in thinking"?[15] It seems that Aristotle would have agreed with this.

It must have been language that suggested to man the notion of creator God, that is of a God who creates by his word as much as by his hands—although, a more theologically informed position would also maintain the reverse, namely, that it was God the Logos who imparted in man both the ability to *technē* and to *logos*. Thus, techno-logy would ultimately originate in God's original act of creation.

Therefore, we could speak of two epoch-making moments in the evolution of humanity with respect to such techno-theo-logy: The first technological achievement is man—that is, that being who, by the use of tools, fashions himself as a human over against the animal and the natural world. The second technological achievement is narrated in Mary Shelley's *Frankenstein*. That is, not as one may assume, the animation of a corpse, but rather the self-deification of man—who, by the use of techno-science, makes himself a god. Mary Shelley aptly names Dr. Frankenstein "Victor" after God's name "the potent Victor" in Milton's *Paradise Lost*. Furthermore, the suggestive subtitle of *Frankenstein* "The Modern Prometheus" echoes Kant's hailing a hero of technological innovation, Benjamin Franklin, as "the Prometheus of modern times."[16]

Freud, writing of the technological advances of his time, suggests that they should be understood as the means by which humanity strives to attain those very characteristics humans have always attributed to their gods (e.g., omniscience, omnipresence, and so on). Thanks to technology, Freud argues, "[man] has become a god himself"—what he

---

[14] Martin Heidegger, *Parmenides* (trans. André Schuwer and Richard Rojcewicz; Bloomington: Indiana University Press, 1992), p. 80.

[15] Martin Heidegger, *What Is Called Thinking?* (trans. J. Glenn Gray; New York: Harper & Row, 1968), p. 16.

[16] Immanuel Kant, *On the causes of earthquakes on the occasion of the calamity that befell the western countries of Europe towards the end of last year. In Kant: Natural Science*, ed. Eric Watkins. Cambridge: Cambridge University Press, 2012. (1:472).

calls more explicitly "a prosthetic God."[17] Derrida, echoing Freud, speaks of "artifacts and prostheses" that "tend to become more animistic, magical, mystical,"[18] so much so as to allow us to speak of religion as "the theological machine, the 'machine of making gods.'"[19] Thus, he proposes that "instead of opposing them, as is almost always done, [religion and technology] ought to be thought together, as one and the same possibility: the machine-like and faith."[20] It is within this techno-theo-logical framework that we can understand Bergson's enigmatic conclusion to his essay on religion:

> Mankind lies groaning, half crushed beneath the weight of its own progress. Men do not sufficiently realize that their future is in their own hands. Theirs is the task of determining first of all whether they want to go on living or not. Theirs the responsibility, then, for deciding if they want merely to live, or intend to make just the extra effort required for fulfilling, even on their refractory planet, the essential function of the universe, which is a machine for the making of gods.[21]

From our modern perspective, we may feel justified in taking pride in our mechanical world (i.e., of a world understood precisely as a machine) for having rescued us from the superstitions of a bygone age when the workings of the world, shrouded in mystery, could only be seen as magical. Yet, language reminds us of what we would conveniently prefer to forget, namely, the common ancestry of the magical and the mechanical. Linguistically, these two terms originated from the same root, that of the Proto-Indo-European *maghana*, a word that signifies "that which enables," that which gives power over the natural (the machine) or the supernatural (magic)—assuming that such a distinction is even meaningful. Machines are as magical as magic is mechanical. In some instances, as in the story of the Golem of Prague, the magical and the mechanical are united again through a demonstration of force, the supplementation of might,[22] and the will to power.

Technology and logotechny

Richard Kearney's theopoetics offers an alternative to the techno-theo-logical alliance between the divine machine and the mechanical god as outlined so far. His hermeneutical reading of the scriptural text pays close attention to a different "making," that of *poiesis*, exemplified by poetry, human and divine. "Theopoetics," he claims at the outset of his

---

[17] Sigmund Freud, *Civilization and Its Discontents* (trans. James Strachey; New York and London: W.W. Norton, 1961), p. 44.
[18] Jacques Derrida, "Faith and Knowledge: The Two Sources of 'Religion' at the Limits of Reason Alone," in *Religion* (ed. Jacques Derrida and Gianni Vattimo; Stanford, CA: Stanford University Press, 1998), p. 56.
[19] Ibid., p. 51.
[20] Ibid., p. 48.
[21] Henri Bergson, *The Two Sources of Morality and Religion* (trans. R. Ashley Audra and Cloudesley Brereton; Notre Dame, IN: University of Notre Dame Press, 1977), p. 317.
[22] The English word "might" is etymologically linked to both magic and the machine.

chapter, "names the notion that the divine (*theos*) manifests itself as creative making (*poiesis*)." By focusing on those scriptural passages from Genesis, Proverbs, and the Wisdom of Solomon, among others, in which divine creation is best understood not in terms of manufacture but rather as an artwork, Kearney effects a reversal of crucial implications for theology. His interpretation of divine creation moves away from the *logos* about *technē* (techno-logy) in favor of a *technē* of *logos*; from the subordination of language to production to a production in service of language. I borrow the term *logotechny* from the Greek in order to signify the reversal of the technological. In Greek *logotechnia* means simply "literature" and it denotes any literary work, such as poetry, novel, theater, and so on. The example of "theopoetic art" analyzed by Kearney in his chapter, Rublev's *Trinity*, offers us a clear statement as to how Kearney understands theology's true vocation—which is, at the same time, theology's provocation—to retrieve and rethink (the anatheistic challenge) God's relation to humanity and humanity's relation to God as an art beyond the artisan. In his concluding words:

> Why do we need art to recover God after God? Why look to poetry and painting rather than doctrine and theology? Why is Creation a matter of making as well as revealing? Because, we believe, poetics is the first bridge between word and flesh.

My task in this chapter is to sketch the theological presuppositions that make Kearney's theopoetics possible. To this effect, I propose three ideas closely interrelated: nothingness, freedom, and desire. This conceptual trinity is, like the Holy Trinity, a unity—for all three are unified by the notion of *creation*: "In the beginning God created the heaven and the earth" (Gen. 1.1).

We began with a philosophical exegesis of the concept of nature (*physis*). That was a necessary task, even though its purpose was not clear then. It was a necessary task as it shall now allow us to contrast and juxtapose nature to creation. Nature *is not* creation. The Scriptural idea of creation underscores the world's contingency, for there was a time that the world neither existed nor had to exist. There was a time that time was not. Furthermore, the creation of the world "in the beginning" (Gen. 1.1) dispels any illusions of eternity and allows for the mystery of time and history to be reevaluated and vindicated. And because, unlike nature, creation is neither eternal nor divine, it can now be known (hence the inception of modern science). The following anecdote from one of Lacan's seminars provides us with further corroboration:

> I remember that one evening when I was dining at the home of a descendant of one of those royal bankers who welcomed Heinrich Heine to Paris just over a century ago, I astonished him by telling him—he remains astonished up to this day, and is still clearly not ready to get over it—that modern science, the kind that was born with Galileo, could only have developed out of biblical or Judaic ideology, and not out of ancient philosophy or the Aristotelian tradition.[23]

---

[23] This story is told in relation to Lacan's analysis of the *creatio ex nihilo* in *The Ethics of Psychoanalysis: 1959-1960* (*The Seminar of Jacques Lacan*, Book VII [ed. Jacques-Alain Miller; trans. Dennis Porter; New York and London: Norton, 1992]), p. 122.

At the same time, creation, precisely by its beginning, cannot be anything else than a creation in freedom and out of freedom. Freedom is first and foremost exemplified in creation's gratuitousness. The *ex nihilo* of the creation indicates that "there is no possible question that could go back behind this God who created in the beginning ... No question can go back behind the creating god, because one cannot go back behind the beginning."[24] That is because, according to Bonhoeffer, the beginning "is completely free."

> In other words the Creator—in freedom!—creates the creature. The connection between them is conditioned by nothing except freedom, which means that it is unconditioned.[25]

In this assertion, Bonhoeffer follows the Patristic tradition of the Church for which the creation of the world was always unconditioned and ungrounded, precisely in order to safeguard the freedom of God's creative act. Every compromise on this score, usually erring on the side of Platonism (cf., Origen, Schelling) meant

> that God was a creator by necessity and not freely. Without creating the world God would remain unfulfilled, he would not be God. The notion of God and the notion of creation thus overlap, and paganism makes its appearance disguised under the form of Christian doctrine.[26]

It is precisely this kind of disguise that one encounters, for example, in Schelling's positing of an eternal yearning or craving (*Sehnsucht*) in God that necessitates God's self-manifestation in the "creation" of the world.[27] Going further than the ontological necessity, Schelling does not hesitate to speculate the world's becoming as "morally necessary" (*eine sittlich-notwendige Tat*).[28]

Since creation in general—that is, both the world and humanity—was not necessary, nor determined by any hidden necessity for God, but came about as an act of His freedom, they too are participants in that gift. That means that creation (and every human being along with it) is free to become itself. "The manner in which *what* something is (given/gift, being/eternal being) emerges from *how* something

---

[24] Dietrich Bonhoeffer, *Creation and Fall: Dietrich Bonhoeffer Works*, Volume 3, ed. John W. de Gruchy, trans. Douglas Stephen Bax. Minneapolis: Fortress Press, 2004. (DBWE 3), pp. 31–32.
[25] Ibid., p. 32.
[26] John D. Zizioulas, *The Eucharistic Communion and the World* (ed. Luke Ben Tallon; New York: Continuum, 2011), p. 158. For Zizioulas too one could "locate the heart of the problem and the crucial difference [between Christianity and Greek philosophy] in the question of whether the world has had a *beginning* or not" (p. 157, emphasis in the original).
[27] F.W.J. Schelling, *Philosophical Investigation into the Essence of Human Freedom* (trans. Jeff Love and Johannes Schmidt; Albany: SUNY Press, 2006), p. 28. With good reason, Schelling avoids the term "creation" for the term "procession" (*Folge*) that further confuses the life of God ad intra as Trinity with his creative work ad extra.
[28] Ibid., p. 65. Perhaps in his attempt to affirm human freedom, Schelling undermined God's.

is (well being/bad-being)."[29] What we have here is a revolutionary idea that breaks with the essentialism of classical philosophy, and particularly of Neo-Platonism, and anticipates by some ten centuries the existentialist primacy of existence (the how) over essence (the what). The primacy of existence and existents—be they He who exists superabundantly as the principle of existence or those who exist (literally, *ek-sist*) as derivative beings—avoids and indeed transforms the anonymity of being (what Levinas has called the *il y a*). Existence is made personal. This has an epistemological consequence: essence (the *what, quid est*, quiddity) can be known only through an existent (in Maximus the Confessor's vocabulary, the *tropos* of hypostatic being). Here the ground is prepared for the famous Kierkegaardian principle of the incarnation that reverses the classical hierarchy by ranking the particular higher than the universal and affords to the particular an infinite value—indeed the value of infinity. It can indeed be expected as a matter of course that wherever the ex nihilo of creation is not properly thematized, then an essentialist metaphysics are in order. Christian theologians (from Maximus the Confessor to Eriugena to Kierkegaard) in situating their thought vis-à-vis creation, think constantly of the origin, of the beginning, that is of the *nothing*—to which, ironically, a theologian is not supposed to have recourse.[30] Yet, Christian thought is made possible by a constant encounter with this very question: "Why there is something rather than nothing?" As Vigilius Haufniensis writes: "The Christian view takes the position that non-being is present everywhere as the *nothing* from which things were created."[31] Creation was indeed made of nothing (*ex nihilo*), but the nothing shows through.

Bonhoeffer forbade us to ask the question "why did God create the world?"—for the why asks after a cause, it expects a be-cause, and if both God's and the creation's freedom is to be maintained, then not only should this question remain without an answer but it should not even be posited as a question. Nevertheless, we could perhaps ask a slightly different question: "What kind of God could be the creator God?" That is, what could creation tell us about a creator God? This question prompts us to add to the two concepts that we have already discussed—namely, freedom and nothingness—a third one: desire. And it is by this third concept that theopoetics becomes, in Kearney's words, "theoerotics."

> But greater than curiosity is desire. For in forming the human, God bore witness to a gap within divinity, a sabbatical crack or fracture from which the life-drive of eros could emerge as desire for its other. God created because he desired a play mate. Someone to consort with, as we know from Hosea, Isaiah and the Song of Songs. Or as the contemporary Jewish philosopher, Emmanuel Levinas, put it: "*Dieu a créé l'homme car on s'amuse mieux à deux.*" Creation is a love affair. Theopoetics is theoerotics.

---

[29] John Gavin (reading John Scottus Eriugena's Periphyseon V, 63) in *A Celtic Christology: The Incarnation According to John Scottus Eriugena* (Eugene, OR: Cascade Books, 2014), p. 93.

[30] At least according to Heidegger, who in his polemical remarks against Christianity assumes that a Christian on account of his or her belief on a creator God is unable to think the primordial nothing, thus a "Christian philosophy is a round square and a misunderstanding." See, *An Introduction to Metaphysics* (trans. Ralph Manheim; New Haven, CT: Yale University Press, 1987), p. 7.

[31] Søren Kierkegaard, *The Concept of Anxiety* (trans. Reidar Thomte; Princeton, NJ: Princeton University Press, 1980), p. 83 (my emphasis).

This "gap within divinity," the *chora* around which (*peri*) the perichoretic event takes place, is the core of Trinitarian mystery itself. A God conceived as identical with His substance, as a selfsame ipseity, exclusive of any alterity, that is, a God after the manner of religious monotheism (Judaic or Islamic) or philosophical monism (Parmenidean or Plotinean) leaves the differentiating ground of multiplicity together with space and time unaccountable. This ultimately means that such a conception of God fails to ground creation. In fact, it would have been impossible to justify the reason and the manner according to which such a strictly monotheistic God could create the world to begin with. For Christianity, on the other hand, God can create, that is, God can not only posit the world as His other, as that which is not-God, but He can also posit it as something intrinsically good, precisely because the otherness of the creation is a manifestation *ad extra* of the otherness in God Himself who exists ecstatically as the perichoretic communion of the enhypostasized difference of the Trinitarian Persons. A substantial God cannot but be as monistic as static. Such a God, however, cannot, by definition, be creative.

By this we have already arrived at Kearney's visual example of theopoetics: Andrei Rublev's Holy Trinity. The freedom of a God who is free to exist because He *ek-sists*, that is, because He "exits" and "stands beyond" Himself; a God who is free from His own being or essence; a freedom indicated by the "gap within divinity," by the no-thing of the perichoretic *chora*; finally, a nothing that knows nothing "of that narcissistic self-regard—a self-loving-love, a self-thinking-thought, a self-causing-cause"—all of these motifs (freedom, nothing, eros) are embodied in Kearney's reading of Rublev's icon. Didn't the naturalism of the Greeks know of eros? A student of ancient philosophy may object. Doesn't eros after all belong to *physis* as what is natural and aiming at the propagation of nature? *That* eros, what Lyotard has called in his *Libidinal Economy* "Nicomachean Erotics"[32] is precisely too natural, that is to say, too symmetrical, equally subservient to biological and political needs; it is an economic eros that grants satisfaction inasmuch as it demands it. Ultimately, it is a technological eros, to recall Levinas's remark that "machines ... echo the impatience of desire."[33] Not so with the eros that freely begets creation. In Rublev's icon the movement of eros is in the eyes: the gaze of each angel "deflects" from the one to the other and to the third in a continuous movement that never comes to a halt. Trinitarian eros is not inscribed within an economy of self-satisfaction but within a community of difference and deferment.

I would like to bring this brief response to a close by quoting the words from another meditation on Rublev's icon of erotic theopoetics:

> The created self, made in God's image, is unmistakeably and irreducibly erotic, and its desirousness is not something to be eradicated. To be as a created subject is to be a locus of desire; it is not a lie to say "I"—unless that "I" is trapped in the terms of functional and symmetrical gratifications, held back from the radical delight in the otherness of the other's desire that is rooted in the love of the Trinity.[34]

---

[32] Jean-François Lyotard, *Libidinal Economy* (trans. Iain Hamilton Grant; Bloomington: Indiana University Press, 1993), pp. 155–165.

[33] Emmanuel Levinas, *Existence and Existents* (trans. Alphonso Lingis; The Hague: Martinus Nijhoff, 1978), p. 91.

[34] Rowan Williams, "The Deflections of Desire: Negative Theology in Trinitarian Disclosure," in *Silence and the Word* (ed. Oliver Davies and Denys Turner; Cambridge: Cambridge University Press, 2002), p. 133.

Index

Abraham 148, 151–2, 154, 156, 158–60
Absolute 26, 32
acts 108, 140, 142
adonnée 57, 75
advent 50
Alighieri, Dante 127–33, 136, 138, 141–2
alumbrados 90
Álvarez, Baltasar 91
Alvarez de Paz, Diego 91
ambivalence 58
anamnesis 130
anatheism 143–60, 166
Anaximander 33, 46
Anselm 27, 122
apocalypse 108–9, 111, 127–30, 132–3, 136
Aquinas, Thomas 33, 37, 39, 102
Areopagite, Dionysius the 32
Arianism 129
Aristotle 33–4, 38, 42, 44, 139, 149–50, 161–2, 164
arrival 49
Athanasius 143
atheism 110, 135, 152–3, 162
Augustine 27, 37–8, 44–5, 57, 61, 133, 153
Avellaneda, Diego de 91

Barthes, Roland 94
Baumgarten, A. G. 42, 57
Beharrlichkeit 43, 47, 50, 58
Bergson, Henri 44, 165
Bérulle, Pierre de 33
Blake, William 127–9, 131–2, 136, 140
Boeve, Lieven 71
Bonaventure, St. 82
Bonhoeffer, Dietrich 135, 167–8
Bonz, Marianne Palmer 140, 142
Brentano, Franz 38
Brooks, David 135
Brown, Norman O. 137–8, 141
Bruno, Giordano 34

Canfield, Benet of 33
Caputo, John 135
carnality 104–7, 110, 112, 114–21, 123–4, 154
Carson, Anne 159
Catholic Principle 101–5, 107, 109–10, 112–15, 117, 119, 123
causa sui 32, 44, 57–8
Chardin, Teilhard de 154
charity 63–7
Church 99–125, 129–30, 136, 140, 142, 157, 159, 167
Clauberg, Johannes 57–8
claustrales 92
Colossians 100, 106
conatus in suo esse perseveranda 43ff, 58
Copernicus, Nicolaus 34
Corinthians, First Letter to the 53, 108, 111
Corinthians, Second Letter to the 53
creation 119, 139–40, 143–50, 152, 154, 157–60, 164, 166–9
Cusa, Nicholas of 27, 34

De Sales, Francis 33
Derrida, Jacques 49, 123, 165
Descartes, René 24, 26–7, 34, 42, 122
desire 145, 166, 168–9
desolation, spiritual 80, 83–4
destiny 49, 61
devil 140, 158
Diocletian 110
Diotima 27
Docetism 114–15, 117, 141
Dostoyevsky, Fyodor 153
Dubarle, Dominique 37, 40, 55
Dulles, Avery 71, 79
Duns Scotus, John 27, 33, 38–9

Eckhart, Meister 157
Egan, Harvey 81

Index

Eliade, Mircea 136
Endean, Philip 82
enframing 59, 61
ens commune 39
ens creatum 43
ens entium 38
ens in quantum ens 41, 58
ens rationis 43
ens reale 58
ens supremum 38
Ephesians 148
Ephrem of Syria 143
epic 127–33, 139–40, 142
Eriugena, John Scotus 168
Erlebnis 75
esse in actu 39
Eucharist 129–30, 151, 157
event 72, 82, 105–8, 111, 113–14, 116, 123–4, 137, 152, 156, 169
excess 106, 154
Exodus, Book of 37

Fénelon, François 33
flesh 72, 82
Franklin, Benjamin 164
freedom 166–9
Freud, Sigmund 150, 153, 164–5

Gadamer, Hans-Georg 102
Galilei, Galileo 125, 166
Genesis 136, 144–8, 156, 166
gift 28–9, 48–51, 56–7, 59, 64–7
Gnosticism 104, 106–7, 110–11, 115, 117
Goclenius, Rudolph 42, 58
Golem 148, 165
Gonzalez Dávila, Gil 92
grace 111, 153
Greisch, Jean 37
Gschwandtner, Christina 63–5

Hauerwas, Stanley 109
Hegel, G.W.F 24–6, 44, 127, 132, 142, 152
Heidegger, Martin 24, 38, 43, 45, 56–8, 60–1, 62, 104, 127, 140, 162–3
heresy 106, 114, 127–8, 157
hermeneutics 104–6, 114, 116–17, 120, 131, 151, 154, 159–60, 165
hierarchy 100–4, 106, 115, 118, 156, 168
Hildegard of Bingen 159

history 99–103, 105–6, 109–10, 113–19, 121–4, 128, 132, 138–40, 144, 154, 166
Hobbes, Thomas 42
Hodgson, Marshall G.S. 138
Homer 130–1, 139
Hopkins, Gerard Manley 150–1, 153
Hosea 145, 168
Husserl, Edmund 56

icon 72, 82, 106–8, 124, 147–9, 155–60, 169
idol 72, 82, 102, 104, 106, 124, 148
idolatry, double 61
illeity 65–7
infinite 31–5
Ipsum Esse Subsistens 32–3, 37, 39
Ipsum Intelligere 32
Iranian Revolution 137
Isaiah 107, 116, 148, 168
Islam 136–8, 141, 169

James, Henry 95
James, Letter of 54
Jennings, Theodore 135
Jesus Christ (Yeshua) 100–1, 104–11, 116–18, 121–3, 128–30, 132, 137, 141, 148, 151, 157, 160
John, Gospel of 51–4, 115, 147
John of Damascus 156
John of the Cross 153
Joyce, James 107, 127–33, 136–8, 140, 142
Jubilee year 107–8, 110–11, 116–17

kairos 101, 106, 111, 151
Kant, Immanuel 43, 47, 57–8, 122, 163–4
Kearney, Richard 111, 123
Keats, John 152
Keller, Catherine 143
kenosis 62, 154, 158
kerygma 70
Kierkegaard, Søren 102, 127, 152, 168
kingdom of God 28–9, 104, 106–12, 114–18, 120–1, 123, 139, 144–5, 148, 158
Kugel, James L. 109
Küng, Hans 102

Lacoste, Jean-Yves 70, 76–7, 82–3, 85
Lazarus 110, 152

Leahy, D.G. 132–3
Levinas, Emmanuel 31, 32, 65–7, 77, 103, 123, 145, 153, 158, 168–9
love 64–7
Loyola, St. Ignatius 69, 78–85, 87
Luke, Gospel of 27, 52–4, 60, 73, 107, 110, 116, 140, 142, 160
Luther, Martin 103, 127
Lyotard, Jean-François 169

Mann, Thomas 145
Marion, Jean-Luc 72, 82–3, 85, 87, 106
Mark, Gospel of 53, 71, 106–7
Marno, David 92–3
Marx, Karl 153
Matthew, Gospel of 28, 53, 107, 116
Maximus the Confessor 168
Mercurian, Everard 91
metaphysica 39, 41–51, 53, 57, 59–60
metaphysics 103, 106–7, 110, 117, 121, 153–4, 168
microeschatologies 111
Milton, John 127–9, 131, 136, 138–40, 142, 164
Moses 137
Muhammad, Prophet 137, 141
mythology 110–11, 161

Nabert, Jean 124
Nadal, Jeronimo 90
Nancy, Jean-Luc 62
nature 161–2, 166, 169
negation 132, 152–3
Neoplatonism 105, 110, 168
Neusner, Jacob 136
Newman, John Henry 129
Niebuhr, Reinhold 135
Nietzsche, Friedrich 38, 40, 44, 47, 60, 111, 127, 132, 153
nihilism 60–4, 132
nothingness 166–8
Nyssa, Gregory of 27, 32–3

Obama, Barack 109, 135
O'Malley, John 93
onticity 41
ontology, Christic 38, 55
ontology, theologal 38
ontotheology 112, 117, 132

Origen 162, 167
Orsi, Robert 96
orthodoxy 99
Other, face of the 66

panentheism 34
pantheism 34
Pascal, Blaise 154
Paul, St. 100, 102, 108–9, 111, 115, 123, 127, 129, 140
perichoresis 147–8, 157–60
phenomenology 120, 127
Philippians, Letter to the 45, 52–3, 60
Pilate, Pontius 107, 110
Plantinga, Alvin 122
Plato 26–7, 31, 33, 161, 167
Plotinus 27, 33
Porete, Marguerite 100
presence 44–5
present 50–1
Proclus 27, 31
promise 104–5, 107–8, 111–13, 115, 137, 151–3
Protestant Principle 103–4, 114
Proust, Marcel 150
Proverbs 144, 146, 166

Qur'an 137–8, 141

Rahner, Karl 32, 69, 79–82
recogidos 92
recogimiento 90
revelation 70–7, 128
Ricoeur, Paul 149
Rohr, Richard 158–9
Rublev, Andrei 144, 147, 154–60, 166, 169

sacrament 103–4, 113–14, 116, 151
sacrifice 49, 60, 129–30
saturated phenomenon 56, 72, 74–5, 82, 87, 96
Schelling, Friedrich 127, 167
Schleiermacher, Friedrich 32
Schrijvers, Joeri 76
Scullion, Sr. Mary 99, 109
secularism 135, 138, 142, 150, 153
secularization 63
Shakespeare, William 136–7
Shelley, Mary 164

Simplicius 45, 162
Sluhovsky, Moshe 90
Socrates 153
sola scriptura 100–2
Song of Songs 145, 168
Spinoza, Baruch 42, 100
Spirit 99–106, 109–18, 121–4, 130, 133, 136, 152, 155–9
Suárez, Francisco 40, 57
subsistence 43
substance 43, 58, 103–5, 108, 110, 114, 146, 169
summum ens 38

Taylor, Mark C. 8, 135
technology 164–6, 169
Thales 161–2
theopoetics 106, 112, 114, 117–18, 123–4, 143–60, 165–6, 168–9
Tillich, Paul 102–5, 110, 114
Timpler, Clemens 42, 58
Tintoretto 108
Toner, Jules 78–9

Torres, Miguel de 91
trace 66
Tracy, David 123–4
tradition 100–7, 112–18, 122–3, 127–9, 131–2, 137–42
transubstantiation 103
Trinity 147–8, 154–60, 166, 169

Vatican 100, 102, 105, 118
Vattimo, Gianni 62–4
Virgil 140–1
vocative 23–4

weakening 63
Weber, Max 153
Winters, Margie 99–101, 109, 111, 113–14, 116–18
Wisdom of Solomon 144, 166
Wolff, Christian 42, 57

Xavier, St. Francis 92–3

Žižek, Slavoj 135

CPSIA information can be obtained
at www.ICGtesting.com
Printed in the USA
LVHW020710130222
710998LV00004B/254